Unions, Wages, and Inflation

Greg Saltzman

DANIEL J. B. MITCHELL

Unions, Wages, and Inflation

THE BROOKINGS INSTITUTION
Washington, D.C.

Library of Congress Cataloging in Publication Data:

Mitchell, Daniel J B
    Unions, wages, and inflation.
    Includes bibliographical references and index.
    1. Wages—United States. 2. Inflation (Finance)—
United States. 3. Collective bargaining—United States.
4. Labor economics. 5. Trade-unions—United States.
I. Title.
HD4975.M49   331.2′973   79-3776
ISBN 0-8157-5752-2
ISBN 0-8157-5751-4 pbk.

9 8 7 6 5 4 3 2

THE BROOKINGS INSTITUTION is an independent organization devoted to nonpartisan research, education, and publication in economics, government, foreign policy, and the social sciences generally. Its principal purposes are to aid in the development of sound public policies and to promote public understanding of issues of national importance.

The Institution was founded on December 8, 1927, to merge the activities of the Institute for Government Research, founded in 1916, the Institute of Economics, founded in 1922, and the Robert Brookings Graduate School of Economics and Government, founded in 1924.

The Board of Trustees is responsible for the general administration of the Institution, while the immediate direction of the policies, program, and staff is vested in the President, assisted by an advisory committee of the officers and staff. The by-laws of the Institution state: "It is the function of the Trustees to make possible the conduct of scientific research, and publication, under the most favorable conditions, and to safeguard the independence of the research staff in the pursuit of their studies and in the publication of the results of such studies. It is not a part of their function to determine, control, or influence the conduct of particular investigations or the conclusions reached."

The President bears final responsibility for the decision to publish a manuscript as a Brookings book. In reaching his judgment on the competence, accuracy, and objectivity of each study, the President is advised by the director of the appropriate research program and weighs the views of a panel of expert outside readers who report to him in confidence on the quality of the work. Publication of a work signifies that it is deemed a competent treatment worthy of public consideration but does not imply endorsement of conclusions or recommendations.

The Institution maintains its position of neutrality on issues of public policy in order to safeguard the intellectual freedom of the staff. Hence interpretations or conclusions in Brookings publications should be understood to be solely those of the authors and should not be attributed to the Institution, to its trustees, officers, or other staff members, or to the organizations that support its research.

Foreword

INFLATION has become a dominant economic issue. Policymakers have struggled to control rising prices by traditional demand-restraint tactics, by guidelines, and by direct controls. None of these have done much to restrain rising prices, partly because policymakers have also pursued other—and conflicting—economic objectives. The failings of economic policy have focused the attention of researchers and the general public on the mechanisms of inflation.

The labor market is often cited as a source of inflationary pressure. Wage guidelines and controls with numerical norms foster the impression that inflation can be limited through action in the labor market. And within the labor market, the unionized sector is generally singled out for special scrutiny.

In this volume, Daniel J. B. Mitchell explores the general characteristics of wage determination under collective bargaining. He finds that union wages are pushed up above nonunion levels and that union wage setting is less influenced by governmental demand-restraint policies than nonunion wage setting. After examining the evidence of "wage imitation" and pattern-following in some major contract negotiations, he concludes that the government cannot strongly affect wages throughout the economy by influencing a few union negotiations. His view is that collective bargaining is not an initiating source of inflation, but rather one of the mechanisms that perpetuate inflation after prices start to rise for other reasons. He suggests that guidelines can play a limited role in easing the transition from a high to a low rate of inflation, but urges caution in invoking them because he believes that economists have been prone to adopt oversimplified models of unions and union wage determination, models that can lead to inaccurate forecasts and ineffective policies.

Daniel J. B. Mitchell is a professor at the Graduate School of Management of the University of California at Los Angeles and director of the UCLA Institute of Industrial Relations. He completed this study while on leave from UCLA as a senior fellow at the Brookings Institution. He is coauthor (with Arnold R. Weber) of another book dealing with wage

vii

determination, *The Pay Board's Progress: Wage Controls in Phase II,* published by Brookings in 1978.

Many persons were helpful during the preparation of this volume. The author is grateful to Harry P. Cohany and Alvin Bauman of the U.S. Bureau of Labor Statistics for valuable data, and to Daniel Quinn Mills, Albert Rees, and Arnold R. Weber, who commented on a draft of this volume as members of a reading committee. The portion of chapter 4 that was presented to the Brookings Panel on Economic Activity and appeared in *Brookings Papers on Economic Activity, 3:1978* benefited from the comments of panelists Marvin Kosters and Michael L. Wachter (as discussants) and of the panel cochairmen, Arthur M. Okun and George L. Perry. Frederic Meyers, Paul Bullock, Paul Prasow, and Walter A. Fogel of UCLA made useful suggestions on working papers that were eventually incorporated into the study. Comments were also received from Jerome M. Staller, Loren Solnick, Charles Myers, Ross E. Azevedo, and James P. Luckett. Thomas A. Gray, Amy E. Kessler, and Jesse M. Abraham provided research assistance. The manuscript was edited by Elizabeth H. Cross; its factual content was verified by Cynthia M. Browning under the supervision of Penelope S. Harpold. The index was prepared by Florence Robinson, and the manuscript was typed by Monica M. Yin, Kathleen Elliott Yinug, and Margaret H. Su.

The institution is grateful to the Alfred P. Sloan Foundation for financial support of this project, and to the National Science Foundation for support of the Brookings Panel on Economic Activity. The views expressed here are the author's alone and should not be ascribed to the Alfred P. Sloan Foundation, the National Science Foundation, or to the trustees, officers, or other staff members of the Brookings Institution.

BRUCE K. MAC LAURY
President

April 1980
Washington, D.C.

Contents

Text Tables

Appendix Tables

I

Introduction

DO ES collective bargaining really make any difference in the determination of wages? Is it simply a style of wage setting with no significant effect on the eventual result? Does it contribute to inflation? These questions have long been of concern to labor economists and industrial relations researchers. Apart from any public policy considerations, they are interesting questions in themselves. However, public policy to deal with the economic effects of collective bargaining, especially those related to inflation, is critical. In the 1970s inflation became a major political and economic issue. And twice in the decade efforts were made by the federal government to influence wage settlements directly, both times as part of an anti-inflation program.

It is not surprising that economic policymakers have sought to supplement the traditional monetary and fiscal tools with programs of direct intervention in wage and price decisions. Fighting inflation with monetary and fiscal restraint is costly. Restraint in aggregate demand affects chiefly real output; it has little effect on inflation, especially in the short run. But inflation is also costly, although its costs are more difficult to define than the loss of real output associated with demand restraint. Inflation's costs are increased uncertainty in the economic outlook, increased transaction costs, especially in long-term relationships, and the distortion of the social and legal rules of behavior that are predicated on stable prices.[1] Thus if supplements to monetary and fiscal restraint do not take up the economic slack, demand-restraint policies are ultimately likely to be implemented.

Inflation, by definition, is a continuous rise of prices. Yet when inflation is discussed, the conversation often shifts to wages. In their official pronouncements, union officials regard this shift as unfair and declare that wage setting typically responds to price setting rather than the other way around. (The private views of union leaders are hard to obtain.) But the fact that labor compensation represents a significant proportion of total costs in the private sector and of outlays in the public sector is diffi-

1. Arthur M. Okun, "Inflation: Its Mechanics and Welfare Costs," *Brookings Papers on Economic Activity, 2:1975*, pp. 351–90.

cult to contest.[2] Clearly, wage developments have an important role in price determination and government outlays. But it is also clear that price inflation plays an important role in the determination of wage increases.

The emphasis on wages goes beyond the simple observation that wages are an important component of costs. Most models of pricing behavior are based on either profit maximization or a markup approach. In either case, prices will reflect costs passively, even if the firm can exercise monopolistic power. But economists suspect that a more exogenous element is behind wage determination.[3] Notions of "equity" permeate discussion of wages. Equity is difficult to define; sometimes it carries an absolute connotation (a decent minimum income) and sometimes a relative connotation (traditional wage differentials). In its relative form, the concept of a "just" wage increase is as important as the just wage itself. If in fact wages and wage increases are influenced by notions of equity, wage determination takes on an exogenous aura—that is, it appears to be affected by factors beyond simple supply and demand considerations.

Considerations of equity may influence an employer, even without outside constraints. But such considerations are certainly more likely to be influential when some external force is operating. In the United States a limited number of workers are affected by legal constraints such as minimum wage laws. Equity considerations may be reflected in another aspect of government policy, namely, the pay schedule of civil servants.[4] But in the private sector, the predominant external pressure on employers to

2. In 1977 labor compensation amounted to 67 percent of domestic corporate product, 53 percent of the total purchases of goods and services, and 33 percent of the expenditures of all levels of government. *Survey of Current Business,* vol. 58 (July 1978), pp. 32, 39.

3. Wage rigidity—a form of exogenous wage behavior—was a central element in the Keynesian theory of economic fluctuations, the theory that has conditioned a great deal of modern thought on macroeconomics. Richard Kahn, "Some Aspects of the Development of Keynes's Thought," *Journal of Economic Literature,* vol. 16 (June 1978), pp. 553–55.

4. It has been argued, for example, that equity considerations tend to make municipal government wages at the bottom of the pay scale relatively high compared with the private sector, with the reverse tendency occurring at the top. Walter Fogel and David Lewin, "Wage Determination in the Public Sector," *Industrial and Labor Relations Review,* vol. 27 (April 1974), pp. 410–31; David Lewin, "Aspects of Wage Determination in Local Government Employment," *Public Administration Review,* vol. 34 (March–April 1974), pp. 149–55; and Daniel J. B. Mitchell, "Collective Bargaining and Wage Determination in the Public Sector: Is Armageddon Really at Hand?" *Public Personnel Management,* vol. 7 (March–April 1978), pp. 83–85.

abide by equity standards comes from unions through collective bargaining. Unions do not unilaterally set wages in collective bargaining negotiations, but they can impose costs on employers who attempt to ignore equity. They are thus an outside influence on wage determination, which does not exist where employers make unilateral decisions.

In fact, when the federal government has directly intervened in wage and price setting as part of an anti-inflation program (whether by controls or guidelines), the effort has implicitly centered on wages, especially on collectively bargained wages. The wage-price guideposts of the Kennedy and Johnson administrations were in reality a wage guidepost coupled with an injunction to price setters to follow costs. If wage increases had exceeded the 3.2 percent guidepost, the cost injunction would have passed the inflationary pressure into prices. The same can be said of the wage-price controls established in 1971. Except in the unionized construction industry, wage increases were subject to a 5.5 percent standard established by the Phase II Pay Board, whereas price controls were rules for markups over costs. Both the guideposts and the formal controls were structured to focus attention primarily on union agreements. The guideposts, because they were not compulsory and included no formal monitoring arrangement, were directed at "visible" wage setters, which were inevitably major union contracts involving large numbers of workers. The program of controls established by the Pay Board in 1971 was also designed to focus the most attention on units containing large numbers of workers.[5]

But the fact that a particular policy was followed or that a particular model was adopted does not prove that the policy was appropriate or that the model was correct. Whether private sector collective bargaining is inherently inflationary is therefore a crucial question for investigation. In dealing with it, however, this study does not address other aspects of inflation. In particular, whether certain aspects of price setting are inflationary is not covered. Nor is the determination of monetary and fiscal policy considered.

5. On the Phase II wage controls program, see Arnold R. Weber and Daniel J. B. Mitchell, *The Pay Board's Progress: Wage Controls in Phase II* (Brookings Institution, 1978). A summary can be found in Daniel J. B. Mitchell, "Phase II Wage Controls," *Industrial and Labor Relations Review,* vol. 27 (April 1974), pp. 351–75. On the guideposts, see John Sheahan, *The Wage-Price Guideposts* (Brookings Institution, 1967).

What Makes Collective Bargaining Controversial?

The practice of collective bargaining has been part of the American scene since the 1930s and 1940s in many industries and began even earlier in others. Yet this institution, which is essentially a procedure for wage determination and the general establishment of work-place rules, often evokes heated emotions. When polls are taken of public attitudes toward unions, invariably a large proportion of the public favors the idea of unions. But when specific aspects of union behavior such as strikes impinge on the public consciousness, solutions such as compulsory arbitration of labor disputes are usually viewed as desirable. In the 1930s and 1940s the public endorsed unions but much preferred AFL-style unions to their "radical" CIO counterparts. In the 1950s the public endorsed unions but was uneasy about charges of corruption and undemocratic practices. In the 1970s the public was disturbed by strikes of government employees. Even though there has been general support for collective bargaining as an institution, widespread doubts about the quality of union leadership remain.[6]

Union officials have naturally been defensive about public attitudes and have often blamed unfair or uninformed press coverage. But the uneasiness with which collective bargaining is viewed is deeply embedded in modern American history and the nature of the U.S. economic system. From the historical viewpoint, collective bargaining on a large scale is a recent phenomenon. Some unions, of course, originated in the middle and late nineteenth century, especially in traditional crafts such as printing, railroads, and construction. But even for skilled workers in that early

6. Various Gallup polls suggest this dichotomy. When asked about general attitudes toward unions, 60–75 percent of those responding typically express approval. Hazel Gaudet Erskine, "The Polls: Attitudes toward Organized Labor," *Public Opinion Quarterly*, vol. 26 (Summer 1962), pp. 283–84. But on specifics the results are contradictory. During the famous sit-down strikes in the automobile industry in the 1930s, 56 percent of the public favored the employer; 63 percent said they favored craft over industrial unions. In 1948, 70 percent favored compulsory arbitration to settle labor disputes. In 1977, 47 percent of those polled regarded the honesty and ethical standards of labor union officials as low or very low, though only 18 percent felt that way about business executives. George H. Gallup, *The Gallup Poll: Public Opinion 1935–1971* (Random House, 1972), vol. 1, pp. 48–49, 539; and *The Gallup Opinion Index*, Report 150 (January 1978), pp. 20, 26.

period, employer recognition—if it came at all—was usually grudging and temporary. The unions' first efforts to organize were in no sense protected by law and were generally viewed suspiciously by the legal system as potential threats to the social order. Moreover, the organization of unskilled and semiskilled factory workers was often left to radicals and utopians whose efforts were usually unsuccessful and whose occasional successes were short-lived.

The depression of the 1930s fostered a change in the attitudes of workers toward unions. In some cases workers organized themselves with little assistance from the existing union establishment. And substantial changes in public policy toward unionization occurred. The Norris-La Guardia Act of 1932 limited the role of federal courts in union organizing and industrial relations. The National Industrial Recovery Act of 1933, a centerpiece of New Deal legislation, provided an ill-defined right to organize until the act was declared unconstitutional. Finally, the Wagner Act of 1935, which established the National Labor Relations Board, supplied the outline for the contemporary system of rules for union elections, recognition, and conduct of bargaining.

Employers who resisted the provisions of the Wagner Act found themselves only a few years later enmeshed in the wage controls and dispute-settling apparatus of World War II. These wartime programs had the effect of cementing existing union gains and extending union organizational successes. Unionization of the labor force increased from less than 7 percent in 1930 to almost 25 percent in the mid-1950s. The development of collective bargaining was therefore sudden and dramatic and was closely linked to changes in public policy. Such changes are bound to cause social distress. Passage of the Taft-Hartley Act in 1947, which placed restrictions on certain union activities, can be viewed as a reaction to this sudden dislocation.

There is a more profound reason for the controversy that surrounds collective bargaining and unionization. American ideology stresses individualism. Unions stress collective action. Free markets and free enterprise are part of the American value system. Some readers will question the degree to which markets are "free" in reality, but that is really beside the point. The prevailing belief is that markets ought to be free and competitive, and unions are seen as deviating from that ideal in that they are engaged in fixing the price of labor. The left-wing views of some of the CIO's leadership until the purges of the 1940s reinforced the popular image of unions as organizations opposed to free enterprise. Yet the successful practice of collective bargaining requires mutual recognition by labor and management of their respective roles.

Finally, production workers are not accorded high social status in contemporary society. In the private sector, professional, technical, and clerical workers are not generally unionized; they are unionized mainly where blue-collar organization has spilled over to other occupational categories. In certain cases where the blue-collar–white-collar distinction is especially blurred (for instance, clerks in retail supermarkets), unionization has spread beyond the traditional production-worker core.[7] In the public sector, wherever professional, technical, and clerical organization has occurred the covered workers often prefer that their organizations refer to themselves as "professional associations" rather than "unions" and remain independent of the AFL-CIO.[8] Unions are seen as representatives of low-status people and are therefore not held in high esteem. The concentration of unions in the blue-collar sector is not inevitable—in some European countries other categories of employees are extensively organized—but has been the tendency in the United States.

Employers' attitudes have helped condition public perceptions. Employers resent the constraints that unionization imposes on their internal employment policies. Obviously the attitudes of employers cover a wide spectrum. Some are fiercely antagonistic toward unions; others accept them. Nonunion employers generally resist unionization, perhaps simply on the grounds "that living without a union is a sound business decision."[9] In the bitter battle over the proposed labor reform bill in 1978, the latent antagonism between employers and organized labor showed clearly.

In this background on public attitudes toward unions and bargaining

7. Marten Estey, "The Grocery Clerks: Center of Retail Unionism," *Industrial Relations,* vol. 7 (May 1968), pp. 249–61.

8. After studying a sample of aerospace engineers, one author concluded that "the majority of all engineers want an organization which represents them in their job and professional interests, but show little interest in an organization that cooperates with established unions or that looks like a union." Archie Kleingartner, "Professionalism and Engineering Unionism," *Industrial Relations,* vol. 8 (May 1969), p. 235.

9. Peter J. Pestillo, "Learning to Live Without the Union," in Industrial Relations Research Association, *Proceedings of the Thirty-first Annual Meeting* (Madison, Wis.: IRRA, 1979), p. 234. In contrast, American resistance to unionization has no counterpart among Western European employers. Everett M. Kassalow, "Industrial Conflict and Consensus in the United States and Western Europe: A Comparative Analysis," in Industrial Relations Research Association, *Proceedings of the Thirtieth Annual Winter Meeting* (IRRA, 1978), p. 120.

the economic effects that unions may have are nowhere mentioned. Obviously, these effects are important—indeed, they are the subject of this book. But it is also important to recognize that in much of the controversy surrounding unions other factors are at work. Economists have been studying unions for many years; the flowering of unions led to the flowering of labor economics. Yet in the heat of public battles over labor legislation, the economists' view is usually submerged in the argument.

Perhaps it is best that the economic viewpoint is largely neglected when specific labor legislation is debated. While there is a general consensus among scholars on some of the economic effects of unionization, it would be difficult to relate these views to the fine points of labor regulation and regulatory administration. Nor do economists have any special expertise in such vague, though important, concepts as "industrial democracy." However, unions do affect the workings of the labor market sufficiently to influence the formulation of both microeconomic and macroeconomic policy. Over the next ten or even twenty years, it is doubtful that there will be any changes in labor law sufficient to change the basic characteristics of unions and collective bargaining. It is thus important to consider the implications of these basic characteristics for the achievement of such economic goals as price stability.

Three Basic Economic Issues

Many interesting questions could be asked about the impact of collective bargaining, but the inflation focus of this study directs investigation to three issues: (1) the relative wage effects of unions; (2) the response of collectively bargained wages to general economic conditions; and (3) the degree to which wages are determined through processes of wage imitation and patterns and the implications of these phenomena. In this section, the background of the three issues is described. The next major section will discuss the significance of these issues for inflation and other matters of social concern.

Relative Wage Effects

Probably the first question economists asked about unions was whether they raised wages. At first, the answer may seem obvious: the function of unions is to improve wages and if they were unable to deliver this service to their members they would not survive. But the issue is much more complex. Raising wages is a relative matter. If it is said that unions raise wages, this presumably implies that wages are higher than they would otherwise be. But the methodology by which one determines what wages would otherwise be is not immediately evident.

Collective bargaining is exactly what its name implies: a bargaining process. If the rules of the game are followed, management will offer somewhat less than it expects to pay and labor will ask for more. The outcome is not simply a splitting of the difference—there is limited evidence that the management offer typically moves up less than labor's demand moves down.[10] But the end result is that labor is seen to have "won" a concession, even if the final outcome differs little from what might have been determined unilaterally by a nonunion employer. The precise rules of the bargaining process are not officially prescribed by current labor law. But the law tends to frown on management tactics that involve putting an initial offer on the table and holding to it firmly.[11] Thus even a weak union might hold the allegiance of its members with apparent "successes" at the bargaining table, whether it actually raised wages or not.

The issue of whether unions raise wages is further confused by the growing complexity of typical union contracts. Besides basic wage rates, such contracts usually specify a range of fringe benefits (some of which are difficult to cost or evaluate), work rules, grievance procedures, safety standards, seniority systems for promotions and layoffs, and so forth. In principle, a researcher might try to reduce these various outcomes of bargaining to an index and then ask whether unions raise the composite index.[12] But it is evident that the proliferation of contractual provisions makes more difficult the process by which a *worker* might try to evaluate whether a union has improved his welfare. Note that making comparisons with reference groups of other workers—a concept embedded in the in-

10. Roger L. Bowlby and William R. Schriver, "Bluffing and the 'Split-the-Difference' Theory of Wage Bargaining," *Industrial and Labor Relations Review,* vol. 31 (January 1978), pp. 161–71.

11. See Morris D. Forkosch, " 'Take It or Leave It' as a Bargaining Technique," *Labor Law Journal,* vol. 18 (November 1967), pp. 665–75.

12. For an example of such an index, see Paul F. Gerhart, "Determinants of Bargaining Outcomes in Local Government Labor Negotiations," *Industrial and Labor Relations Review,* vol. 29 (April 1976), pp. 331–51.

dustrial relations literature—is complicated by fringe benefits and other features of modern labor relations.[13]

The fact that union contracts are multifaceted also raises empirical issues. Usually, researchers use a simple wage measure or perhaps a wage-plus-fringe-benefit measure to assess the impact of unions.[14] It is possible that unions could improve other aspects of the labor-management contract, from the viewpoint of the worker, without raising measured wages or compensation. In fact, some economists now stress the value of the nonwage element of the contract: grievance procedures, seniority, job satisfaction, and the like.[15] The outside observer might thus have difficulty in detecting or accurately measuring the overall union effect using a wage index as the sole measure of influence. In principle, the bias could go either way. Unions could improve nonwage issues without comparable improvements in wages, or they could trade nonwage benefits for wages. However, evidence presented later in this volume suggests that unions do raise measured compensation. Hence any impact they have on nonwage items comes on top of the compensation effect.

Cyclical Wage Effects

Assume for the moment that unions do raise the wages of their members. If this assumption is valid, there is no reason to suppose that the absolute wage impact is a simple constant. That is, the union-nonunion wage difference might be estimated to be, say, 20 percent in one period but in another period to have increased to 25 percent or decreased to 15 percent. Such changes could be associated with changes in the economic climate surrounding the negotiating unit—for instance, an increase in import competition for the final product. Or they could be associated with a change in the institutional setting such as a shift in the degree of rival union competition or cooperation. Finally, they could be

13. It has been noted that firms can nominally follow wage patterns and in fact adjust effective compensation by varying fringe benefits. Bevars Mabry, "The Economics of Fringe Benefits," *Industrial Relations*, vol. 12 (February 1973), pp. 95–106.

14. For example, see Albert E. Schwenk and Martin E. Personick, "Analyzing Earnings Differentials in Industry Wage Surveys," *Monthly Labor Review*, vol. 97 (June 1974), pp. 56–59.

15. R. B. Freeman, "Job Satisfaction as an Economic Variable," *American Economic Review*, vol. 68 (May 1978), pp. 135–41. Other references can be found in this article.

connected with the ups and downs of the business cycle and the rate of inflation. Business cycles appear to influence such features of industrial relations as strike activity, success rates of unions in representation elections, and complaints filed about unfair labor practices.[16] It would be surprising if wage determination was somehow unaffected by the forces that influence these other indicators of the state of industrial relations.

Price inflation might also be associated with changes in union-nonunion wage differentials, especially if the institutional differences in union and nonunion wage determination are considered. For example, the union sector is characterized by long-term contracts, which may slow the reaction to unanticipated price inflation. On the other hand, cost-of-living escalators in the union sector—a rarity in nonunion wage determination—might at times speed up the union response to inflation. These differences in relative response can exist even though both union and nonunion wages are strongly influenced by price developments.

Patterns and Wage Imitation

Specialists in industrial relations have long pointed out a special feature of union wage determination, the phenomenon of wage imitation. This concept has been applied in a firm's internal wage structure. For example, it is often said that wage differentials in a firm or bargaining unit tend to be rigid across occupations and job classifications as a result of internal wage comparisons.[17] It is also said that jobs across firms or bargaining units are themselves linked in "wage contours."[18] And there is a more general sense of wage imitation, often called "pattern bargaining," that suggests linkages between fairly diverse groups of union contract negotiations.

Because wage changes are linked by forces other than collective bar-

16. See chapter 4 for further discussion of these effects.

17. Wage "inequities" in bargaining units and resulting worker dissatisfaction are sometimes used as organizing devices by unions. See Mark W. Leiserson, "Wage Decisions and Wage-Structure in the United States," in E. M. Hugh-Jones, ed., *Wage-Structure in Theory and Practice* (Amsterdam: North-Holland, 1966), pp. 18–19. Once the union feels wage inequities have been eliminated, the then-existing differentials tend to be perpetuated. George H. Hildebrand, "External Influences and the Determination of the Internal Wage Structure," in J. L. Mey, ed., *Internal Wage Structure* (North-Holland, 1963), p. 289.

18. John T. Dunlop, "The Task of Contemporary Wage Theory," in John T. Dunlop, ed., *The Theory of Wage Determination* (St. Martin's, 1964), pp. 16–20.

gaining, it is difficult to specify models of wage imitation as empirically testable hypotheses,[19] although efforts have been made to do this. A major difficulty is that wage changes throughout the economy are likely to be intercorrelated even in the absence of unions.

For example, the business cycle and price inflation affect most wage-determination units. If simple correlation of wage changes is the operative definition of wage imitation, it is evident that virtually all wages are set in "patterns," even in the nonunion sector. But if deliberate imitation is part of the definition, evidence must be sought for ways in which information on wages is exchanged across units (a wage must be known before it can be imitated) and for mechanisms through which imitation occurs. The issue is not so much whether the wage-imitation phenomenon exists but how important and widespread it is and whether it has implications for public policy.

Finally, there are many data problems in research on wage patterns and imitation. Available data are frequently in the form of average earnings rather than occupational wage rates or even average wage rates. Thus the data will be affected by differences in employee mix, the proportion of overtime hours worked, and so on. Also, the theory of wage contours does not stop at the neat industry definitions set forth in the standard industrial classification code, the code so often used for earnings statistics. Of course, collecting data on a wage contour basis would require a precise operational definition of a contour and assurance that the contour would remain stable.

Public Policy Concerns

The three issues raised—relative wage effects, cyclical wage effects, and patterns—are all of potential concern to public policymakers. Each issue has implications for the interrelation of wage determination and inflation as well as for labor-market efficiency and income distribution. The inflation issue will receive concentrated attention in this book, but the other issues are also of interest.

19. For discussion, see Daniel J. B. Mitchell, "Wage Determination," *Labor Law Journal,* vol. 28 (August 1977), pp. 483–88. An example of an attempt to filter out these expected correlations from general economic conditions can be found in Y. P. Mehra, "Spillovers in Wage Determination in U.S. Manufacturing Industries," *Review of Economics and Statistics,* vol. 58 (August 1976), pp. 300–12.

Relative Wage Effects

A determination that unions affect wage levels is a prerequisite to the study of other economic issues. For example, it would be strange to state that unions do not have the capability of raising wages but that collective bargaining is somehow inflationary. Discretion in union wage setting is a necessary, though not sufficient, condition for any inflationary impact. It would be quite possible for some unions to be unable to influence wage levels significantly and yet still hold the allegiance of their members by providing other services. But in this circumstance, the union wage and the wage that the employer sets unilaterally are assumed to be identical. This hypothetical employer might conceivably have a cyclical response in wage determination that differed from other industries and could also be a pattern follower or even a pattern setter. But these characteristics could not be attributed to unionization if the union were impotent in matters of wage determination.

How much unions affect wages is significant for resource allocation as well as for inflation. If unions raise wages, economic theory suggests that the result should be a lessened demand for labor by the employer (or employers) affected. This lessening is the result of a combination of influences. A boost in wages could induce the employer to substitute other factors of production for his unionized labor, such as lower-wage labor. For example, an employer might subcontract with other firms to have certain functions (previously performed by unionized workers) performed by outside workers. Or if the enterprise included nonunion plants (or lower-wage union plants), work might be shifted there.

Of course, unions will resist these substitution possibilities. Clauses banning subcontracting may be incorporated in the contract at union insistence. Such demands are not uncommon, especially since subcontracting was ruled a mandatory subject of bargaining.[20] Unions may also resist capital substitution by insisting on work rules governing manning requirements. Many examples can be cited. Limits on gang sizes were used when containerization and other technical change threatened longshoremen. Resistance to the elimination of the firemen on diesel or electric freight trains was a major issue for many years. But pressure for factor

20. Discussion of the law on the duty to bargain can be found in A. Howard Myers and David P. Twomey, *Labor Law and Legislation,* 5th ed. (Cincinnati: South-Western Publishing, 1975), pp. 233–43.

substitution sometimes overcomes union resistance. And unions have on some occasions engaged in "productivity bargaining," in which restrictive work rules are traded for other forms of benefits.[21]

Where resistance to substitution is the union's chosen path, internal remedies may not be sufficient to prevent decreased employment. In a partially unionized industry, a widening of the union-nonunion wage differential gives a labor-cost advantage to nonunion firms, which can then undercut their unionized rivals in the product market. Unions may respond by trying to organize the nonunion firms—not always an easy task. On occasion, if employment prospects are grim, union concessions on wages may occur. Examples can be found in textiles in the mid-1950s, meatpacking in the late 1950s and early 1960s, and construction in the mid-1970s.[22] However, when employment opportunities are generally rising, unions may be willing to tolerate a relative shift to nonunion employment. In bituminous coal, for example, the rise in energy prices was sufficient to increase job opportunities in union mines substantially in the 1970s. This tendency was enhanced by falling productivity, which was apparently due in part to stricter safety standards. Employment effects did not constrain the United Mine Workers in collective bargaining when new jobs were opening up.

As noted, unions can avoid direct nonunion competition by unionizing an entire industry, thereby "taking wages out of competition." However, if the industry concerned operates in world markets, as either an exporter or an importer, the market is international; then the entire industry cannot be unionized and the prospect of substitution remains. There has been talk about international collective bargaining in which unions in different countries would coordinate their efforts. But aside from some limited examples that cross the U.S.-Canadian border there is little likelihood of

21. Academic and government interest in productivity bargaining increased as a result of the encouragement of productivity bargaining under British incomes policy in the 1960s. Lloyd Ulman, "Under Severe Restraint: British Incomes Policy," *Industrial Relations,* vol. 6 (May 1967), especially pp. 248–60.

22. A classic study of such concessions is George P. Shultz and Charles A. Myers, "Union Wage Decisions and Employment," *American Economic Review,* vol. 40 (June 1950), pp. 362–80. Although such wage cuts do occur, unions are extremely sensitive about them. For example, in the meatpacking case, see Hervey A. Juris, "Union Crisis Wage Decisions," *Industrial Relations,* vol. 8 (May 1969), pp. 247–58, and the angry response to this article from the union involved, James H. Wishart, "Criticism and Comment: Union Crisis Wage Decisions," *Industrial Relations,* vol. 9 (February 1970), pp. 243–47.

such bargaining in the foreseeable future.[23] Faced with international competition on the export side, there is little unions can do, other than moderate their wage demands, if foreign orders decline. But if import competition is a problem, unions can seek government protection in the form of quotas or tariffs, with the former usually preferred.[24]

Finally, unions face the possibility of substitution away from unionized labor via consumer preferences. A boost in labor costs, if passed into prices, tends to shift consumer demand to other goods. In some instances, unions might be able to offset even this effect by obtaining government subsidies, as in the case of public transit. But in general the portion of elasticity of labor demand that comes from the elasticity of industry product demand is very hard to escape.

From the economist's viewpoint, labor-market inefficiency arises from a combination of labor-demand elasticity and a union wage differential. When the demand for labor is highly inelastic (big wage increases produce little reduction in labor demand), little economic inefficiency is generated by a large union wage differential. Wage costs are simply passed through to consumers, which is largely an income transfer from consumer to worker. When there is significant elasticity of labor demand in the face of a union wage differential, inefficiency is generated because labor is underutilized in the unionized firm and possibly other factors of production are overutilized. There is also an "artificially" induced underconsumption of the firm's product and overconsumption of competitors' products and even substitute products from other industries.

No one has ever tried to directly measure the costs of such inefficiencies in the union sector. But there is some evidence that the important short-run effects are chiefly redistributions of income and that the inefficiencies are small relative to these redistributional effects. Studies have suggested that unions usually face inelastic demand curves.[25] For a given union wage differential, the combination of an inelastic demand for

23. See Herbert R. Northrup, "Why Multinational Bargaining Neither Exists Nor Is Desirable," *Labor Law Journal,* vol. 29 (June 1978), pp. 330–42. On the U.S.-Canadian case, see Daniel J. B. Mitchell, *Essays on Labor and International Trade* (UCLA Institute of Industrial Relations, 1970), pp. 86–90.

24. For a discussion of the labor and trade issue, see Daniel J. B. Mitchell, *Labor Issues of American International Trade and Investment* (Johns Hopkins University Press, 1976), pp. 4–10. Unions should prefer quotas to tariffs, because once the quota is exhausted, foreign labor costs become irrelevant to domestic wage determination.

25. See R. B. Freeman and J. L. Medoff, "Substitution between Production Labor and Other Inputs in Unionized and Non-Unionized Manufacturing," discussion paper 581 (Harvard University, Institute of Economic Research, October 1977).

union labor and a more elastic demand for nonunion labor would minimize inefficiency in the economic sense. Employment in the union sector would not decline much because of the wage advantage. Displacement of workers (or reduction in hiring) would be small and would have only a slight (downward) effect on wages in the nonunion sector. This observation must be partially offset by the observation that unions facing more inelastic demand curves might be able to achieve larger increases in wages than those employers would unilaterally establish.

Over the longer term, however, the issue of employment displacement must be taken more seriously. It is usually thought that long-run demand curves are more elastic than short-run curves. Possibilities of both factor and product substitution expand with the time horizon. The predicted result of this process will vary with the observer's model of union wage behavior.

In the past, various economic models have been proposed.[26] One version presents the union as essentially a labor-supplying firm and proceeds to analyze its behavior following the general outlines of the theory of the firm. In early elaborations of this model, the union was said to maximize the wage bill (wages per worker times number of workers), providing an analogy to profit maximization for the firm. However, the wage bill seems an arbitrary target since union members cannot be viewed as analogous to shareholders.

Although more sophisticated models have been developed from this approach, chapter 3 presents a more useful alternative, which incorporates management resistance to union demands. The outcome of the union-push–management-resist model of collective bargaining is less predictable in the long run than in the short run, when management resistance is likely to minimize labor-market inefficiency and employment displacement. Over the long haul, however, there is nothing to suggest that the union-nonunion wage differential remains trendless. The bias from the balance of forces might be upward or downward. In this regard, the tendency (illustrated in chapter 2) of union earnings to rise relative to nonunion earnings since the mid-1950s at least suggests a gradual accretion of relative union power, that is, an upward bias.

Obviously factors other than relative wages can be cited as causes of the relative decline in employment in sectors where union members are

26. For further references to these models in the industrial relations literature, see Daniel J. B. Mitchell, "Union Wage Policies: The Ross-Dunlop Debate Reopened," *Industrial Relations,* vol. 11 (February 1972), pp. 46–61.

most commonly found. The shift to a service economy might be attributed to changes in public tastes, perhaps associated with rising real incomes. Rising import penetration in certain manufacturing sectors might be attributed to such factors as postwar recovery in Europe and the spread of modern technology to low-wage countries. The possibility remains, however, that changing wage differentials have played a role in the trend toward declining unionization of the labor force.

In the debate on import limitation it has been the unions that have most vociferously raised the issue of whether a shift to a service economy—a nation of "hamburger stands," as the AFL-CIO graphically called it—is a desirable long-term trend.[27] Union leaders have questioned whether the types of jobs created in a service economy will be as desirable as those the present labor market provides, and whether U.S. national defense interests can be served without an "industrial base." These are complex issues well beyond the scope of this book. However, it seems undesirable to accelerate the shift artificially, even if it is an underlying trend. And from the viewpoint of the union movement, it is certainly not desirable for the employment base in heavily unionized sectors to decline relative to the overall work force.

Cyclical Wage Effects

Labor economists have always been interested in the response to business cycle pressures. Dunlop, in his classic study of trade unionism examined the responsiveness of union wages to the slide into the Great Depression.[28] The early interest was probably sparked by the question of whether wages were rigid downward, an important element of Keynesian economics. In fact, even in the pre-Keynesian classical view (and in more recent neoclassical and monetarist views of the business cycle) downward wage rigidity implied that contractions in demand would lead to unemployment. This is not the same as saying that flexible wages would eliminate unemployment, only that rigid wages are part of the mechanism through which unemployment is created in these models. But regardless of the model chosen, since unions permit the worker a voice in wage determina-

27. The quotation is from a statement by the chief economist of the AFL-CIO, Nathaniel Goldfinger, in *Trade Adjustment Assistance,* prepared for the House Committee on Foreign Affairs, 92 Cong. 2 sess. (Government Printing Office, 1972), pp. 52–53.

28. John T. Dunlop, *Wage Determination Under Trade Unions* (Macmillan, 1944), pp. 130–37.

tion, union wages would be more likely to exhibit rigidity (or less downward flexibility) during a depression than wages in general.

The price surge after World War II suggested to some observers that union wage determination might also retard wage growth despite sudden inflationary pressures. That is, union wages might be "sticky" in both directions. In the 1940s there were instances of relative wage slippage and subsequent contract reopenings to adjust to labor-market pressures. In more recent years, the development of the multiyear contract has added to interest in cyclical wage response. If wages are determined in advance for long periods, they cannot react to changes in real economic circumstance. Even if escalator clauses are included, wages in long-term contracts can respond only to price inflation according to the escalation formula. This special characteristic of the union sector is explicitly reflected in the empirical analysis of contractual wage change in chapter 4.

Cyclical wage effects are interrelated with the general arguments concerning cost-push inflation that were popular in the late 1950s and early 1960s.[29] The cost-push view was offered as an alternative to the traditional demand approach to inflation. The cost-push approach is based on the belief that inflation was caused by an "exogenous" upward pressure that is often identified with administered price and wage setting. This view might be proposed without explicit relation to monetary and fiscal policy. A more sophisticated version suggests that monetary policy is constrained by political factors to hold down unemployment and therefore would validate exogenous inflationary pressures. That is, inflation would lead to monetary expansion rather than the other way around.[30]

The troubling aspect of the cost-push view has always been the degree to which it insists on viewing wage and price setting as exogenous. It seems unrealistic to posit a totally detached system of wage and price determination. (The same can be said, it might be noted, for the determination of monetary and fiscal policy.) However, the cyclical view provides an interpretation of cost-push inflation that does not require completely exogenous wage-price behavior but that does allow behavior not closely linked with demand pressure. The cyclical view suggests that wage behavior is linked to past economic circumstances, which may have changed. Past unanticipated inflation therefore gradually works its way into wages. The process is gradual because not all contracts are available for renego-

29. Richard Perlman, ed., *Inflation: Demand-Pull or Cost Push?* (Heath, 1965).
30. John R. Hicks, "Economic Foundations of Wage Policy," *Economic Journal,* vol. 65 (September 1955), pp. 389–404.

tiation at any one time. In subsequent periods, those who fell behind
begin to catch up, even though inflation may have subsided or a recession
may be under way. Thus one way to view cost-push is simply as a lagged
process, in which the lags are quite long.

From a public policy viewpoint, the implication of the lagged interpretation of cost-push is that inflation fighting through demand restraint will
be a painful process. In the labor market in particular, at any time some
wage setters are reacting to past conditions. Changing current conditions
will have only limited influence on their decisions. For example, some
observers interpreted the Nixon administration's difficulty in slowing inflation in 1969–71 as being caused by wage catch-up for the inflation of
the earlier period.[31]

The cyclical view helps deal with the difficult question of whether collective bargaining causes inflation. Few would argue that collective bargaining and stable prices could not coexist under some circumstances;
they did so in the early 1960s. Few would argue that collective bargaining
caused the price inflation of the late 1960s, an inflation that can easily be
traced to traditional demand factors associated with the Vietnam buildup
and the Great Society domestic programs. The interesting question raised
by the cyclical view is not whether collective bargaining causes inflation,
but whether it contributes to the perpetuation of inflation.

Perhaps the distinction between causation and perpetuation is of interest only to economists trying to reconcile traditional theory with observed
fact. Does it really matter what the initial causes of inflation were in the
mid-1960s when that inflation remains in the 1970s? But the cyclical approach has value beyond such reconciliation. It helps interpret pressure
on wages in times of controls, formal or informal. For example, the Phase
II Pay Board provided exceptions to its general 5.5 percent standard for
catch-up pay raises in explicit recognition of labor-market lags.[32]

The cyclical approach also gives a further dimension to the old question of who benefits and who loses during periods of inflation. Once it is
recognized that different sectors of the labor market react differently to
economic circumstances, the issue of inflationary income redistribution
must be taken beyond the usual creditors versus debtors dichotomy. In
particular, evidence presented in chapters 2 and 3 suggests that the infla-

31. See Marvin Kosters, "Wages, Inflation and the Labor Market," in William
Fellner, ed., *Contemporary Economic Problems, 1976* (American Enterprise Institute for Public Policy Research, 1976), pp. 131–32.
32. Weber and Mitchell, *The Pay Board's Progress*, pp. 73–78.

tion and recession of the mid-1970s had a relative redistribution effect away from nonunion workers and toward union workers.

Patterns and Wage Imitation

Suppose unions are (misleadingly) viewed as firmlike monopolies that have a one-shot effect on wages when first formed and thereafter simply maintain a wage differential. Then the possibility of causal connection between collective bargaining and inflation is removed by assumption.[33] The addition of a cyclical reaction in wage determination suggests a lagged process, though one in which inflation could ultimately be dampened by the application of demand restraint. But the further addition of imitative wage behavior could lead to enduring inflation or even to accelerating inflation. Again, it all depends on what models are accepted, on what assumptions are made, and on the economic and other factors that impinge on wage determination. Some of the early commentators on wage imitation believed it to be a source of inflationary pressure; others were content to provide general descriptions.[34]

Even the most extreme critics of imitative wage behavior would be unlikely to claim that by itself such behavior would move a noninflationary economy into an inflationary phase. But some models of the process suggest that an inflationary spark from some other source might induce a wage reaction through wage imitation that would perpetuate or even accelerate inflation. A system in which units of wage determination judge their wage desires and status by what others are earning could easily be unstable. If unit A looks at B and observes an increase in B's wages, A will demand a comparable increase. If A obtains its comparable increase, this might stimulate a second round in the next period in unit B,

33. This type of argument, based on the union-as-monopoly view, can be found in Milton Friedman, "What Price Guideposts?" in George P. Shultz and Robert Z. Aliber, eds., *Guidelines, Informal Controls, and the Market Place* (University of Chicago Press, 1966), p. 22. Friedman argues that in the mid-1930s government policies strengthened both labor- and product-market monopoly power, causing cost-push inflation. But thereafter, he believes, no comparable episodes occurred.

34. Arthur M. Ross coined the phrase "orbits of coercive comparison" to describe the wage imitation phenomenon; *Trade Union Wage Policy* (University of California, Institute of Industrial Relations, 1948), p. 53. Ross can be classified as a friend of collective bargaining who simply described wage imitation. On the other hand, Charles E. Lindblom, who viewed collective bargaining as socially disruptive and inflationary, regarded wage imitation as part of the inflation problem; *Unions and Capitalism* (Yale University Press, 1949), pp. 87–89.

especially if B was initially trying to pull ahead of A. And so a mutual cycle, which could be accelerating, could be set up. After a few periods, the origins of the initial increase in B would be a matter of passing historical interest. The issue would then become one of breaking the cycle if the rate of wage increase was incompatible with price stability.

Wage imitation models can be analogous to the usual exposition of the wage-price spiral in which wages push up prices and prices pull up wages. The "wage-wage" model effectively adds a second spiral. But, as noted, the model can be embellished to provide not only self-perpetuating inflation but even self-accelerating inflation. Suppose wage comparisons are made on an absolute wage basis and initially both A and B are satisfied with their status relative to each other. Wage inflation can then continue at a constant rate in both units without provoking worker dissatisfaction. But if one unit decides to change its relative status and the other does not acquiesce, the model can become explosive. Unit A obtains a larger increase than in the previous round and determines to hold its advantage. Unit B then matches the increase in an attempt to catch up. Unit A requires a still larger increase in the next period to restore its newly acquired advantage. As the competition intensifies, wage inflation spirals upward. It has been argued that wage-wage processes produced just this result in the construction industry in the late 1960s and early 1970s, ultimately requiring sectoral wage controls to bring about agreement on relativities.[35] For the economy as a whole, however, it should be stressed that the mere fact that such models can be constructed does not prove their validity.

Although wage imitation might be viewed as inflationary—if models along the lines sketched above are accepted—it can also take a benign form. Inflationary views of wage imitation require interaction between bargaining units. That is, A watches B and B watches A. Alternatively, if A watches B but B does not watch A (or anyone who watches A), pattern bargaining simply implies that workers in unit A can be regarded as part of unit B. A settlement in unit A would have multiplier, or "ripple," effects extending to B, but no feedback effects.

Even if collective bargaining is the sole cause of this one-way imitation, all that can be said is that collective bargaining and unionization effectively reduce the number of wage-determination units in the economy. Such a reduction neither perpetuates nor accelerates inflation. However,

35. For an empirical exploration, see D. Q. Mills, "Explaining Pay Increases in Construction: 1953–1972," *Industrial Relations,* vol. 13 (May 1974), pp. 196–207.

it could be important to inflation fighting by controls or jawboning. If the "key" pattern-setting units can be identified, anything that affects the outcome of their wage determination process can be assumed to spread to other workers. The significance of this influence depends on the extent of the pattern. Statements by public officials have sometimes implied that pattern bargaining within the union sector provides an important handle for government anti-inflation efforts.[36]

It is also frequently said that the union sector is widely imitated in the nonunion sector, thereby extending the effective sphere of collective bargaining well beyond the unionized fourth of the labor force.[37]

Despite these assertions, there are many uncertainties concerning these influences. For example, suppose it is true that one key settlement has widespread influence on other settlements. First, are the outcomes of the key settlements themselves interrelated? That is, if a government anti-inflation policy could influence one settlement, would it influence all of them? And if there is public intervention in a wage settlement, will the imitators who normally follow it remain passive? For the nonunion sector, is the influence from the union sector significant beyond narrow industry or enterprise lines? Are bank employees—to take an example of an industry with little unionization—ultimately as strongly influenced by union settlements as, say, nonunion white-collar workers in the automobile industry? The implications for public policy depend on the answers.

Summary

For many reasons, the topic of collective bargaining remains controversial. The current system of industrial relations arose in the 1930s, a

36. See, for example, the statements of Barry Bosworth, director of the Council on Wage and Price Stability, in June 1978 about the assumed importance of the (then) upcoming Teamsters' negotiations, in Hobart Rowen, "Bosworth Says U.S. Fumbles Rail Talks," *Washington Post,* June 16, 1978.

37. For example, Dunlop argued that technical, professional, managerial, and clerical salaries in the late 1970s would largely follow the patterns set by "leading wage settlements." See his comments in a symposium on an earlier paper in *Industrial and Labor Relations,* vol. 31 (October 1977), p. 15. In a report on the inflation outlook the Council on Wage and Price Stability, though noting dissent in the literature, presented an equation "based on the premise that nonunion wages are a function of the unemployment rate and union wage increases." *A Quarterly Report of the Council on Wage and Price Stability with a Special Report on Inflation,* no. 13 (GPO, 1978), pp. 45–46.

period of great social ferment and change, and the views expressed about unions in public opinion polls and other forums are colored by forces other than unions' economic impact. But this does not mean that their economic impact should be ignored.

Economists have for many years been concerned about the possible inflationary effect of the wage-determination process. Views on this subject are diverse. The concern that is expressed usually focuses on the collective bargaining sector and has been reflected in such expressions of public policy as the wage-price guideposts of the Kennedy-Johnson years, the wage-price controls program of 1971–74, and the guidelines program of the Carter administration.

While many interesting questions about the impact of unionization might be posed, a study concerned with the interrelation between inflation and collective bargaining must address three major topics. The first is what relative wage effects may be attributed to unionization. Precise magnitudes are less important than whether union wages in general are above what employers would unilaterally determine, for unless there is some evidence of this, it is difficult to justify any discussion of collective bargaining as a source of inflation. The second topic is the response of union wages to economic conditions such as business-cycle developments and price inflation. If there are systematic differences in the wage responses of the union and nonunion sectors to these economic factors, a case can be made for examining the union response to see whether it is inflationary. Alternatively, if the union and nonunion sectors respond to economic circumstances in much the same fashion, it is difficult to argue that collective bargaining (as opposed to wage determination generally) plays a significant role in the inflation process.

Finally, the interconnection of wages through imitative processes and pattern following has been ascribed to the collective bargaining sector in the industrial relations literature. This type of phenomenon could have inflationary consequences or it could be harmless. Much depends on the model used to describe the process. Wage imitation can be benign if it involves a one-way causal flow in which patterns are set by key wage determiners that are not themselves influenced by wages in follower units. But if there is feedback, the system might perpetuate or even accelerate inflation.

II

The Institutional and Economic Background

WAGE DETERMINATION has often been of special concern to anti-inflation policy, and the collective bargaining sector typically has received disproportionate attention. Subsequent chapters will explore the three major issues identified in chapter 1: relative wage effects, cyclical wage effects, and wage imitation. However, before discussing them, some background on the collective bargaining sector and its main characteristics will be presented.

The Relative Size of the Union Sector

As shown in table 2-1, the Bureau of Labor Statistics reported a total union membership of 19.4 million in 1976. If the employee associations, which are primarily in the public sector and which prefer not to be called "unions," are included, the figure rises to 22.5 million. These membership estimates represented 24.5 percent and 28.3 percent of total employment in nonfarm establishments. The estimates would be somewhat higher if the membership figures included single-firm, unaffiliated unions and municipal associations. Since unionized workers tend to earn more than their nonunion counterparts, the proportion of payroll going to union workers is higher than the membership proportions suggest. But it is clear that the union sector, however defined, is a minority component of the labor force.[1]

1. Data on union and association membership are from U.S. Bureau of Labor Statistics press release, "Labor Union and Employee Association Membership—1976," USDL 77-771 (September 2, 1977). In 1974 there were 475,000 members of single-firm, unaffiliated unions and 235,000 members of municipal employee associations; BLS, *Directory of National Unions and Employee Associations, 1975,* bulletin 1937 (Government Printing Office, 1977), p. 63. The new employment cost index of the BLS suggests a payroll weight for the union sector in the private, nonfarm economy of about 35 percent (data supplied by the BLS).

Table 2-1. *Union Membership Trends, 1930–76*

Year	Total union membership, excluding Canada[a] (thousands)	Union membership as percent of labor force	Union membership as percent of nonfarm employment
	Unions		
1930	3,401	6.8	11.6
1940	8,717	15.5	26.9
1945	14,322	21.9	35.5
1950	14,267	22.3	31.5
1955	16,802	24.7	33.2
1960	17,049	23.6	31.4
1965	17,299	22.4	28.4
1970	19,381	22.6	27.3
1975	19,473	20.5	25.3
1976	19,432	20.1	24.5
	Unions and associations		
1970	21,348	24.7	30.0
1975	22,298	23.5	28.9
1976	22,463	23.2	28.3

Sources: Bureau of Labor Statistics press release, "Labor Union and Employee Association Membership—1976," USDL 77-771 (September 2, 1977); and *Handbook of Labor Statistics, 1975—Reference Edition*, bulletin 1865 (Government Printing Office, 1975), p. 389.

a. Includes membership in Canal Zone, Puerto Rico, and other areas (excluding Canada) and members of locals affiliated directly with the AFL-CIO. Excludes members of single-firm and local unaffiliated unions.

The degree of collective bargaining coverage varies considerably. In general, production workers are more likely to be covered than other types of employees. Men are more likely to be covered by union agreements than women. Durable manufacturing, transportation, public utilities, and coal mining are often considered the heartland of industrial unionization. Many construction workers are unionized. However, there are exceptions to these generalizations. Retail trade is often considered basically a nonunion sector, but in many cities food stores and department stores are unionized. The office machine and computer industry is part of durable manufacturing and yet is mostly nonunion.

There is a striking difference between the growth rate of union membership in the quarter century after the Korean War and the growth rate in the years before that conflict. Unionization peaked in the mid-1950s after a period of rapid growth that began in the 1930s. While some researchers have questioned the estimates of membership available from the Bureau of Labor Statistics, the shift from a period of growth to one of relative decline is apparent from any data source.[2]

For purposes of this study, the reasons for the shift are less important than the statistical fact. Academics have long debated the issue. It has been argued that white-collar workers are especially resistant to unionization and that unions have largely covered the organizable sector.[3] Many have cited changes in the composition of the labor force as being unfavorable to the spread of unionization.[4] Others have resisted this interpretation.[5] The growth of white-collar unionization in the public sector and its extent in some European countries could be cited as counterarguments. Unions have complained in recent years of sophisticated management techniques for impeding drives to organize nonunion workers. And the union "win rate" in representational elections held by the National Labor Relations Board has shown an unmistakable downward trend.[6]

The change in union growth patterns has two important consequences for statistical analysis. First, the basic pattern of unionization across industries was established thirty or forty years ago, or even earlier. Thus models of union wage effects which assume that unionization in the 1960s and 1970s reflected the choice of current workers are suspect. In general, the probability that an individual worker is or is not covered by a union contract is a function of the industry in which that worker is employed.

2. Other sources of estimates of union membership are discussed in Leo Troy, "Trade Union Membership, 1897–1962," *Review of Economics and Statistics*, vol. 47 (February 1965), pp. 93–113; C. E. Ferguson and William J. Stober, "Estimates of Union Membership from Reports Filed Under the Labor-Management Reporting and Disclosure Act," *Southern Economic Journal*, vol. 33 (October 1966), pp. 166–86; A. J. Thieblot, Jr., "An Analysis of Data on Union Membership," working paper 38 (Washington University, Center for the Study of American Business, 1978).

3. See C. Wright Mills, *White Collar: The American Middle Classes* (Oxford University Press, 1951), chap. 14, for a classic study of this resistance.

4. See Leo Troy, "Trade Union Growth in a Changing Economy," *Monthly Labor Review*, vol. 92 (September 1969), pp. 3–7; Marten S. Estey, "The Impact of Labor Force Changes on Labor Relations," *Annals of the American Academy of Political and Social Science*, vol. 333 (January 1961), pp. 1–4; and William J. Moore and Robert J. Newman, "On the Prospects for American Trade Union Growth: A Cross-Section Analysis," *Review of Economics and Statistics*, vol. 57 (November 1975), pp. 435–45.

5. An "anti-saturationist" viewpoint can be found in Irving Bernstein, "The Growth of American Unions, 1945–1960," *Labor History*, vol. 2 (Spring 1961), pp. 131–57.

6. Unions won 67.6 percent of NLRB elections in fiscal year 1955. By 1976 the figure had fallen to 48.1 percent. See National Labor Relations Board, *Annual Report, 1955* (GPO, 1956), table 13, p. 170; *Annual Report, 1976* (GPO, 1976), table 13, p. 236.

The attitudes of current workers toward unionization are likely to be dominated by events that occurred long ago.

Second, there are good reasons to confine statistical studies on the effects of collective bargaining to the period after the Korean War. It was then that unionization stabilized. Labor and management in already unionized industries could concentrate on developing their bilateral relationships. Moreover, the union movement itself stabilized. The rival AFL and CIO merged into a single organization and created machinery to settle disputes between competing unions over jurisdiction.[7] The aftershocks of the expulsion of certain left-wing unions from the CIO in the late 1940s had largely disappeared by the mid-1950s.[8] Also, the basic legal framework for regulating collective bargaining and labor-management relationships had been set out in the Wagner Act of 1935 and the Taft-Hartley Act of 1947. Although these laws have since been modified, there has been much greater continuity since the Korean War in legal regulation of labor-management relationships than before the war.[9]

The Collective Bargaining Agreement

The outcome of the collective bargaining process is a written agreement covering a specified time period. This agreement will cover not only wages and benefits—the aspects with which economists are generally concerned—but also a wide variety of other provisions. Most contracts contain provisions for the arbitration of grievances and contract interpretation.[10] These procedures represent a form of private jurisprudence generally supported by the formal legal system.[11]

7. For a discussion of this machinery, see David L. Cole, "The AFL-CIO's Internal Disputes Plan," *Monthly Labor Review,* vol. 92 (September 1969), pp. 12–15.

8. See F. S. O'Brien, "The Communist-Dominated Unions in the United States Since 1950," *Labor History,* vol. 9 (Spring 1968), pp. 184–209.

9. It would be wrong to suggest that the time since the Korean War has been one of tranquillity for the labor movement. Among the unsettling factors was the expulsion from the AFL-CIO of the Teamsters and other unions on charges of corruption in the 1950s.

10. A survey of 1,570 private agreements covering 1,000 or more workers in 1976 showed that 99 percent specified some form of grievance procedure and most provided for arbitration of grievances that could not be otherwise settled. See Bureau of Labor Statistics, *Characteristics of Major Collective Bargaining Agreements, July 1, 1976,* bulletin 2013 (GPO, 1979), table 8.1, p. 82.

11. See Paul Prasow and Edward Peters, *Arbitration and Collective Bargaining: Conflict Resolution in Labor Relations* (McGraw-Hill, 1970), chap. 13, for a dis-

Union contracts reflect the ongoing relationship between the employer and the employee. They define work rules, procedures to be followed in layoffs and promotions, safety standards, and so on. Union contracts are indicative of long-term relationships. They usually cover more than one year, a practice that has been assisted by the cost-of-living escalator clause, which allows the parties to deal with the uncertainties of inflation.[12] Besides the employer-employee relationship, union contracts will also specify aspects of the union-employer relationship. They often include, for example, such "union security" arrangements as the union shop (newly hired workers must join the union within a specified time) and the checkoff (union dues are deducted from paychecks and forwarded to the union by the employer).

The fact that union agreements imply long-term relationships is of special importance to the interpretation of cyclical union wage behavior. Evidence presented in chapter 4 suggests that fluctuations in real economic output are less strongly reflected in union wage changes than in nonunion wage changes. It is not surprising that parties to a long-term contract may ignore short-term economic changes.

Impasses

The Bureau of Labor Statistics has estimated that about 195,000 collective bargaining agreements were in effect in 1975. If it is assumed that contract duration averages two and a half years, roughly 80,000 contracts would expire annually. Yet in 1975 only 5,031 strikes were reported, and of these, only 2,688 arose from the renegotiation of contracts.[13] Despite the publicity that accompanies them, strikes are certainly not the automatic consequences of negotiations.

---

cussion of judicial policy toward arbitration. The NLRB's policy toward arbitration has also been supportive although it has wavered in how much the NLRB would defer to the decisions of private arbitrators where statutory rights are concerned. See Kenneth J. Simon-Rose, "Deferral Under *Collyer* by the NLRB of Section 8(a)(3) Cases," *Labor Law Journal*, vol. 27 (April 1976), pp. 201–16.

12. The survey of contracts cited above reveals a positive association of contract length and the presence of an escalator. Only 1 percent of the forty-five contracts with durations of twelve months or less had escalators; 53 percent of the contracts with durations of thirty-six months had such clauses. Bureau of Labor Statistics, *Characteristics of Major Collective Bargaining Agreements*, table 3.18, p. 40.

13. Bureau of Labor Statistics, *Directory, 1975*, p. 77; and BLS, *Analysis of Work Stoppages, 1975*, bulletin 1940 (GPO, 1977), p. 20.

On the other hand, the commonly cited statistics on the small fraction of work time lost to strikes can be misleading. In 1975, a light bargaining year, only 0.16 percent of work time was lost to work stoppages. About 88 percent of this total stemmed from stoppages in which renegotiations were involved. It is known that in 1975 about 2.5 million workers were covered by major contracts due to expire or reopen; this represents about 24 percent of the total number of workers covered by major agreements.[14] If similar proportions had prevailed for all other union workers, the total number of workers under all expiring contracts would have been roughly double the reported figure.[15] If potential workdays for these employees were 250 a year, the work time lost to stoppages was about 2 percent.[16] Thus the total annual time lost because of work stoppages for employers that are actually negotiating is small, but not as insignificant as the 0.16 percent estimate suggests. Perhaps of greater relevance is the fact that about one-fifth of the workers who might have been under contract expirations or reopenings did become involved in a work stoppage.[17]

Ultimately, it is the strike threat that gives weight to union demands. Without unions, of course, employers would be constrained by labor-market conditions and considerations of employee morale. It is conceivable that a union could influence employers' behavior by articulating these issues without threatening to strike. But unions have been more than mere articulators, especially in the private sector. Employers are aware of the potential costs of strikes, costs that may vary according to the individual employer's situation. These cost considerations influence employers' behavior.

Of course, strikes also impose costs on workers. Some unions maintain strike funds to defray these costs and change the perceived balance of

14. Lena W. Bolton, "Bargaining in 1975: Oil, Maritime, Postal Talks Top Light Agenda," *Monthly Labor Review*, vol. 97 (December 1974), p. 24.

15. Over 10 million workers were included in the major union sector from which the expiration estimate was taken. Roughly twice that number were reported to be union members.

16. Total expirations are estimated by multiplying known expirations (2.5 million workers) by the ratio of all union members to major-union members. Workdays for the total membership are estimated by multiplying membership by 250 days (50 weeks a year times 5 days a week). Workdays lost to renegotiation disputes were 27.3 million in 1975. Bureau of Labor Statistics, *Analysis of Work Stoppages, 1975*, table 9, p. 20.

17. About 1.1 million workers were involved in such strikes in 1975. The ratio method described in the previous footnote suggests that about 5 million workers were covered by expiring or reopening contracts. Ibid., p. 20.

power. However, strike benefits are typically much smaller than the earnings lost.[18] Only two states offer unemployment insurance benefits to "primary" strikers (those actively engaging in a strike as opposed to those indirectly made idle by it). Moreover, in some industries management has established "mutual assistance pacts" so that struck employers are aided by their nonstruck competitors, increasing their ability to withstand a prolonged strike.

Impasses therefore involve considerable costs to both sides if stoppages occur. This helps explain the trend toward long-term contracts. Multiyear agreements reduce the frequency of contract negotiations and thus the risk of impasses and stoppages. In many instances, the influence of stoppage costs far exceeds other considerations in reaching a settlement. The employment-wage trade-off emphasized by some economic models of union wage determination is far less perceptible and is likely to be dwarfed by strategic bargaining considerations and the costs that both parties can impose. Thus the importance of the strike threat as a bargaining weapon also helps explain why business cycles exert less pressure on union wages than on nonunion wages.

Bargaining and the Labor-Management Relationship

Public attention is focused on collective bargaining mainly at contract expiration time—the day-to-day interaction during the life of the contract goes unnoticed. Since wage and benefit changes are most often made during contract negotiations, it is the outcomes of the formal process of bargaining that are of greatest concern in this study.[19]

Bargaining practices vary considerably. Negotiations may be carried on at several levels simultaneously. The degree of participation of various interest groups on both the labor and management sides may also vary,

18. A 1972 survey revealed an average weekly benefit of $25. See Sheldon M. Kline, "Strike Benefits of National Unions," *Monthly Labor Review*, vol. 98 (March 1975), pp. 17–23.

19. Sometimes unscheduled wage and benefit changes may occur during the life of the contract as a result of arbitration decisions, changes in the nature of particular jobs, and so forth. Changes in earnings (as opposed to changes in wage rates or in benefit rates) may occur because of differing combinations of overtime and straight-time hours. Changes in average earnings may also be due to alterations in the demographic or skill mix of the work force.

even within a particular firm or unit.[20] In general, however, a common practice is for some kind of internal consultative arrangements to be established on both sides. These arrangements permit participation of low-level union and management officials in the formulation of bargaining positions.[21]

There have been numerous attempts by economists to model the bargaining process.[22] Although some of these studies were enlightening, the details of how bilateral bargaining produces a particular outcome remain elusive to economic theory. However, two important elements emerge from the literature. First, the fact that labor and management are tied in a long-term relationship makes collective bargaining different from the sort of bargaining involved in one-shot transactions. The buyer and the seller of a used car may never see each other after they negotiate. But in collective bargaining there are incentives to continue the relationship on a stable basis, as well as incentives to score points, create impressions, and establish precedents that will be useful in the future, even if they have no immediate value.

Second, while an overt exchange of information occurs during bargaining—that is, the parties formally state their positions—a more subtle exchange of information also takes place. Each side must try to discover the other side's final resistance point. Management needs to know at what point the union would be compelled to call a strike. Labor needs to know

20. For example, in the early 1960s contracts in the steel industry were negotiated through a special "Human Relations Committee" which bypassed preexisting structures. See David E. Feller, "The Steel Experience: Myth and Reality," in Industrial Relations Research Association, *Proceedings of the Twenty-first Annual Winter Meeting* (Madison, Wis.: IRRA, 1969), pp. 152–59. Political forces in the Steelworkers union led to a shift back to more formal arrangements. See Robert M. MacDonald, "Collective Bargaining in the Postwar Period," *Industrial and Labor Relations Review*, vol. 20 (July 1967), pp. 560–61.

21. Low-level union officials can be expected to represent membership priorities and preferences. See Edward E. Lawler III and and Edward Levin, "Union Officers' Perceptions of Members' Pay Preferences," *Industrial and Labor Relations Review*, vol. 21 (July 1968), pp. 509–17.

22. For example, Carl M. Stevens, "Regarding the Determinants of Union Wage Policy," *Review of Economics and Statistics*, vol. 35 (August 1953), pp. 221–28; J. Pen, *The Wage Rate Under Collective Bargaining* (Harvard University Press, 1959); Carl M. Stevens, *Strategy and Collective Bargaining Negotiation* (McGraw-Hill, 1963); Pao Lun Cheng, "Wage Negotiation and Bargaining Power," *Industrial and Labor Relations Review*, vol. 21 (January 1968), pp. 163–82; Bevars DuPre Mabry, "The Pure Theory of Bargaining," *Industrial and Labor Relations Review*, vol. 18 (July 1965), pp. 479–502; and Richard E. Walton and Robert B. McKersie, *A Behavorial Theory of Labor Negotiations* (McGraw-Hill, 1965).

at what point management would decide to accept a strike or even provoke one. Obviously such needs can lead to bluffing and false information.[23] But even with bluffing, both parties have an interest in avoiding a costly conflict and accidental impasses based on false information. The bargaining process is apt to be dominated by strategic considerations and estimates of conflict costs and of the propensity for conflict of the other party. These considerations obscure other economic circumstances and help explain the relative insensitivity of union-sector wages to real economic fluctuations.

Bargaining Structures

Collective bargaining practices vary in accordance with such factors as the historical development of unions within an industry (for example, craft versus industrial unions) and the economic characteristics of the industry. Sometimes groups of employers will bargain together as a unit. Examples can be found in industries characterized by small employers, such as trucking, longshoring, construction, and apparel. Small employers may group together because they believe they have more bargaining power as a united front. But unions in these industries also have an incentive to induce employers to group together so that they can coordinate their own wage policies. Multiemployer bargaining is also found in some industries with large employers, such as steel and railroads.[24]

Bargaining may also take place at the enterprise level. These arrangements are found in such industries as automobile manufacturing, farm machinery, and flat glass. Presumably, firm-level rather than industrywide bargaining can encompass a greater diversity of employer interests than

23. Empirical studies have suggested that different levels of bluffing take place during bargaining and that the final settlement is usually closer to the initial management offer than to the initial union demand. However, studies are available only for the public sector. Roger L. Bowlby and William R. Schriver, "Bluffing and the 'Split-the-Difference' Theory of Wage Bargaining," *Industrial and Labor Relations Review*, vol. 31 (January 1978), pp. 161–71; and Daniel S. Hamermesh, "Who 'Wins' in Wage Bargaining?" *Industrial and Labor Relations Review*, vol. 26 (July 1973), pp. 1146–49.

24. Such bargaining arrangements can change. For example, immediately after World War II, the rubber industry practiced multiemployer bargaining, but this practice soon ended. Robert A. Winters, "Aspects of Joint Bargaining in the Rubber Industry," *Industrial and Labor Relations Review*, vol. 3 (October 1949), pp. 3–16.

could be accommodated in a multiemployer framework.[25] But even in firm-level bargaining there can be a range of practices running from uniformity to diversity. The "big three" automobile firms sign contracts that are similar in outline. But smaller automobile companies (which now means only American Motors but in the past included other firms) have been permitted greater deviation from the pattern of the big three.

Collective bargaining may also take place at the plant level, and the degree of coordination between plants may vary. Such arrangements can be found in aerospace, cement, and chemicals.[26] But no matter what type of bargaining structure is followed, a certain amount of tension is inevitable. If bargaining is highly centralized, complaints of neglect of local interests may arise. In some cases, the economic incentive to "take wages out of competition" through centralized and coordinated bargaining may be compromised by local pressure. Therefore, unions that bargain at the firm or industry level often feel it necessary to allow their constituent local unions considerable autonomy.

In some industries, especially those in which unionization has had a long history, workers are organized by crafts. Prominent examples include construction, printing, and railroads.[27] In the construction industry especially, competition between craft unions has been cited as a cause of wage instability.[28] For that reason, a separate program of wage controls

25. Employers' perceptions of their communality of interests may change, leading to a switch from or to multiemployer bargaining. For example, in glassware and flat glass, multiemployer bargaining was replaced by firm-level bargaining. Trevor Bain, "Flat Glass: 'Industrial Peace' Revisited," *Industrial Relations,* vol. 8 (May 1969), pp. 259–68; Richard H. Slavin, "The 'Flint Glass Workers' Union' vs. the Glassware Industry: Union Management Policies in a Declining Industry," *Labor History,* vol. 5 (Winter 1964), pp. 29–39; and Gerald G. Somers, "Pressures on an Employers' Association in Collective Bargaining," *Industrial and Labor Relations Review,* vol. 6 (July 1953), pp. 557–69.

26. If there is more than one major union in an industry, plant-level bargaining may be encouraged. In aerospace, the Machinists and the Auto Workers are the major unions, and their attempts to coordinate bargaining efforts have not always been successful.

27. There have been some notable consolidations of craft unions in printing and railroads, especially as employment opportunities have declined. However, economic pressures for such consolidations may be resisted. Aaron W. Warner, "Technology and the Labor Force in the Offshore Maritime Industry," in Industrial Relations Research Association, *Proceedings of the Eighteenth Annual Winter Meeting* (IRRA, 1966), p. 139.

28. There is also evidence that the industry is more strike prone than others. This tendency appears even after standardization for a number of variables measuring union structure. Myron Roomkin, "Union Structure, Internal Control, and Strike Activity," *Industrial and Labor Relations Review,* vol. 29 (January 1976), pp. 198–217.

was developed for that industry during the 1971–74 controls period to deal with wage differences and imitation.

The wide variety of bargaining structures suggests that diverse wage outcomes may be expected in response to economic circumstances in different industries. These differences may show up in both short-run responses and long-term trends. The reader is therefore cautioned that generalizations about union versus nonunion wage determination cover a multitude of individual situations. Even if it is true that on the average union wages are rising faster than nonunion wages in a particular period or that union wages are higher than nonunion wages, there can be wide divergences from the average in individual units or industries.

Controls, Jawboning, and Guidelines

Much of what is usually described as "labor law" involves regulating the conduct of labor-management relations and collective bargaining rather than the outcomes of the process. For example, the National Labor Relations Board regulates such aspects of labor-management relations as the determination of bargaining representatives and the permissible range of tactics during negotiations. However, the federal government has periodically attempted to regulate or influence the outcomes of wage bargaining for anti-inflation purposes.

Since the 1930s there have been three episodes of legally sanctioned wage controls, all during military conflicts. There have also been attempts at informal "jawboning"—attempts to restrain wage settlements by presidential persuasion rather than by legal authority. During the Kennedy and Johnson administrations a numerical guidepost of 3.2 percent was propounded for wage increases by the Council of Economic Advisers. In early 1978 the Carter administration established a program of wage "deceleration" operated by the Council on Wage and Price Stability. This program was followed in October 1978 by a numerical guideline for wage increases of 7 percent.

Although all these efforts fall under the general heading of direct intervention, a wide spectrum of options for design and administration is represented. During World War II economic circumstances changed drastically. The federal government's share in the absorption of GNP rose from 5.7 percent in 1939 to 42.5 percent in 1944. At the same time, labor-force availability was strained by the rapid growth of the armed forces and the military draft. Controls were exercised over wages as part of a general effort to allocate employment resources and to avoid work stoppages as well as for anti-inflation purposes. In the national emergency, the public was willing to put up with bureaucratic directives and the inconveniences of formal and informal rationing. The two subsequent efforts at mandatory wage control—during the Korean and Vietnam conflicts—were considerably less elaborate in structure, in part because public toleration of inconvenience and disruption could not be relied upon to the same degree.[29]

Wage controls during the Korean War were directed mainly at fighting inflation. The more limited nature of the military effort made the need for direct allocation of resources less pressing. As a result, the wage control authorities were less likely to be concerned with nonwage issues, such as union security, and are remembered for their decisions about innovations in wage setting, such as deferred adjustments.[30]

Although the controls of both the Korean War and World War II relied on regulations and publicly announced criteria in evaluating wage increases, the Korean War controls generally were less involved in the details of each case. The authorities were more concerned about which of the various regulations fitted particular situations. After the Korean War controls expired in 1953, controls were not imposed again until 1971. The 1971–74 program contained aspects of both the regulatory and the case-by-case approach.

In the construction industry a case-by-case approach, which placed emphasis on local craft wage differentials, was followed. For other industries, a regulatory model was established based on a numerical guideline for wage increases of 5.5 percent. The other industries program went through a series of phases, but the incompatibility of the regulatory and

29. A brief discussion contrasting the three controls programs can be found in Milton Derber, "The Wage Stabilization Program in Historical Perspective," *Labor Law Journal,* vol. 23 (August 1972), pp. 453–62; and detailed discussion in Daniel Quinn Mills, *Government, Labor, and Inflation: Wage Stabilization in the United States* (University of Chicago Press, 1975). The distinction between World War II controls, with their allocative functions, and those of the Korean War is made in John Kenneth Galbraith, *A Theory of Price Control* (Harvard University Press, 1952), chap. 4.

30. During World War II the National War Labor Board played an important role in continuing the process of unionization that had begun in the 1930s. For example, see M. J. Fox, Jr., and Anita Jewel, "Maintenance of Membership and the Unionization of Gulf Coast Petroleum Refineries," *Labor Law Journal,* vol. 21 (April 1970), pp. 222–30; and William G. Caples, "Development and Problems of Bargaining Structure in the Steel Industry," in Arnold R. Weber, ed., *The Structure of Collective Bargaining: Problems and Perspectives* (Free Press, 1961), pp. 181–82.

the case-by-case approaches was never resolved.[31] While the design of direct intervention programs and the choice between the two options were partly a matter of administrative convenience and political constraints, they also reflected implicit models of the wage-determination system. In subsequent chapters, the discussion will return to these models.

Economic Background of the Post–Korean War Period

Since the Korean War the American economy has undergone widely varying levels of economic activity and rates of inflation. Tables 2-2 and 2-3 summarize the highlights of these changes in economic conditions. For convenience, the tables include two periods, 1953–58 and 1958–64, identified by Frank Pierson in his well-known study on the economic effects of collective bargaining through the mid-1960s.[32] Pierson viewed 1953–58 as a period of consolidation in the collective bargaining sector. The year 1953 marked the termination of the Korean War wage controls. Unlike the 1930s with their industrial relations turmoil or the 1940s with their total mobilization, the mid-1950s permitted the collective bargaining sector to operate relatively free of exogenous shocks from governmental intervention. Organized labor's newly developed muscle at the bargaining table could be flexed freely, at least in some industries. In contrast, 1958–64 seemed to some observers a period of management consolidation.

Obviously the selection of particular subperiods has an arbitrary quality. Economic events seldom flip on and off in discrete time intervals. Nevertheless, some time divisions can be illuminating. It seems reasonable to divide the years following the period covered by Pierson into two

31. For example, during Phase III of the controls beginning in early 1973, a committee was set up to stabilize wages in the food industry following the construction industry approach. However, the case volume implied by case-by-case processing and the inability of the labor and management representatives to agree on a common framework led to a grudging acceptance of the old Phase II rule with its numerical standard. See Albert Rees, "Tripartite Wage Stabilizing in the Food Industry," *Industrial Relations,* vol. 14 (May 1975), pp. 250–58; and William M. Vaughn III, "Wage Stabilization in the Food Industry," in John T. Dunlop and Kenneth J. Fedor, *The Lessons of Wage and Price Controls—The Food Sector* (Harvard University, Graduate School of Business Administration, 1977), pp. 145–94.

32. Frank C. Pierson, *Unions in Postwar America: An Economic Assessment* (Random House, 1967), pp. 39–51.

Table 2-2. *Annualized Rates of Change in Selected Indicators, 1953–76*
Percent

Period	Consumer price index	Compensation per hour[a]	Unit labor costs[a]	Output per hour[a]	Real compensation per hour[a]
1953–58	1.6	4.6	2.5	2.1	3.0
1958–64	1.2	4.1	0.9	3.2	2.9
1964–71	3.9	6.0	4.0	2.0	2.1
1964–68	2.9	5.6	2.8	2.8	2.6
1968–71	5.2	6.6	5.6	1.0	1.3
1971–76	7.1	8.3	6.7	1.5	1.1
1971–73	4.8	6.8	4.3	2.4	1.9
1973–76	8.6	9.3	8.3	0.9	0.6
1953–76	3.3	5.7	3.4	2.2	2.3

Sources: Calculated from data appearing in *Monthly Labor Review*, vol. 101 (April 1978), pp. 85, 100; and *Economic Report of the President, January 1978*, pp. 300, 313.
a. Nonfarm business sector.

Table 2-3. *Unemployment Rate for the Civilian Labor Force, 1953–76*
Percent

Year	Unemployment rate		Year	Unemployment rate	
	Civilian labor force	White males, aged 35–44		Civilian labor force	White males, aged 35–44
1953	2.9	1.8	1965	4.5	2.3
1954	5.5	3.6	1966	3.8	1.7
1955	4.4	2.6	1967	3.8	1.6
1956	4.1	2.2	1968	3.6	1.4
1957	4.3	2.5	1969	3.5	1.4
1958	6.8	4.4	1970	4.9	2.3
1959	5.5	3.2	1971	5.9	2.9
1960	5.5	3.3	1972	5.6	2.5
1961	6.7	4.0	1973	4.9	1.8
1962	5.5	3.1	1974	5.6	2.4
1963	5.7	2.9	1975	8.5	4.5
1964	5.2	2.5	1976	7.7	3.7

Sources: Bureau of Labor Statistics, *Handbook of Labor Statistics, 1975*, pp. 145, 153; and *Handbook of Labor Statistics, 1977*, bulletin 1966 (GPO, 1977), pp. 107, 115.

distinct eras. The years 1964–71 encompass the Vietnam buildup, the general stimulation of the economy that accompanied the military effort, and the recession that was later induced by restrictive demand policy to dampen the resultant inflation. While changes in aggregate demand and traditional economic policy can be invoked to explain economic trends during 1964–71, the next period selected—1971–76—was instead characterized by a series of exogenous shocks to the wage and price determination system. Mandatory wage-price controls were in effect during 1971–74. And the economy suffered from price pressures stemming from worldwide crop shortages and the crystallization of a foreign oil cartel.

In recent years, concern over inflation has become a dominant issue of economic policy. To an economist of the mid-1960s, this concentration would seem peculiar. Used to the Phillips curve, economists tended to view inflation and unemployment as closely linked, so that concern about one was the reverse of concern about the other. It was simply a matter of estimating the trade-off between the two evils. Thus Pierson could write in the mid-1960s: "If a rise in consumer prices in the range of 3 percent per annum and a level of unemployment in the range of 5 percent are deemed tolerable, government fiscal and monetary policies would probably not need to be supplemented by more explicit measures."[33] By the late 1970s the possibility of achieving either 3 percent inflation or 5 percent unemployment—even one at a time—seemed remote. While unemployment might still respond to traditional demand expansion or restraint, inflation apparently could be strongly influenced by forces outside the domestic economy.[34] And when related to domestic causes, inflation seemed beset with lags in adjustment to demand that bordered on self-perpetuation.

Two unemployment rates are shown in table 2-3 to indicate the wide labor-market fluctuations between 1953 and 1976. The overall civilian labor force unemployment rate covers all noninstitutionalized individuals aged sixteen and over. This is the rate usually reported in the press, the rate that receives the most public attention. However, it has been argued that changes in the demographic composition of the labor force have given the official rate an upward bias as a measure of labor-market pressure. Specifically, the growth in the proportion of young workers and females in the labor force has caused the unemployment rate to rise because these workers, for one thing, are less strongly attached to the

33. Ibid., p. 123.
34. For example, Popkin estimated that 3.7 points of the 8.2 percentage point rise in prices from the fourth quarter of 1972 to the fourth quarter of 1973 was the direct result of world commodity inflation. Joel Popkin, "Commodity Prices and the U.S. Price Level," *Brookings Papers on Economic Activity, 1:1974*, p. 256.

labor force than prime-age males.[35] Although the merits of this proposition cannot be discussed here, it is noteworthy that the more narrowly defined unemployment rate shown in table 2-3—that for white males thirty-five to forty-four years old—gives a similar picture of relative fluctuations in the tightness of the labor market. For example, both series indicate that 1975 represents the worst recession year of the period, with 1958, 1961, and 1954 coming in second, third, and fourth. On the other hand, the narrowly defined unemployment rate suggests a greater degree of upward pressure on wages in the late 1960s and again in 1973 relative to the mid-1950s than the official unemployment rate indicates. However, as noted in chapter 4, unemployment rates are sufficiently intercorrelated to make it difficult to distinguish their relative performance when used in statistical wage equations.

Since table 2-2 illustrates the wide range of inflation rates experienced during the various subperiods through 1976, it answers one question immediately. The system of collective bargaining was basically unaltered over the entire period shown. Yet inflation during one prolonged period, 1953–64, was less than 2 percent a year. Thus it is evident that collective bargaining is compatible with low rates of inflation. To put it more strongly, there is nothing in collective bargaining that prevents the existence of reasonable price stability. For this reason, the statement that collective bargaining is a primary cause of inflation must be rejected. However, the table by itself says nothing about the degree to which collective bargaining may influence the speed with which continuing inflation can be brought under control.

A second conclusion can be drawn from table 2-2. A broad measure of the rate of change in compensation for the nonfarm business sector is provided. Compensation per hour represents the total of all wages and fringe benefits paid (including legally required fringes such as social security taxes). When divided by output per hour, it produces a comprehensive measure of unit labor costs. And when divided by the consumer price index, it provides a measure of real wage gains. It is often said that productivity increases are the long-term basis for real wage gains and that over the long run prices behave as if they were markups over unit labor costs. These statements are supported by the table. Over the whole period

35. For a discussion of this point, see George L. Perry, "Changing Labor Markets and Inflation," *Brookings Papers on Economic Activity, 3:1970,* pp. 411–41; and Carolyn Shaw Bell, "The Economics of Might Have Been," *Monthly Labor Review,* vol. 97 (November 1974), pp. 40–42.

(1953–76) real compensation per hour rose 2.3 percent and productivity 2.2 percent a year. Consumer prices rose 3.3 percent and unit labor costs 3.4 percent a year.[36]

However, table 2-2 also shows that for shorter periods the relationships between wages, productivity, unit labor costs, and prices are quite loose. In some periods prices may rise faster than unit labor costs; in others, more slowly. And in some periods real wage gains might exceed productivity improvements; in others they might fall behind. The lack of a simple, short-run linkage between prices and labor costs is one of the chief problems in arranging "social compacts" between government and labor on inflation. Government cannot guarantee to union leaders that a slowdown in wages will automatically be accompanied by a price slowdown. Nor can it guarantee to business that a price slowdown will lead to an offsetting reduction in unit labor costs.

Divergent Sectoral Wage Trends

Table 2-2 is highly aggregative and thus obscures sectoral wage adjustments. Of particular interest for this study are relative wage movements in the union and nonunion sectors. Unfortunately, for the time period covered only limited data are available for analyzing these two sectors. If broad coverage of the labor market is desired, the only data source available on a detailed industry basis is average hourly earnings. Hourly earnings as reported by the Bureau of Labor Statistics do not include fringe benefits such as pension and health and welfare plans. Another deficiency is that earnings data are affected by changes in the mix of overtime and regular hours and of high- and low-paid workers. Finally, the Bureau of Labor Statistics does not separate union and nonunion establishments in presenting its earnings data. Nevertheless, the earnings data can be used to indicate general trends, especially when combined with other data

36. The two assertions in the text are closely related. Let Y = national income or product, P = a price deflator, W = hourly labor compensation, and H = hours worked. Let k = ratio of total labor compensation to national income, that is, $k = (WH)/Y$. If this expression is multiplied on both sides by Y and divided on both sides by P and by H, the result is $W/P = k(Y/P)/H$. And if k (labor's "share" of national income) remains relatively stable, the real wage, W/P, will be proportionate to productivity, $(Y/P)/H$. If both sides of the new expression are inverted and multiplied by W, then $P = U1/k)$, where $U = WH/(Y/P)$, or unit labor costs. Thus if k is relatively constant, P will behave as a markup over (move proportionately with) unit labor costs.

Table 2-4. Annualized Rates of Change in Average Hourly Earnings, by Measure of Unionization, Selected Industries, 1953–76

Percent

Period	Contract file		Compensation survey		Current population survey		
	Industries with above-average unionization rates	Industries with below-average unionization rates	Industries with above-average unionization rates	Industries with below-average unionization rates	Industries with above-average unionization rates	Industries with below-average unionization rates	All industries
1953–58	4.4	3.9	4.4	3.6	4.6	3.6	4.1
1958–64	3.3	3.2	3.1	3.3	3.3	3.3	3.2
1964–71	5.3	5.3	5.2	5.4	5.2	5.5	5.3
1964–68	4.4	4.6	4.2	5.0	4.2	5.0	4.6
1968–71	6.6	6.1	6.5	6.0	6.7	6.3	6.3
1971–76	8.5	7.2	8.0	7.2	8.3	7.1	7.7
1971–73	7.8	6.1	7.1	6.3	7.2	6.2	6.7
1973–76	9.0	8.0	8.7	7.8	9.0	7.7	8.4
1953–76	5.3	4.8	5.1	4.8	5.3	4.8	5.0
Addendum:							
Number of industries, 1958–76	34	59	49	39	34	35	93
Number of industries, 1953–58 and 1953–76	26	33	35	21	26	19	59

Sources: See appendix A. Definitions of and sources for the three measures of unionization—the contract file, the compensation survey, and the current population survey—are given in the text and footnotes 37–40.

sources. And data availability dictates the use of hourly earnings as the principal source of information.

Table 2-4 provides tabulations of annualized changes in hourly earnings for a group of ninety-three industries for periods beginning after 1958. (For periods beginning before 1958, data for fifty-nine industries are available.) Although the data cannot be broken down by union and nonunion establishment, individual industries can be identified as having relatively high or low proportions of unionized workers in total employment (relatively high or low unionization rates). The table divides the sample into industries with above-average and below-average unionization rates. This is as close as it is possible to come to a statistical distinction between the union and nonunion sectors for a broad range of industries over a long period of time in the private nonfarm economy.[37]

Detailed data on unionization by industry are not readily available. However, three sources of estimates were used to prepare table 2-4. These sources, along with the ninety-three-industry sample, will be used throughout the rest of this book. The first source, called the "contract file," is based on a computerized listing of "key and nonkey" collective bargaining agreements maintained by the Bureau of Labor Statistics. Key agreements are those covering 1,000 or more workers (not all of whom are necessarily union members). The BLS believes its file on these larger agreements is relatively complete. Also included are the nonkey listings for smaller agreements covering fewer than 1,000 employees. These files are not complete. However, data are available at the three-digit SIC level on workers known to be covered by union agreements, and these can be divided by employment in the industries to produce unionization rates. The unionization data used for the contract file portion of table 2-4 were drawn from a 1977 computer printout.[38]

Two other sources of data on unionization rates were drawn from a

37. Industries included in the sample are listed in appendix A by standard industrial classification (SIC) code. Earnings data for these industries are reported on a monthly basis in Bureau of Labor Statistics, *Employment and Earnings*, relevant volumes. The ninety-three industries represented about 65 percent of total payroll employment in the private nonfarm sector in 1976. However, the industry sample tends to underrepresent the service and trade sectors because of lack of historical data.

38. The printout was made available to the author by the Bureau of Labor Statistics. Union coverage data were divided by payroll employment in 1976 to produce unionization rates. The earlier date for the employment data was chosen since the BLS estimates of agreement coverage are entered at the time the contract is signed. Hence the coverage data are implicitly lagged.

study by Freeman and Medoff.[39] One of these series is based on a biennial survey of compensation conducted by the Bureau of Labor Statistics,[40] the primary purpose of which is to track trends in the wage and benefit expenditures of private employers at an aggregate level. (Only manufacturing and nonmanufacturing breakdowns are presented in official publications.) However, the computer tapes containing the survey provide a three-digit industry code designation for each establishment in the survey and indicate whether a majority of workers in the establishment were covered by a collective bargaining agreement. It is thus possible to identify establishments as union or nonunion and to compute industry unionization rates. The annual sample of establishments in any particular industry tends to be quite small. Freeman and Medoff partially compensate for the small industry samples by combining data for 1968, 1970, and 1972.

An alternative source of unionization used by Freeman and Medoff was the current population survey, which is the basic source of monthly data on such widely used economic indicators as the unemployment rate. The surveys for May include data on union membership of employed persons as well as on the industry of employment, using the three-digit census industry code. To broaden the sample, the authors combined the surveys for May 1973, 1974, and 1975 in calculating unionization rates. Note that the concept employed in the current population survey is union membership rather than contract coverage. Some union members may not be covered by union contracts and some nonmembers may be. Finally, it should be noted that data were available from the compensation survey for only eighty-eight of the ninety-three industries covered by table 2-4; the current population survey data covered only sixty-nine industries.

The data sources on unionization differ from each other by industry. They also differ from estimates of unionization at more aggregate industry levels used in earlier studies. Some of these differences are due to discrepancies in the concepts used and the periods covered. However, it must be recognized that each data source has its own drawbacks and that at the detailed industry level considerable inaccuracies are likely. By deriving estimates from all three sources, a test of the robustness of the propositions

39. Richard B. Freeman and James L. Medoff, "New Estimates of Private Sector Unionism in the United States," *Industrial and Labor Relations Review*, vol. 32 (January 1979), pp. 143–74.

40. Freeman and Medoff refer to this series as the EEC survey (expenditures for employee compensation survey); it is called "the compensation survey" throughout this book.

advanced in the text can be made that no single source could provide. Hence subsequent empirical estimates in this and later chapters will present the alternative results based on the three measures of unionization.

In table 2-4 the rate of change in average hourly earnings from each of the three data sources is shown for industries characterized by above-average and below-average unionization rates. The periods of estimation are the same as those in table 2-2. The figures, which are the simple averages of the earnings changes in each industry grouping, reveal considerable differences between the groupings. Particularly striking is the fact that over the entire period 1953–76 earnings in the heavily unionized sector (no matter how defined) rose noticeably faster than in the lightly unionized sector. Economic models of unionization often posit a one-shot union impact on wages with at most a cyclical variation after the initial effect. However, table 2-4 suggests that theories which predict or are based on a constant union-nonunion differential are suspect. It appears instead that a long-term trend toward a widening of the differential has been at work. Such a widening is hard to reconcile with the view that unions can be regarded as analogous to monopolies in standard price theory. Textbook monopolies hold prices above marginal cost, so a shift in an industry from competition to monopoly would produce a one-shot price-raising effect. Evidently the union-nonunion earnings differential has not behaved this way, and models of collective bargaining must be capable of encompassing trends.[41]

Table 2-5 highlights the trend shown in table 2-4 by presenting the data in real terms, that is, deflated by the consumer price index. Of special interest is the trend in real earnings during the last subperiod, 1971–76, when productivity growth was generally slower than in previous years. Yet though real earnings changes in both the heavily and lightly unionized sectors show a corresponding slowdown in growth, it is evident that the brunt of the slowdown in productivity was borne by the lightly unionized sector. It is therefore important to be cautious about accepting broad generalizations that the inflation of the 1970s and the productivity slowdown hurt labor. Average real wage growth did suffer during this period,

41. For an example of the union-as-monopoly view, see Milton Friedman, "What Price Guideposts?" in George P. Shultz and Robert Z. Aliber, eds., *Guidelines, Informal Controls, and the Market Place* (University of Chicago Press, 1966), pp. 21–22. It should be noted that the widening trend shown in table 2-4 could be due to factors correlated with unionization rather than to unionization itself. This issue is discussed in chapter 3.

Table 2-5. *Annual Percentage Change in Real Hourly Earnings, by Measure of Unionization, Selected Industries, 1953–76*

Percent

Period	Contract file		Compensation survey		Current population survey		All industries
	Industries with above-average unionization rates	Industries with below-average unionization rates	Industries with above-average unionization rates	Industries with below-average unionization rates	Industries with above-average unionization rates	Industries with below-average unionization rates	
1953–58	2.8	2.2	2.8	2.0	3.0	2.0	2.5
1958–64	2.1	2.0	1.9	2.1	2.1	2.1	2.1
1964–71	1.4	1.3	1.2	1.5	1.3	1.6	1.4
1971–76	1.3	0.2	0.9	0.2	1.1	0.1	0.6
1953–76	1.9	1.4	1.7	1.4	1.9	1.4	1.6

Sources: Same as table 2-4.

but the heavily unionized sector appeared to be more insulated from the adverse trend than the lightly unionized sector.[42]

According to table 2-4, 1953–58 exhibited a marked widening of the gap between earnings in the heavily and lightly unionized sectors. When unionization is taken from the current population survey data, the widening is about 1 percentage point a year. When the contract file is used, the estimate is about 0.5 percentage point. In contrast, data for the next period, 1958–64, suggest that the gap remained constant. There is some support in the industrial relations literature analyzing this period for the notion of a consolidation of union bargaining power in the first period followed by a hardening of management's stance in subsequent years.

1953–58 and 1958–64

After the Korean conflict ended, the economy was sluggish. There was general uncertainty about the economic outlook. Inflationary expectations, which seem so ingrained in the 1970s, largely did not exist. This is not surprising in view of the relative price stability that accompanied price controls after 1951. Moreover, many people in the mid-1950s remembered the depression and the major decline in prices of the early 1930s. Over half of the respondents to a national survey indicated in June 1954 that they expected the price level five years in the future to be the same or lower.[43]

On the wage side, the possibility of actual wage cuts seemed real. The director of the Federal Mediation and Conciliation Service earnestly advised the parties on the need for adding contractual devices to their agreements that could be used to cut wages if necessary.[44] There were indeed wage cuts in some industries, especially in textiles, where military demands had led to excessive peacetime capacity. And in textiles, shoes, and apparel, production was gradually moving south, accompanied by considerable discussion of the problems of "runaway" shops.[45] Low-wage

42. As noted, the hourly earnings data omit fringe benefits such as pension and health and welfare plans, which are associated with unionization. Had it been possible to include these benefits in table 2-4, the gap between compensation trends in the two sectors would have been widened.

43. See George Katona and Eva Mueller, *Consumer Expectations: 1953–1956* (University of Michigan, Survey Research Center, 1956), p. 37.

44. See "The Cole Wage-Reduction Proposal," *Labor Law Journal*, vol. 4 (March 1953), p. 165.

45. In some instances, apparel unions attempted to resist the southward movement by providing financial assistance to ailing northern firms. "The Labor Month in Review," *Monthly Labor Review*, vol. 77 (August 1954), p. III.

competition from the South began to undermine northern union wage scales. Import competition in labor-intensive industries was also beginning to be felt.

Despite the deflationary climate, some industries were able to raise wages and prices. As noted, the industries that exhibited the fastest rates of earnings increases were in general more highly unionized than others. Not surprisingly, the economics literature soon began to debate the question of "administered" price and wage setting and "cost-push" inflation.[46]

The literature does contain elements that support the view that the period immediately after the Korean War was one of consolidation of union bargaining power. The major automobile producers appeared to have trouble coordinating their bargaining strategies. Significant concessions were obtained by the Auto Workers, especially in fringe benefits.[47] There was also much discussion of steel price and wage determination as a result of the mid-1950s experience. One author argues that steel prices were artificially depressed by the price controls that ended in 1953. Thereafter, the oligopolistic industry used bargained wage increases as a coordinated signal for price increases. According to this view, workers and employers could thus engage (for a time) in a mutually beneficial interaction.[48]

There is also casual evidence that management's attitude hardened in 1958–64.[49] Greater cooperation existed between the large automobile

46. For example, see Richard T. Selden, "Cost-Push versus Demand-Pull Inflation, 1955–57," *Journal of Political Economy*, vol. 67 (February 1959), pp. 1–20. A review of this literature can be found in Martin Bronfenbrenner and Franklyn D. Holzman, "Survey of Inflation Theory," *American Economic Review*, vol. 53 (September 1963), pp. 593–661.

47. In 1953 the union persuaded General Motors to reopen its five-year agreement (with two years yet to run) on the grounds that a contract should be a "living document." The other firms soon followed. In 1955 the UAW made a breakthrough in obtaining supplemental unemployment benefits from Ford after an attempt at management coordination had failed. Generally, the union perfected its strategy of choosing one of the big three firms as the target, making the target company vulnerable during a strike to loss of sales to its competitors. Also, union members at the other firms would remain employed and able to support the strike financially. See Joseph P. Goldberg, "A Review of American Labor in 1953," *Monthly Labor Review*, vol. 77 (February 1954), p. 123; and William H. McPherson, "Cooperation Among Auto Managements in Collective Bargaining," *Labor Law Journal*, vol. 11 (July 1960), pp. 607–14.

48. This interpretation can be found in M. A. Adelman, "Steel, Administered Prices and Inflation," *Quarterly Journal of Economics*, vol. 75 (February 1961), pp. 16–40.

49. See Herbert R. Northrup, "Management's 'New Look' in Labor Relations," *Industrial Relations*, vol. 1 (October 1961), pp. 9–24.

companies than in the earlier period. A major strike took place in the steel industry, which has been attributed by some observers to increased management resistance to further wage gains.[50] "Featherbedding" on the railroads became an important area of contention between labor and management, ultimately involving a presidential commission and the Congress.[51] In several industries, including railroads, rubber, airlines, and printing, management developed "mutual assistance pacts" and "strike insurance" arrangements whereby struck firms would receive financial or other assistance from their nonstruck competitors.[52] Finally, the development of a system of wage-price guideposts by the Kennedy and Johnson administrations may have increased management resistance to union wage demands in some industries.[53]

50. According to the Adelman hypothesis cited above, once the industry attained its optimal price level, the mutually beneficial interaction between labor and management came to an end. And the recession of the late 1950s and greater import competition encouraged management to take a tougher position.

51. The railroad firemen became the symbol of management's efforts to alter work rules, although other jobs and rules were also in contention. Morris A. Horowitz, "The Diesel Firemen Issue on the Railroads," *Industrial and Labor Relations Review,* vol. 13 (July 1960), pp. 550–58; Philip Arnow, "Findings of the Presidential Railroad Commission," *Labor Law Journal,* vol. 14 (August 1963), pp. 677–85; and Marvin J. Levine, "The Railroad Crew Size Controversy Revisited," *Labor Law Journal,* vol. 20 (June 1969), pp. 373–86. Under a 1972 agreement, firemen were retained for passenger and yard service and as trainees for the position of engineer.

52. The airline pact has probably received the widest publicity because its operation had to be approved by the Civil Aeronautics Board. Unions protested its operation to the board repeatedly. In 1978 they achieved their goal of drastically limiting the allowable scope of such pacts in the airline industry through congressional action. On the airline experience, see Vernon B. Briggs, Jr., "The Mutual Aid Pact of the Airline Industry," *Industrial and Labor Relations Review,* vol. 19 (October 1965), pp. 3–20; and Marvin J. Levine and L. W. Helly, "The Airlines' Mutual Aid Pact: A Deterrent to Collective Bargaining," *Labor Law Journal,* vol. 28 (January 1977), pp. 44–55. More general discussion of such pacts can be found in John S. Hirsch, Jr., "Strike Insurance and Collective Bargaining," *Industrial and Labor Relations Review,* vol. 22 (April 1969), pp. 399–415; and Sam Marshall, "Curbing Mutual Aid Pacts," *American Federationist,* vol. 86 (February 1979), pp. 9–12.

53. The guideposts are discussed in John Sheahan, *The Wage-Price Guideposts* (Brookings Institution, 1967). Some econometric work has indicated that a depressing effect on wage increases was in evidence during the guidepost period. See George L. Perry, "Wages and the Guideposts," *American Economic Review,* vol. 57 (September 1967), pp. 897–904; and the comments on Perry's paper in *AER,* vol. 59 (June 1969), pp. 351–70. However, industrial relations experts were skeptical that any actual influence had been felt. See John T. Dunlop, "Guideposts, Wages, and Collective Bargaining," and Frederick R. Livingston, "Comments," in Shultz and Aliber, *Guidelines,* pp. 84, 261.

1964–71 and 1971–76

Table 2-4 indicates that in 1964–68 earnings in the lightly unionized sector rose more rapidly than in the heavily unionized sector. In 1968–71 a reversal of this tendency occurred; earnings in both sectors accelerated but those in heavily unionized industries showed a relative gain. When the unionization rate used to dichotomize the ninety-three industries represented in table 2-4 is based on the contract file, the earnings of the heavily unionized sector appear to have kept up with the earnings of the lightly unionized sector over the entire 1964–71 period. But data based on the other two measures of unionization suggest that as of 1971 heavily unionized earnings were still somewhat "behind." Nevertheless, the most interesting question raised by the table is what caused the change in the relative pace of earnings growth in the two sectors. Why did earnings in the heavily unionized sector first slip relative to those of the lightly unionized sector and then speed up?

One important economic factor to affect wage determination in the mid-1960s was an acceleration in the rate of price inflation. Another factor was the increase in real demand pressure that accompanied the military buildup in Vietnam and the expansion of Great Society domestic programs. Monetary and fiscal policy became more expansionary. A number of empirical studies have suggested that union and nonunion wages react differently to changes in economic conditions.[54]

The demand pressures that built up in the mid-1960s could be expected to have a greater effect on nonunion wages than on union wages. There is considerable evidence (see the next chapter) that unionization is associated with higher wages, even after standardizing for other wage-raising characteristics. If union wages are above the levels employers would unilaterally set, it can be assumed that there is generally a queue of workers awaiting vacancies and that incumbent workers are reluctant to quit their jobs since comparable opportunities would be hard to find.[55]

54. Evidence on these different reactions will be developed more fully in chapter 4. For other studies, see Michael L. Wachter, "Cyclical Variations in the Interindustry Wage Structure," *American Economic Review*, vol. 60 (March 1970), pp. 75–84; and Adrian W. Throop, "The Union-Nonunion Wage Differential and Cost-Push Inflation," *American Economic Review*, vol. 58 (March 1968), pp. 79–99.

55. Modern theories of the labor market suggest that employers make a trade-off between turnover and payroll costs in setting wage levels. Employers for whom turnover costs are high will pay higher wages than employers for whom such costs are low. The higher the wage for a given job, the lower the expected rate of turnover

Thus a modest decrease in the number of job seekers and a modest increase in the number of job opportunities throughout the economy would have little effect on union wages. Unionized employers would see a shortening of the queue for vacancies but no serious labor shortages. In contrast, nonunion employers would find that their unilaterally determined wage levels were associated with excessive turnover and recruitment difficulties. Hence they would be more sensitive to labor-market pressure and more likely to raise wages as demand increased.

The union sector is also characterized by long-term contractual arrangements, which inhibit quick adaptation to changed economic circumstances. Nonunion employers can make wage changes at their discretion, another factor influencing the relative responsiveness of wages to demand pressure in the two sectors. But some unions have escalator clauses that do permit wages to respond to price inflation, and the wages of some union workers were increased during the life of their contracts as a by-product of the price inflation that rising demand pressure created. However, because prices were relatively stable after the mid-1950s, the popularity of escalator clauses diminished. In some unionized industries, such as steel, metal cans, and railroads, escalator clauses were dropped from contracts. Other industries, such as tires, telephone communications, and coal mining, had never had such clauses. Even where escalator clauses do exist, they have generally provided less than full protection against inflation.[56] Their basic formulas are often not generous enough to protect the real wage fully, and they are sometimes subject to "caps" and "corridors," which further limit the payout.[57] Artful negotiators can play an

---

(and associated turnover costs) will be. For a review of this literature, see Daniel J. B. Mitchell and Ross E. Azevedo, *Wage-Price Controls and Labor Market Distortions* (UCLA Institute of Industrial Relations, 1976), pp. 33–53.

56. This fact has not always been appreciated by economists. For example, Kareken implicitly treats the existence of escalators as equivalent to perfect inflation expectations. See John H. Kareken, "Inflation: An Extreme View," *Federal Reserve Bank of Minneapolis Quarterly Review*, vol. 2 (Winter 1978), p. 12.

57. The basic formula generally specifies a flat cents-per-hour increase per increment in the consumer price index (for example, 1 cent for each 0.3 index point increase). The actual payout will therefore depend on the base year chosen for the index by the parties (if index points are used) and whether the formula is based on index point increments or percentage point increases. (One cent for each 0.3 index point is more generous than 1 cent for each 0.3 percentage point increase whenever the consumer price index is greater than 100.) A cap is an absolute limit on the amount payable by the escalator, regardless of the basic formula. A corridor is a provision stipulating that a certain amount of inflation must occur before payout begins.

astounding variety of games with escalators so that union leaders can claim victory in obtaining such clauses while management limits the risks of tying wages to uncertain future price developments.[58] In the mid-1960s the degree of escalation in the union sector was insufficient to keep union wages rising at the same pace as nonunion wages.

As inflation continued in the late 1960s, earnings in the heavily unionized industries began to increase faster than those in the lightly unionized industries. This was partly due to the "realization" by collective bargaining negotiators that inflation was likely to be higher in the future than they had anticipated. It also represented pressure from union negotiators to catch up with the unanticipated inflation that had occurred during the life of contracts expiring in the late 1960s. Finally, government demand policy pushed the economy into a recession in 1970–71 to combat inflation. Nonunion wages could have been expected to be more sensitive to the increase in economic slack than union wages in the early 1970s, just as they were more sensitive to the decrease in slack in the mid-1960s.

The realization that inflation would be a continuing problem led to union demands for expanded escalator protection, which continued throughout the 1970s. Escalators were installed for the first time in the telephone (1971), coal (1974), and tire (1976) industries. Where escalators had previously existed, unions demanded improved formulas and the removal of escalator limitations.[59]

In general, inflation seemed to heighten tension in industrial relations.

58. In industries such as construction where advance bidding is common, employers have a special need to know in advance what their wage costs will be, so escalator clauses are rare. An example of an artful escalator in the manufacturing sector is the 1976 contract between the Electrical Workers (IUE) and General Electric. Wages were to rise 1 cent for each 0.3 percentage point (not index point) increase in the consumer price index up to a limit of 7 percent price inflation. If the inflation rate rose above 9 percent, the formula would resume paying off. But no credit would be given for the corridor between 7 and 9 percent inflation. "Wage Highlights," *Current Wage Developments,* vol. 28 (July 1976), p. 1.

59. For example, in the aerospace industry a cap on the escalator clause led to an accumulation of what the unions regarded as unpaid escalator money when contracts expired in 1971. In a partially face-saving move, the Auto Workers had succeeded in obtaining a pledge from one of the companies that this "missing" money would be part of the 1971 offer. Since the offer was bound to be greater than the unpaid escalator money, the pledge had little economic meaning. But it turned out to have substantial legal meaning and ultimately led to the overturning by a federal court of a Pay Board decision cutting back the 1971 aerospace contracts. See Arnold R. Weber and Daniel J. B. Mitchell, *The Pay Board's Progress: Wage Controls in Phase II* (Brookings Institution, 1978), pp. 250–51.

Table 2-6. *Work Stoppages, 1961–76*

Year	Number of complete stoppages (1)	Days idle as percent of work time (2)	Number of stoppages arising from wage and benefit issues[a] (3)	Number of stoppages arising from issues other than wages and benefits[b] (4)	Number of stoppages arising from contract renegotiations (5)
1961	3,367	0.11	1,690	1,677	1,517
1962	3,614	0.13	1,858	1,756	1,747
1963	3,362	0.11	1,605	1,757	1,459
1964	3,655	0.15	1,761	1,894	1,613
1965	3,963	0.15	1,983	1,980	1,802
1966	4,405	0.15	2,297	2,108	1,942
1967	4,595	0.25	2,480	2,115	2,157
1968	5,045	0.28	2,980	2,065	2,667
1969	5,700	0.24	3,287	2,413	2,770
1970	5,716	0.37	3,239	2,477	2,916
1971	5,138	0.26	2,920	2,218	2,635
1972	5,010	0.15	2,456	2,554	2,179
1973	5,353	0.14	2,936	2,417	2,717
1974	6,074	0.24	3,960	2,114	3,593
1975	5,031	0.16	2,880	2,151	2,688
1976	5,648	0.19	3,200	2,448	3,075

Source: Bureau of Labor Statistics, *Analysis of Work Stoppages*, various issues, 1962–77.
a. Includes "other contractual matters."
b. Includes union organization and security, job security, plant administration, other working conditions, inter- or intra-union matters, and not reported.

The literature began to include discussion of an alleged increase in rejections by the rank and file of contracts that union leaders had negotiated. Interpretations of the available data differed, however.[60] It is clear that the frequency of strikes rose in the late 1960s and remained high thereafter. Table 2-6 summarizes data on strike frequency during the period 1961–76. Both the frequency measure (number of strikes) and days idle

60. William E. Simkin, "Refusals to Ratify Contracts," *Industrial and Labor Relations Review*, vol. 21 (July 1968), pp. 518–40; Donald R. Burke and Lester Rubin, "Is Contract Rejection a Major Bargaining Problem?" *Industrial and Labor Relations Review*, vol. 26 (January 1973), pp. 820–33 (comments appear in the April 1975 issue). It has been suggested that the rejection rate is influenced by the business cycle and that the tightening of the labor market in the mid-1960s caused the rate to increase. See Charles A. Odewahn and Joseph Krislov, "The Relationship Between Union Contract Rejections and the Business Cycle—A Theoretical Approach," *Nebraska Journal of Economics and Business*, vol. 12 (Summer 1973), pp. 23–35.

as a percentage of total work time show evidence of an increase in industrial unrest.[61]

Again, the data lend themselves to various interpretations. Unrest developed in several sectors of society during the late 1960s (college campuses, inner city neighborhoods), and some of it may have spilled into the industrial relations system. Young people entered the labor force in large numbers, which could have contributed to the propensity to strike or reject contracts.[62] Inflation clearly provoked tension in some cases, but it is impossible to estimate its overall effect or to distinguish that influence from others.

During 1971–76 the gap between the earnings of the heavily and lightly unionized sectors continued to widen. In some cases in the early 1970s, pressure to catch up with inflation from the late 1960s remained. For example, in the West Coast longshore case decided by the Pay Board in 1972, catch-up accounted in part for the large wage increase requested. West Coast longshoremen had worked under an exceptionally long five-year agreement negotiated in 1966, which contained no escalator clause. Their next contract was delayed by a strike and Taft-Hartley injunction.[63] But catch-up pressure does not completely explain the 1971–76 period. The differences between rates of earnings growth in those years are simply too large, no matter which of the three measures of unionization of table 2-4 is used. Rather than catch-up, the figures suggest resumption of a relative trend in the two sectors.

Of course, 1971–76 saw some unusual events. Mandatory wage and price controls were in effect in 1971–74 and could have had different effects on the heavily and lightly unionized sectors. Controls expired in early 1974, giving the nonunion sector a chance to catch up from any wage lag

61. Work time is sensitive to the number of workers under expiring contracts, a number that can vary substantially from year to year.

62. It was estimated that, in 1970, 35 percent of the members of the Steelworkers union were under the age of thirty and that the union's turnover rate was one-third of the membership every two years. John L. Gurney, "Union Conventions: United Steelworkers of America," *Monthly Labor Review*, vol. 93 (December 1970), p. 33. However, the strike record in the steel industry was good (low) throughout the period covered by table 2-6. There were no major national strikes after the protracted work stoppage in 1959. Youth and turnover do not automatically create a stormy strike picture.

63. Under the Taft-Hartley Act of 1947, the President can obtain injunctions in national emergency disputes providing for an eighty-day cooling-off period. For details of the West Coast longshore case, see Weber and Mitchell, *The Pay Board's Progress*, pp. 182–91.

it may have suffered. And available evidence suggests a continuation of the differing trends even after 1976.[64]

In the latter part of the 1971–76 period, economic circumstances were favorable for a relative gain in earnings in the heavily unionized sector. A severe recession occurred, a development more likely to retard wage growth in nonunion establishments than in union establishments. At the same time, price inflation reached new heights. The popularity of escalator clauses had increased in the union sector, so that the wages of a greater fraction of the unionized work force under existing contracts were mechanically linked to prices. Although price inflation influences both union and nonunion workers, including those without mechanical escalators, there is some evidence to suggest that wage setting in the union sector is more price sensitive than in the nonunion sector (see chapter 4).

Divergent Industry Wage Trends

The preceding discussion of general trends in two sectors of the economy may hide the underlying diversity of earnings adjustments in particular industries. To illustrate this diversity, table 2-7 presents the earnings growth experience of thirteen of the industries used for table 2-4.[65] The industries were selected because of the publicity surrounding their negotiated wage changes or because of unusual wage performance.[66]

64. During the twelve months ending December 1977, union wage rates rose 7.6 percent and nonunion rates rose 6.6 percent, according to the employment cost index. In 1978 the comparable figures were 8.0 percent and 7.6 percent. Even the narrowing of the gap in relative advances in 1978 is misleading, however. The employment cost index includes a wider category of occupations than the earnings data of table 2-4 and is distorted by high commissions paid in 1978 to (nonunion) stockbrokers, who had experienced a big increase in sales volume. See Bureau of Labor Statistics press release, "Employment Cost Index—December 1978," USDL 79-147 (February 28, 1979); and "Employment Cost Index Shows Wages and Salaries Rose 1.7 Percent in Fourth Quarter, 1977," *Current Wage Developments,* vol. 30 (April 1978), pp. 66–67.

65. As indicated in table 2-7, earnings data were not available before 1958 for trucking, which was therefore excluded from calculations for the period before 1958 in tables 2-4 and 2-5. For illustrative purposes, however, an estimate of hourly earnings in 1953 for trucking has been included in table 2-7.

66. All but two—meatpacking and electrical equipment—of the industries shown in table 2-7 are included in the heavily unionized sector when the contract file is used to estimate unionization rates. However, the two exceptions appear in the heavily unionized sector when the compensation survey or the current population survey is used.

Table 2-7. *Annualized Rates of Change in Hourly Earnings, Selected Industries, 1953–76*

Percent

Industry	1953–58	1958–64	1964–71	1971–76	1953–76
Cement	5.6	4.0	6.8	9.3	6.4
Tobacco	4.9	3.5	7.1	9.2	6.1
Telephones	4.1	4.2	4.7	12.3	6.0
Building construction	4.2	3.9	7.0	6.4	5.4
Trucking	4.5[a]	4.2	5.6	8.2	5.6[a]
Steel	5.7	2.6	4.2	11.3	5.6
Motor vehicles	3.6	3.9	5.7	8.5	5.4
Bituminous coal	4.1	2.0	5.7	10.2	5.3
Railroads	5.4	2.3	6.5	9.6	5.8
Meatpacking	5.1	3.0	4.8	7.4	5.0
Tires	4.1	3.8	4.3	6.7	4.7
Electrical equipment	4.0	2.9	4.8	7.1	4.6
Men's and boys' suits	2.5	3.3	5.5	6.5	4.5
All industries[b]	4.2	3.2	5.6	7.4	5.0

Source: Appendix A.

a. Earnings not available before 1958. Estimate for 1953 based on a regression of hourly earnings against an index of wage rates for union drivers and helpers and time estimated over 1958–76. The estimate for 1953 was obtained by adjusting the constant so that the 1958 estimate was equal to the actual figure.

b. Based on hourly-earnings index for the private nonfarm sector adjusted for overtime in manufacturing and shifts in interindustry employment.

It is important to make a distinction between industry hourly earnings data and collectively bargained wage rates. First, earnings differ from rates, since they reflect changes in work force composition and the percentage of overtime hours in total hours. Second, some nonunion wages are represented in most of the industries. Third, the industries, as defined by the standard industrial classification code, do not correspond to actual bargaining units. In some cases, bargaining units cross industry lines or do not encompass all components of an industry.[67]

Table 2-7 shows that, while earnings movements are generally correlated, a considerable dispersion in rates of change is normally observed,

67. For example, the contract with Western Electric is linked to the agreements in the telephone communications industry (SIC 481), but Western Electric workers appear under electrical equipment (SIC 36). Motor vehicles (SIC 371) encompasses more than just automobiles and the big three companies' contracts with the Auto Workers, but workers for the big three may be employed in such industries as electrical equipment (SIC 36) or steel (SIC 331). Chapter 4 presents some empirical evidence based on contract wage rates rather than industry earnings.

even over long periods. While earnings in all private nonfarm industries rose at an average annual rate of 5.0 percent during 1953–76, the rate of growth for the particular industries shown in the table ranged from 4.5 percent to 6.4 percent. These differences in growth rates may appear small at first glance, but they can represent substantial shifts in relative earnings status when compounded over a twenty-three-year period. For example, an industry that experiences an average earnings gain 0.5 percentage point above the average for all industries for twenty-three years will raise its relative earnings status by over 12 percent.

Two industries, tobacco manufacturing and cement, show larger gains in hourly earnings than the all-industry average in each of the subperiods presented in table 2-7. This record may be surprising to some readers because of the general obscurity of these industries in the industrial relations literature. Earnings growth in tobacco is centered in the industry's cigarette component, which is highly concentrated. Although the union involved during the period shown, the Tobacco Workers, was not able to unionize one major producer (Reynolds), it has apparently been able to take advantage of the oligopolistic structure of the industry, despite modest productivity gains. In the cement industry, measured industrial concentration at the national level is low. But this index obscures the regional concentration of a product with high transportation costs. Productivity gains have been relatively rapid. And despite some attempts at management coordination, the major union—the Cement, Lime, and Gypsum Workers—has reportedly used whipsaw tactics successfully.[68]

Earnings in telephone communications for 1953–76 show an average annual 1 percentage point gain relative to the all-industries average. The industry is regulated on the price side with labor costs and other costs passed through to subscribers. However, productivity growth has been rapid, offsetting labor-cost increases. Although the impact of a strike on industry output is severely limited by automated telephone equipment, costs are imposed on the operating companies. The major union in the industry, the Communications Workers, appears to have gradually consolidated its position. In 1947 its attempts to achieve national bargaining were rebuffed, but by 1974 this goal had been attained. The only subperiod when earnings slipped significantly below the all-industries average

68. "Cement Industry Settlement Said to Pose Problems for U.S. Stabilizers," *Daily Labor Report,* June 23, 1978, pp. CC1–CC3.

was 1964–71. Lack of an escalator clause contributed to this slippage. By 1971, however, an escalator had become part of the package.[69]

At the other extreme in table 2-7 are the three industries that experienced below-average earnings gains from 1953 to 1976. Import competition could be cited as a possible influence in all three cases, but especially in men's and boys' suits. Also, competition from nonunion sources and southern producers has long been a problem for apparel unions.[70]

During the first two subperiods shown in table 2-7, bargaining in the electrical equipment industry was marked by interunion rivalry on the labor side. At the same time, General Electric followed a hard-line policy in its bargaining.[71] The industrial relations literature suggests that by the late 1960s the various unions had overcome their rivalries and engaged in coordinated bargaining.[72] Yet it is difficult to observe any market shift in the balance of power from the earnings data in table 2-7. Earnings growth in electrical equipment during each subperiod was below the all-industries average.

Folk wisdom in the industrial relations literature up through the mid-

69. The industry was characterized in the 1930s by "company" unions, which impeded the growth of a national labor organization. Elements of independent unionism still exist in the industry, and there is a history of rivalry between these unions and the Communications Workers. Arthur B. Shostak, *America's Forgotten Labor Organization: A Survey of the Role of the Single-Firm Independent Union in American Industry* (Princeton University, Industrial Relations Section, 1962), pp. 64–66. The Communications Workers claim that recent technological changes in the telephone industry have increased the vulnerability of the Bell System to a strike, but this seems doubtful. A. H. Raskin, "Wage Negotiations for the Bell System," *New York Times,* May 18, 1977.

70. One study concluded that unionization in men's clothing had little effect on wages except during the slide into the Great Depression and under the codes of the National Industrial Recovery Act of the 1930s. Elton Rayack, "The Impact of Unionism on Wages in the Men's Clothing Industry, 1911–1956," *Labor Law Journal,* vol. 9 (September 1958), pp. 674–88.

71. Various unions negotiate with General Electric and other firms in the industry. The largest, the Electrical Workers (IUE), was formed when the United Electrical Workers (UE) was expelled from the CIO after charges of communist domination. However, the UE continued as a force in the industry, and interunion relations were marked by personal hostility as well as rivalry. Meanwhile, General Electric followed a bargaining tactic known as "Boulwarism," which involved unilateral, inflexible offers by the company at the bargaining table. See Morris D. Forkosch, " 'Take It or Leave It' as a Bargaining Technique," *Labor Law Journal,* vol. 18 (November 1967), pp. 676–98.

72. For example, the symposium "Coordinated Bargaining" appearing in the *Labor Law Journal,* vol. 19 (August 1968), pp. 512–31; and the electrical case in particular, Abraham Cohen, "Coordinated Bargaining at General Electric: An Analysis" (Ph.D. dissertation, Cornell University, 1973). General Electric's Boulwarism technique also ran afoul of adverse court decisions.

1960s suggested a strong tie between wage settlements in the rubber tire and automobile industries. There is an obvious product-market linkage since original-equipment tires for new cars are an important component of tire sales. Also, the Rubber Workers and the Auto Workers were formerly CIO unions. Even before the mid-1960s, however, there were important differences in contract timing and structure. For example, the automobile industry pioneered in the use of escalator clauses, but the Rubber Workers seemed to prefer short contracts with fixed payments. In any case, it is clear that earnings in tires began to slip relative to those in autos and to the all-industries average beginning in the mid-1960s. This slippage was accompanied by considerable industrial unrest each time contracts with the major rubber companies expired. Lack of an escalator clause may account for some of the relative earnings decline. But it does not fully explain it since at contract expiration time any wage lag caused by unanticipated inflation could have been made up.[73] Management was apparently willing to pay the cost of increased strike activity to obtain savings in wages and benefits. One of the devices used by management was a mutual assistance pact to aid struck companies.[74]

Other factors may have affected earnings changes in the intermediate industries in table 2-7. Demand pressures in the mid-1960s seemed to touch off a wage explosion in the unionized construction industry. The magnitude of the response is often attributed to a wage-imitation structure in an industry that is easily disturbed and lends itself to competitive leapfrogging of wages.[75] Subsequently, wage determination in construction was covered by special controls based on stabilizing wage relativities. Thereafter, downward pressure on wage changes was exerted by the general recession and increased nonunion competition.[76]

Increases in trucking earnings outpaced the all-industries average in three of the four subperiods in table 2-7 and matched the average in the

73. In the 1976 negotiations, after a protracted strike, the Rubber Workers did gain an escalator clause—a major goal of the union. "Wage Highlights," *Current Wage Developments,* vol. 28 (September 1976), p. 1.

74. Cooperative management efforts appeared to break down in the 1979 negotiations, however. Firestone agreed to follow the pattern set by other companies and pull out of the pact. "Rubber Is the Next Big Problem," *Business Week* (April 23, 1979), pp. 120, 122.

75. Models of this type of behavior are discussed in chapter 5. See also Daniel Quinn Mills, *Industrial Relations and Manpower in Construction* (MIT Press, 1972), chap. 3.

76. Not only did nonunion contractors enlarge their share of the market, but union contractors began establishing nonunion subsidiaries as well. Tim Bornstein, "The Emerging Law of the 'Double Breasted' Operation in the Construction Indus-

fourth. Government regulation of entry and pricing in the industry undoubtedly played a part in these gains. It has also been suggested that, as the Teamsters shifted from regional to national bargaining, the union was able to exploit employers' differences and lack of cohesion and at the same time push them into larger groupings.[77]

Of the remaining industries in table 2-7, four exhibit a slowdown in earnings growth relative to the all-industries average in the 1958–64 period: steel, coal, railroads, and meatpacking. As noted earlier, steel and railroads may support the proposition that management's position hardened in the late 1950s. Steel experienced a prolonged strike in 1959, and in railroads a major battle was fought—partly in the political arena—over work rules. Coal is not usually cited as an example of management hardening, but coal prices generally declined from 1958 to 1964 and coal production remained below the 1957–58 levels until 1965. While the United Mine Workers is sometimes known as a union that deliberately traded off employment for higher wages,[78] employers may not have been so willing. The rapid rise in earnings in the coal industry in 1971–76, a period of rapidly escalating energy prices, suggests that wages in that industry are influenced by product-market conditions. The union also underwent political turmoil in the 1970s that increased worker militancy and put upward pressure on wages.[79]

---

try," *Labor Law Journal*, vol. 28 (February 1977), pp. 77–88. The discussion in the text does not explain why construction earnings for the entire 1953–76 period rose faster than the all-industries average. Pierson has suggested, as a partial explanation, that the growth of national construction firms weakened management resistance at the local level (*Unions in Postwar America*, pp. 100–04).

77. Arthur A. Sloane, "Collective Bargaining in Trucking: Prelude to a National Contract," *Industrial and Labor Relations Review*, vol. 19 (October 1965). pp. 21–40; Ralph James and Estelle James, "Hoffa's Impact on Teamster Wages," *Industrial Relations*, vol. 4 (October 1964), pp. 60–76; and Victor J. Sheifer, "Bargaining and Wages in Local Cartage," *Monthly Labor Review*, vol. 89 (October 1966), pp. 1076–84. The Teamsters' sensitivity to regulatory issues can be seen in its strong resistance to proposals for the deregulation of trucking. See, for example, "Deregulation Debate Begins," *International Teamster*, vol. 76 (April 1979), pp. 8–9.

78. Pierson, *Unions in Postwar America*, p. 86.

79. For many years, the United Mine Workers was dominated by its president, John L. Lewis. Lewis's successor, W. A. (Tony) Boyle, was voted out of office in a 1972 election, which was closely supervised by the Labor Department ("Report on the Labor Department's Court-Ordered Supervision of the United Mine Workers," *Daily Labor Report*, special supplement, October 31, 1972). Boyle subsequently went to prison in connection with the murder of an opponent and his family. His successor, Arnold Miller, took over a union beset with factionalism. In particular, the 1977–78 contract negotiations were marked by membership rejections of contracts worked out between the industry and the union's leadership.

In meatpacking, adverse economic conditions appear to have contributed to the relative wage lag in 1958–64 and 1964–71. Changes in technology permitted a decentralization of the industry. Nonunion competition increased in importance. In some instances, wage cuts were negotiated for particular plants to prevent closings.[80] The concern of the two major unions in the industry (later merged) shifted to job security. Special arrangements were negotiated to assist workers dislocated by plant closing or automation.[81]

Earnings growth data for motor vehicles show a surprising acceleration in 1958–64 compared with the earlier period, despite efforts by the big three automobile producers to achieve greater coordination. But the data seem to mask the improvement of fringe benefits in the 1950s, often emphasized by the UAW in its bargaining demands, compared with those of the early and mid-1960s.[82] When fringe benefits are included, motor vehicle earnings growth appears more consistent with a changed ballance of bargaining power in the late 1950s. In at least a portion of the 1964–71 period, the union may not have fully anticipated the acceleration in the rate of price inflation. In the 1967 contract, a cap was placed on the escalator and the frequency of review was shifted from quarterly to annual. The new formula provided for a less generous maximum escalated increase than that under the 1964–67 contract.[83] Subsequently, an uncapped, quarterly escalator clause was resumed.

80. Hervey A. Juris, "Union Crisis Wage Decisions," *Industrial Relations,* vol. 8 (May 1969), pp. 247–58. As noted in chapter 1, the union involved was quite sensitive about these concessions; see the comments of a union spokesman, James H. Wishart, in *Industrial Relations,* vol. 9 (February 1970), pp. 243–47.

81. The automation agreements reached with Armour received considerable public attention in the early 1960s. See "Progress Report of Armour's Tripartite Automation Committee," *Monthly Labor Review,* vol. 84 (August 1961), pp. 851–57. A follow-up report can be found in Harold E. Brooks, "The Armour Automation Committee Experience," in Industrial Relations Research Association, *Proceedings of the Twenty-first Annual Winter Meeting,* pp. 137–43.

82. For most of the ninety-three industries represented in table 2-4, historical fringe benefit data are not available. However, the national income accounts do provide total compensation data (including private and legally required fringes) for workers in motor vehicles and parts. During 1953–58, 1958–64, 1964–71, and 1971–76, total compensation per full-time employee in motor vehicles rose at annual rates of 6.3, 3.7, 6.2, and 10.1 percent. Comparable figures for hourly compensation in the nonfarm business sector were 4.6, 4.1, 6.0, and 8.3 percent. Growth obviously slowed in motor vehicles in 1958–64, but note that these data refer to all occupations, not just to production workers.

83. There was an understanding that any "lost" escalator wages would be reflected in the 1970 contract. "Developments in Industrial Relations," *Monthly Labor Review,* vol. 90 (December 1967), p. 53.

This review of earnings changes in selected industries makes it apparent that explaining disaggregated relative wage movements is much more difficult than characterizing broad sectoral developments. At the disaggregated level, data problems become more severe and underlying causal factors become more subtle. Obviously each of the industries in table 2-7 could be the subject of a lengthy case study. But the table does illustrate two related points. First, it is important not to lose sight of the substantial diversity in earnings movements incorporated in any aggregate measures. Second, despite the diversity, earnings movements in particular industries are sufficiently independent to permit aggregate measures to capture basic trends, which appear to influence many industries at once. In effect, influences on particular industries may "cancel out" when aggregate series are used. It is therefore possible to make useful generalizations about the differences between the heavily and the lightly unionized sectors without these generalizations necessarily being true of each component industry.

Conclusions

The collective bargaining sector has several unique characteristics that must be accounted for in discussions of wage determination. Collective bargaining covers a distinct minority of the work force. The sector expanded rapidly in the 1930s and 1940s, and appeared to peak in the mid-1950s. Since then, the number of workers covered by collective bargaining has declined in relation to total employment.

In the collective bargaining sector, the potential costs of an impasse can be substantial for both parties, and can dominate the considerations of employment-wage trade-offs so popular in economic models of unions and bargaining. Impasse costs are an important incentive for the development of long-term contracts that reduce the frequency of negotiations. Long-term relationships in wage setting imply different responses to business-cycle developments from the union and nonunion sectors, a topic discussed more fully in chapter 4. And because of these long-term relationships, union contracts cover a wide variety of work-rule and industrial-jurisprudence issues as well as wages.

It has been shown that earnings growth rates differed in particular subperiods of 1953–76 in the heavily and lightly unionized sectors. These differences are not surprising in view of the longer horizon likely to characterize the heavily unionized sector in wage setting. What is surprising is the tendency of the growth of earnings in the heavily unionized sector to be more rapid than that in the lightly unionized sector over a long period of time. This statistical fact calls into question models that view the union wage effect as primarily one-shot, with at most an allowance for cyclical wage variations.

Different earnings developments in the heavily and lightly unionized sectors in particular subperiods lend themselves to various interpretations. The industrial relations literature suggests that the mid-1950s were a period of consolidation of union bargaining strength after a period of rapid membership growth. In contrast, the late 1950s and early 1960s are sometimes viewed as years of a hardening of management's bargaining position. The last half of the 1960s is seen by some as a period in which inflation was not fully appreciated in the collective bargaining sector, thereby contributing to catch-up pressures later on. Finally, the 1970s saw such unusual events as wage-price controls and a significant imported inflation, which exacerbated domestic price pressure, and in the mid-1970s, a severe recession. The coincidence of high inflation and recession might be expected to widen union-nonunion differentials, and it apparently did. Obviously other interpretations of earnings movements during the 1953–76 period are possible. In particular industries, the general tendencies apparent in broadly aggregated earnings data may not be visible.

III

The Union Wage Effect

MOST PEOPLE assume that unions secure higher earnings for their members. To economists, this is not an automatic conclusion, however. Many methods are used for fixing wages; collective bargaining is simply one of them. And there is always the possibility that the method of doing something can vary without changing the ultimate outcome.

The issue of the unions' effect on earnings—whether unions cause earnings to be higher than market forces alone would make them—is related closely to the question of inflation and collective bargaining. If union members' earnings were not higher by some definition than they would be without unionization, it would be difficult to argue that unions had much effect on the rate at which earnings levels *changed*. Of course, even if a union wage differential is observed empirically, such a differential does not imply that unions bring about a different rate of earnings change. It simply raises the possibility that an earnings-change effect exists.

There are really two issues. First, do unions have the power to change the earnings levels from the levels that would otherwise prevail? Most observers would acknowledge that the short-run threat of strikes is a potential source of costs to employers. Presumably, there is some "price" that employers are willing to pay to avoid this cost. Of course, employers might calculate that it would be advantageous to invest in efforts to rid themselves of unions rather than raise pay. But if union elimination is not a real option—if it costs "too much"—a concession to buy off the strike threat through higher pay could be the best decision. In the short run, therefore, employers might well be induced to pay higher compensation than they would unilaterally determine.

The crucial second issue is whether such an imposed pay differential can endure over a long period of time. In the textbook perfect-competition model, all firms in an industry are assumed to have identical production functions, costs, and zero profits in the long run. Thus if a union organized some—though not all—employers in a purely competitive industry, it could achieve higher pay only at the cost of negative profits for the unionized sector. Since a firm with negative profits will not stay in business long, the union would ultimately have to choose between giving up the pay differential and giving up the employer.

This dilemma for a union in a perfectly competitive world is not eliminated by unionizing the entire industry at one time unless all entrants who come into the marketplace later are unionized. Otherwise, a lower-paying nonunion sector of new employers will gradually outcompete the original firms. The importance of keeping every firm in an industry unionized has long been recognized and is encapsulated in the union phrase "taking wages out of competition." But in the textbook model of perfect competition, that is more easily said than done.

It is not necessary to move far from this model before situations arise in which permanent pay differentials are possible. For example, transportation costs and locational advantages make it possible for unions to limit their organizational activities to particular areas while allowing a nonunion periphery. Suppose that a given product could be produced and delivered within a city for $3 per unit if there was no union wage pressure. Suppose further that production outside the city involved the same $3 in costs and an additional 50 cents in transportation expense. Initially, all production for the city would take place in the city. A union that succeeded in organizing all employers (and new entrants) in the city could capture the benefits of this 50-cent transportation barrier.

Other limits on the effective sphere of competition can easily be cited. Harbors provide certain locations with a natural advantage in receiving ships. A longshore union can take advantage of this natural barrier to entry in the stevedoring industry.[1] A ship entering one port is not a perfect substitute for a ship entering another port. Similarly, a hotel room in a tourist spot or a center of commerce is not a perfect substitute for accommodations somewhere else.

Geographic and natural limits on substitution are merely examples of barriers to entry. If an industry is characterized by substantial economies of scale or other start-up costs, unionization of the existing firms may provide a margin for a permanent wage differential. Oligopolistic industries with significant entry costs may have such potential for unions. If

1. For example, in 1972, when the Pay Board considered the East Coast longshore cases it was discovered that, despite pattern bargaining, total compensation in the Port of New York was significantly higher than in other areas. This difference was almost entirely due to fringe benefits. An interpretation of this phenomenon is that the union—constrained to pattern bargaining on wage rates—took advantage of New York's higher ability to pay through more generous fringe plans. Details on the longshore case can be found in U.S. Pay Board, "East and Gulf Coast Longshore: Summary and Analysis of PB Forms" (Pay Board, May 2, 1972).

assumptions of perfect information are dropped, such phenomena as product differentiation and brand loyalty must also be considered. In such cases, the consumer demand for the final product as seen by the employer is not a horizontal line, but rather a downward-sloping curve. Whereas in the simple textbook model the union is ultimately faced with choosing no wage differential or no firm, in the real world the choice is more likely to be between more differential and less (but not zero) employment.

The Wage-Employment Trade-off

Given prevailing economic conditions, how do unions determine their wage demands? Alternative models of union behavior have been proposed by economists. Unfortunately, as will be argued below, some of these models fail to recognize that union wage determination is in fact the product of a union-management interaction.

The Union View

A long-standing debate in the literature on union pay determination revolves around the degree of union perception of the trade-off between wages and employment.[2] It originated in an attempt by some observers to create an economic model of the union that would be analogous to the standard model of the firm. In price-theory textbooks a firm is viewed as facing a trade-off between price and quantity—a downward-sloping demand curve. The firm is actually not directly concerned with either price or quantity but does have an indirect interest in them as determinants—when combined with a cost function—of profits. In short, the assumption of profit maximization gives the firm an unambiguous index for choosing a point on the trade-off curve.

The trade-off a union faces is also a demand curve, although it is the derived demand for labor rather than the demand for a product. In this economic environment, the question arises of how the union chooses the

2. For a discussion of this literature, see Daniel J. B. Mitchell, "Union Wage Policies: The Ross-Dunlop Debate Reopened," *Industrial Relations,* vol. 11 (February 1972), pp. 46–61. The leaders in this debate were Arthur M. Ross, *Trade Union Wage Policy* (University of California Press, 1948); and John T. Dunlop, *Wage Determination Under Trade Unions* (Macmillan, 1944). Ross took the view that unions did not perceive such a trade-off and were basically "political" entities. Dunlop took the position that the trade-off was perceived and that unions were "economic" organizations. Other contributors to the debate are cited in the Mitchell paper.

optimal trade-off point. It will be argued below that this may have been the wrong question, but it is worth pursuing for the moment. Unlike the firm, the union has no obvious index to maximize. A quest therefore developed to find something to substitute for profits.

One choice was the wage bill, that is, $E \times H$, where E = hourly earnings and H = hours of employment.[3] Superficially, this is an attractive choice since it is denominated in money (like profits) and contains the two elements of the trade-off, E and H. But on further reflection, there is no reason for preferring an index that is money-denominated over some other index that is not. And there are many functions that contain E and H and that, if maximized, would provide an unambiguous, albeit arbitrary, trade-off selection point. Among these are $E \times H^2$, E^3H, and $E + H$.

Given the arbitrariness of the wage bill as a union goal, researchers turned away from the theory of the firm to the theory of the consumer, in which the consumer is pictured as choosing between alternative products (say, apples and oranges) subject to budget constraint. The consumer is said to have a utility (satisfaction) function permitting him to evaluate alternative patterns of consumption that can be bought within the budget. Utility maximization rather than profit maximization becomes the goal.

In the consumer-theory version, the union is said to have a utility function that contains the two components unions "enjoy," namely, E and H.[4] Presumably H is a good thing from the union viewpoint since it implies more members (an institutional goal) and job security for existing members; E is also a good thing since it is a major component of the income of the union's membership. Moreover, the concept of a utility function is general, unlike that of the precisely defined wage bill. This makes it easy to construct particular functions that cause the hypothetical union to behave in accordance with real-world observation, circular though this approach may be.

Both the wage-bill and the utility-function approaches raise an uncomfortable issue about union preferences. It is difficult to see why any individual union member should be especially concerned in the wage bill. Unlike a stockholder, who derives a proportionate share of profits, the

3. Dunlop, in *Wage Determination*, pp. 36–44, considers various models in which the wage bill is the target. However, he adds the constraint of a membership function and in one instance suggests considering unemployment compensation for displaced workers as part of the wage bill.

4. An example of utility function analysis can be found in Allan M. Cartter and F. Ray Marshall, *Labor Economics: Wages, Employment, and Trade Unionism*, rev. ed. (Irwin, 1972), chaps. 10–11. Other citations can be found in Mitchell, *Union Wage Policies*, p. 48, n. 7.

individual worker's wage bill bears no fixed relation to the aggregate wage bill. It is unclear, therefore, why the union—the aggregate of the members—should be concerned with something that is of no interest to its members individually. If a utility function is postulated to replace the wage bill as a goal, serious conceptual problems arise. It is well known in economic theory (though often ignored) that individual utility functions in general cannot be aggregated into a function that has the same properties as an individual function.[5]

If there is diversity of interests, a given change will improve some individual's welfare at the expense of others. For example, if a vote were taken on a given wage increase, the people who considered themselves most likely to be displaced (as H fell) would vote no; those who expected to be retained would vote yes. With a decision rule such as "majority wins," a determinate outcome will result. But since the outcome makes some people better off and some worse off, whether aggregate utility has increased or decreased is at best in doubt. Yet it is precisely this sort of question that the utility-function approach to union behavior is supposed to answer.

Clearly, the derivation of a utility function for an organization poses some difficult conceptual problems, some of which can be disguised by postulating that the union leadership has a utility function (as if the leaders themselves do not represent conflicting interests and have conflicting interests). But an even more formidable problem remains. For a union to maximize utility when constrained by a trade-off, the union has to be aware of that trade-off.

To the economist used to downward-sloping demand curves the notion of a wage-employment trade-off is axiomatic. But as was pointed out many years ago, the connection is far from obvious to union members or their leaders.[6] To the economist, the trade-off means that if pay were in-

5. The international trade literature makes heavy use of "national" indifference curves, which treat entire countries as if they were individual consumers, despite explicit admissions that a justification for such models is lacking. For example, see Richard G. Lipsey, *The Theory of Customs Unions: A General Equilibrium Analysis* (London: Weidenfeld and Nicolson, 1970), p. 27. Lipsey says "the statement that a given customs union will raise welfare must be taken to mean that it will move the community to a position that is either potentially or actually superior . . . in cases in which it is reasonable to assume the existence of a unique community welfare function. No attempt is made to justify this assumption in general. It is merely noted that, if it is considered desirable to investigate the welfare effects of customs unions, this assumption must be made."

6. Ross, *Trade Union Wage Policy,* pp. 80–93.

creased over what it otherwise would have been, employment would be lower than it otherwise would have been. Unfortunately, what might have been is not directly observable. What has been observed by most workers since World War II is that compensation goes up and that employment fluctuates as a result of changes in orders received by the firm. The link from pay to prices to orders is far from precise, and fluctuations in orders from customers often reflect general economic conditions that have little to do with pay levels in any one unit. Capital is likely to be perceived as being substituted for labor when technology becomes available, not when compensation rises.

One further point is worth noting. Economists tend to view costs, prices, profits, and demand as part of a mechanism. The economist can view the economy as a vast system of equations in which variables interact impersonally. Any one variable influences others, and the impact of a wage increase, in particular, is automatically a labor-demand decrease in a given employment unit. (The partial derivative of pay rates on orders is negative and the partial derivative of pay rates on the capital–labor ratio is positive.) This is a "natural" outcome that simply occurs in the model because it is assumed that firms maximize profits.

From the worker's viewpoint, the links between pay and employment are not passive. When labor costs are passed into prices or capital is substituted for labor, it is because some corporate executive decided to do so. Unions measure employers' behavior against an ethical system in which such phrases as "ability to pay" and "equitable wage adjustment" have genuine meaning. It might be profit-maximizing to pass a pay increase into prices or to automate in response to high wage costs. But such behavior is putting profits ahead of workers' interests and is therefore wrong from the union perspective.

The concept of workers' equity interests (property rights) in their jobs has little meaning in the formal legal system in the United States, especially in the private sector.[7] But it is rich in significance to unionists. If employers behave in ways that injure workers' interests, their behavior is not viewed as passively sliding up a demand curve but rather as a Bad

7. Public sector workers have certain constitutional protections against arbitrary discharge. In at least one case, a private defense contractor was held to have sufficient linkage with government to be subject to the same employee protections. But in general private sector workers have few legal claims to their jobs without a union agreement. See Benjamin Aaron, "The Impact of Public Employment Grievance Settlement on the Labor Arbitration Process," in Joy Correge, Virginia A. Hughes, and Morris Stone, eds., *The Future of Labor Arbitration in America* (New York: American Arbitration Association, 1976), pp. 1–48, especially pp. 21–23.

Thing. Such Bad Things are the direct targets of union demands for manning requirements, work rules, restrictions on subcontracting, and other practices. Economists would say such union efforts are attempts to make labor demand inelastic, but unions see themselves as simply requiring equitable treatment.

In short, the connection between wage increases and employment decreases is not easily observed in many cases and not automatically accepted as inevitable in others. To the extent that the wage-employment trade-off is a reflection of a wage-price-demand response in the product market, perception is especially difficult. Models that assume such perception is general cannot be grounded in reality. Apart from lobbying for favorable government regulations, unions can do little about external demand in the product market. But they sometimes have the power to limit the other source of the trade-off—substitution of capital for labor or nonunion labor for union labor—by means of ad hoc contractual devices. Economists may view such attempts at thwarting profit-maximizing substitutions as inefficiencies. (Note, however, that if wages are above market-clearing levels because of union action, limits on substitution may have second-best justifications even in the standard economic model.) But unions see such restrictions as merely preventing inequities by employers.

The Union-Management Interaction

The view that unions were political entities that did not perceive the wage-employment trade-off evoked considerable controversy when it was initially proposed. Evidence was produced in the form of case studies and anecdotes in which unions appeared to react to economic conditions. The evidence presented was of two types. First, there were stories of unions that made pay concessions when facing adverse economic circumstances.[8] The threat of plant closings in the absence of concessions sometimes will lead to union adaptation. However, there is a substantial difference between a movement along the labor demand curve (the usual trade-off view) and the imminent evaporation of the demand curve. Moreover, if management credibly states that a plant will be closed if a certain concession is not made, the trade-off issue becomes highly visible. No doubts remain about perceptions.

A second type of evidence concerns general actions by unions that help their industries. These include lobbying for import restrictions, sup-

8. George P. Shultz, *Pressures on Wage Decisions: A Case Study in the Shoe Industry* (Wiley, 1951).

porting (opposing) government regulations that increase (decrease) demand for their industry's output, and conducting advertising campaigns.[9] Such behavior usually involves shifting the position of the product demand curve (and the derived labor demand curve) rather than sliding up or down the curve. But unions' perception that more orders bring more employment, greater industry prosperity, and increased "ability to pay" of employers does not say much about their perception of a wage-employment trade-off.

What probably bothers economists most about the unperceptive union is that the goal of a union which believes there is no wage-employment trade-off should be infinite. That is, if E is a good thing and H is a good thing, and there is no trade-off between them, why not demand infinite pay levels? Though warned by the statement of Samuel Gompers, first president of the AFL, that the objective of the union movement *was* unlimited, economists are still bothered by goals that are developed without constraints.[10] This difficulty is easy enough to resolve, however, if it is

9. The United Mine Workers opposed construction of the Saint Lawrence Seaway for many years on the assumption that foreign imports coming through the seaway would compete with domestic coal. When it appeared that the seaway would provide an export market for U.S. coal, the position was reversed. The UMW also established a shipping company in cooperation with coal operators to handle coal exports. "The Labor Month in Review," *Monthly Labor Review,* vol. 79 (October 1956), p. III. Campaigns to encourage purchases of products with union labels—though viewed by some observers as having little effect—also fall into this category of activities to promote employers' prosperity. See Monroe M. Bird and James W. Robinson, "The Effectiveness of the Union Label and 'Buy Union' Campaigns," *Industrial and Labor Relations Review,* vol. 25 (July 1972), pp. 512–23.

10. The statement occurred during a debate between Gompers and Morris Hillquit, a well-known socialist leader.

HILLQUIT: Now, my question is, will this effort on the part of organized labor ever stop until it has the full reward for its labor?

GOMPERS: It won't stop at all. . . .

HILLQUIT: Then the object of the labor union is to obtain complete social justice for themselves and for their wives and for their children?

GOMPERS: It is the effort to obtain a better life every day.

HILLQUIT: Every day and always—

GOMPERS: Every day. That does not limit it.

HILLQUIT: Until such time—

GOMPERS: Not until any time.

HILLQUIT: In other words—

GOMPERS: In other words, we go further than you. You have an end; we have not.

This dialogue (from Commission on Industrial Relations, *Industrial Relations: Final Report and Testimony,* 69 Cong. 1 sess. [Government Printing Office, 1916], p. 1529) is often cited by labor historians to indicate philosophical differences between the AFL and the socialists at the turn of the century. But it has evident relevance for collective bargaining theory.

simply recalled that collective bargaining is a two-party process and that employer resistance is as much a part of the process as union demands.

Employers' goals presumably have a floor. Given labor-market conditions and the internal production processes of the firm, nonunion employers unilaterally set wages at levels that balance direct labor costs, labor supply (including costs of turnover), and, to some extent, equity considerations that affect the morale (and productivity) of the work force. If a union has been successful in bargaining, however, pay levels are set higher than what the employer would unilaterally determine. In a real sense, therefore, the goal of the union is "more" and the counterpart goal of the employer is simply "less."

Both parties to a collective-bargaining situation have potential weapons that may be used to attain objectives. The unions' major weapon is the strike, which inflicts costs on employers. How much of a cost the strike represents varies from situation to situation. In some cases, strikes may be completely effective in shutting down production, leaving the employer with fixed costs to pay and no incoming revenue from the sale of output. Where operations are integrated and inventory costs large, complete shutdowns are relatively easy to accomplish and the costs to employers are particularly severe. But where an employer's plants operate with relative autonomy or where inventories can be built up before a strike, the employer can maintain some production (and revenue from selling output) and can continue to receive some income from selling off inventory. Similarly, if customers have few other sources of supply, so that orders simply remain unfilled until the strike is over, the cost consequences for the employer are less severe than if orders that cannot be filled are lost to competitors. Some employers can maintain production with supervisory crews, especially if their operations are highly automated; others cannot.

Employers sometimes use lockouts to impose loss of income (costs) on their employees in a labor dispute.[11] Of more significance is the fact that a strike by a union imposes costs on its own members. An employ-

11. The law frowns on lockouts except under certain circumstances. For example, lockouts designed to preserve employers' unity in a multiemployer bargaining unit are generally legitimate. If a union attempts to strike just one employer in such a unit, it can be met with a solid front. However, although only two states provide unemployment compensation for strikers, workers who are locked out are eligible for benefits in many jurisdictions. A. Howard Myers and David P. Twomey, *Labor Law and Legislation*, 5th ed. (Cincinnati: South-Western Publishing, 1975), pp. 208–21.

er's decision to accept a strike is as much a weapon as a union's decision to impose a strike. Even where lockouts are of questionable legality, an employer who decides that a strike would be advantageous can usually provoke one.

An important element of labor-management relations is that the union and the employer normally expect to have to get along together after a dispute has been settled. Of course, an employer might consider trying to get rid of a union, thereby inflicting the ultimate cost on the union as an organization. But in general, labor and management are tied together. Employers must consider workers' morale after strikes have ended, and union leaders must consider the tone of their day-to-day dealings with management, since good relations are helpful in coping with problems that may arise during the contract. Neither side, in other words, wants to engender more hard feelings than necessary.

The essential point about collective bargaining is that its strike-cost potential often dwarfs or obscures abstract calculations about labor-demand elasticities, and strategic considerations involving bargaining and potential impasses come to dominate. The larger industrial unions usually develop their bargaining demands through a process of formal or informal consultations with the rank and file and with local officials. The initial "shopping list" of aspirations about wages, fringes, and conditions of work is formulated into a menu of demands, which is eventually presented to management. Union leaders form impressions about which aspirations are truly important and which are of lower priority to the membership. Through the bargaining process, this priority agenda is communicated to management. Management, if it has a long-standing relationship with the union, presumably has established enough rapport with union officials to sense which demands are essential to the union. It learns to distinguish these critical demands from proposals that are presented simply to please some internal union constituency.

A somewhat analogous procedure occurs on the management side. Local problems from first-line management officials are brought together and form part of management's counteroffer. Union officials eventually sense what is essential to management. Both sides are seeking to discover the opposite side's "bottom line"—that is, the package that will avoid a strike. Obviously, there is an element of bluff—the union wants to give the impression that it is more militant (ready to strike) than may be the case, and management benefits if the union believes that it will accept a strike more readily than is the case. The bargaining process can be viewed as an elaborate form of communication, which ultimately focuses on the costs of an impasse.

This does not mean that economic considerations are not discussed at the bargaining table and in other forums. But it is usually management that is most adept at judging such considerations, since it is management that markets the product, deals with competition, keeps the accounts, borrows funds, and so on. Arguments about ability to pay may be put forward in bargaining, but in a world of imperfect information (and a world filled with incentives to misrepresent information) the union may feel that the true test of ability to pay is management's willingness to accept a strike. In short, management resistance is often a proxy for economic considerations.

Since there is management resistance and this resistance is a primary factor in the union's formulation of objectives, it is evident that the "infinite"-pay-objective problem disappears. Clearly, a union would like infinite pay levels if they were costless. But obtaining pay increases is not costless. Generally, the main cost to the union is the risk of a strike, not the hypothetical degree of employment displacement. In the abstract, the union's goals may simply be "more," even if more could ultimately lead to an erosion of the union's employment base. But in reality, management resistance tends to protect the union from the consequences of this abstract desire by refusing to concede beyond some point.[12]

The Failure of Management Resistance and the Union Adaptation

The model of unions presented so far assumes that unions are in a symbiotic relationship with management and can function as political organizations precisely because management plays the role of bargaining unit defender. That is, if the union attempts to push pay levels too high (slides up the labor demand curve too far), it meets resistance from management, which discourages such behavior. It must be recognized, however, that management resistance is not a perfect proxy for the steepness of the wage-employment trade-off. To the extent that this trade-off is simply a reflection of the steepness of the demand curve for the final product, management resistance and the severity of the wage-employment trade-off will be correlated. Upward pressure on labor costs cannot be completely passed to the consumer as long as the absolute value of the elasticity of

12. The emphasis on the importance of dispute costs in collective bargaining is not new in the industrial relations literature. See Neil W. Chamberlain and James W. Kuhn, *Collective Bargaining* (McGraw-Hill, 1965), chap. 7.

demand for the product is greater than zero. In such circumstances price increases will inevitably lead to volume decreases and a reduction in profits. The firm as a profit maximizer has an incentive to resist pay increases that grows with the size of the union demand.[13]

Under some circumstances management's incentive to resist may not be strong enough to restrain union pressure. A small employer, for example, facing a single union that also deals with competitive firms may be an inadequate resister. A prolonged strike might simply put the small employer out of business and transfer its customers to the competition. In the short run, such an employer is mainly interested in not being asked to pay more than the competition. Moreover, if the industry is characterized by fast turnover of enterprises, no individual employer has much incentive to worry about the long term—that is, the absolute wage level and its trend.

Certain unionized components of the apparel industry are prime examples of a situation in which small and often short-lived employers face a union in circumstances where the incentive for management resistance is small.[14] In effect, the apparel unions have the power to bargain themselves out of existence. If union pay rates are set too high, the nonunion

13. Hicks showed that the elasticity of labor demand will be a positive function of the elasticity of product demand, if other influences are held constant. But he also showed that the elasticity of labor demand will be higher if the elasticity of substitution (for factors of production) is higher. This is why the text below suggests that, where other factors can be easily substituted for labor, a union must take special measures to reduce that possibility. See J. R. Hicks, *The Theory of Wages* (St. Martin's, 1963), pp. 241–46.

A related issue is whether the employer's incentive to resist becomes stronger as the union demands larger wage increases. Common sense suggests that it does. And micro price theory indicates that the economic surplus of the firm (revenue − variable costs = profits + fixed costs) is equivalent to the area under the marginal revenue product of labor curve but above the wage rate. Since fixed costs are a constant in the short run, it is clear that the higher wages rise, the more they cut into profits and the greater the management incentive to resist is.

14. Concentration ratios in many sectors of the apparel industry are extremely low and are often overstated due to import competition. This is especially true for women's apparel. For example, the fifty largest firms in the women's dress industry (SIC 2335) accounted for only 28 percent of the value of shipments in the industry and 16 percent of the employees in 1972. Concentration data can be found in U.S. Bureau of the Census, *Census of Manufactures, 1972,* vol. 1: *Subject and Special Statistics* (GPO, 1976), pp. SR2-178–SR2-182. The low rate of capitalization in the apparel industry suggests a high degree of employer impermanence and ease of entry and exit. Apparel ranked at the bottom of a list of twenty-nine industries in capital per worker in 1976. See Bureau of the Census, *Statistical Abstract of the United States, 1978* (GPO, 1978), p. 567. In 1976 apparel had a failure rate per 10,000 operating concerns of 63, whereas the all-industry rate was 35. *The Business Failure Record* (Dun and Bradstreet, Business Economics Division, 1977), pp. 2, 6.

sector and import suppliers will simply absorb more and more of the domestic market. The apparel unions are big enough and unified enough to worry about the overall prosperity of the unionized portion of the industry. Individual employers may be too small to have an industry perspective. Survival requires that the unions develop institutional mechanisms to take account of the highly elastic product demand curve (and therefore labor demand curve) and moderate their own behavior accordingly.[15]

There is no guarantee, however, that unions can always make the necessary institutional adaptations when management resistance is ineffective. Even if they do adapt, the process of adjustment may be slow. It could be argued that the construction trade unions—which often deal with small employers and which face potential nonunion competition—should have behaved more like the apparel unions than they did in the 1960s and early 1970s.[16] During that period, construction unions boosted pay rates considerably faster than unions in other industries and seemingly ignored the inroads being made by nonunion contractors. Pay rates in construction exploded in the late 1960s, were limited during 1971–74 by wage controls, and then exploded again briefly when the controls were lifted. After 1974, pay settlements in union construction were moderate compared with other industries, and in a number of well-publicized instances union concessions were made.[17] In short, the adaptation process in construction, though it ultimately occurred, took at least a decade.

To the extent that the elasticity of demand for labor stems from the

15. One report suggests that union wages in men's apparel were generally not above market levels in nonunion establishments during the period studied. Elton Rayack, "The Impact of Unionism on Wages in the Men's Clothing Industry, 1911–1956," *Labor Law Journal*, vol. 9 (September 1958), pp. 674–88.

16. Construction ranked fourth from the bottom in 1976 when ranked by capitalization of the twenty-nine industries cited above. Average firm size in construction in 1972 for firms with employees was eleven workers. Bureau of the Census, *1972 Enterprise Statistics*, pt. 1: *General Report on Industrial Organization* (GPO, 1977), table 5, p. 144.

17. Roughly 30,000 construction workers in the major union sector received either zero or negative general wage adjustments in 1977. *Current Wage Developments*, vol. 30 (April 1978), p. 64.

Various instances of wage concessions were reported during the period 1975–77 in cities and areas scattered around the country, including Buffalo, western Pennsylvania, Pittsburgh, Detroit, Washington, D.C., New York, Philadelphia, Baltimore, Boston, Los Angeles, Miami, and the state of Washington. *Monthly Labor Review*, February 1975, p. 87; April 1975, p. 78; May 1975, p. 70; May 1976, p. 53; April 1977, p. 85; July 1977, p. 53; and November 1977, p. 56.

possibilities for substitution by employers (capital for labor or non-union labor for union labor), the employer resistance mechanism is automatically attenuated. Consider the following hypothetical example. Suppose a given job pays $6.00 an hour and the union demands a 10 percent wage increase (to $6.60). Suppose further that the employer—unbeknownst to the union—has the option of substituting a machine for this job at a cost equivalent to paying the workers $6.30 an hour. The employer then has an incentive to resist only 30 cents of the 60-cent wage demand. If the union appears to be rigid in its 60-cent demand, the employer can simply accede and then install the machine. Indeed, the employer would offer no more resistance to a 90-cent demand than to a 60-cent demand.

In the substitution case, a union adaptation is also required. However, it can be in the form of revised demands for work rules that limit technological change, clauses barring subcontracting, severance pay or supplemental employment benefits that make layoffs more costly, or some similar device. Apart from substitution, if the union can count on effective resistance to demands that pose problems through the product market channel, the adaptation that the union must make need not change its basic role.

Recapitulation

The conceptual model of union behavior presented above suggests that unions can be usefully divided into two types. "Resistance unions" rely on management resistance when formulating bargaining demands. The primary determinants of their objectives are strategic considerations involving strike costs. Labor demand curve slopes are not directly relevant in explaining their behavior; indeed, resistance unions may act as if they are unaware that there is a sloped labor demand schedule. Effective management resistance means that such awareness is not necessary for the survival of the union or of the bargaining unit. To the extent that pay increases tempt employers to substitute capital or nonunion labor for union workers, ad hoc arrangements to limit such flexibility are likely to be demanded. Resistance unions do recognize that they have a common interest with management in promoting demand for the final product through lobbying for import restrictions, obtaining favorable government regulations, and so on. However, the mere recognition that employer prosperity increases ability to pay should not be taken as a sign that union behavior acknowledges a downward-sloping labor demand curve.

In contrast, where there is no effective employer resistance, unions cannot simply press for more without ultimately endangering their own survival or the survival of the bargaining unit. It may be that for some now-defunct unions the necessary adaptation to this circumstance proved to be beyond the range of institutional feasibility. The term "economic unions" is really applicable to the unions that do meet the challenge presented by inadequate management resistance. Of course, this does not imply that economic unions maximize some particular index such as the wage bill or that composite utility functions really add much to the analysis. What can be said is simply that economic unions recognize a trade-off between wages and employment and that this trade-off acts as a self-imposed brake on their wage demands.

For resistance unions, employer behavior is only a proxy for labor demand conditions. Over a long period of time there is nothing to prevent the wages they negotiate from creeping up from the levels the employer might unilaterally establish. Generally, long-run demand curves (including the demand-for-labor curve) are assumed to have greater elasticity than short-run curves. This is because time is needed to make full use of substitution opportunities in both the product and the labor markets. An upward creep in pay might not be fully projected in employer behavior, partly because employers can make long-run adaptations more easily than short-run adaptations. It is therefore possible that different earnings movements for heavily and lightly unionized industries could continue for a long time—no prediction can be obtained from economic theory, one way or the other. Certainly, the fact that the union sector is shrinking in proportion to the total labor force need not act as a brake on union compensation demands. Even long-term employment trends in particular heavily unionized industries show no significant association with relative earnings movements.

Economic unions do react to the wage-employment trade-off in setting wage objectives. Their behavior is therefore more directly restrained by demand-for-labor considerations. But to the extent that the union sector contains a mixture of resistance unions and economic unions, earnings-change differentials of the type computed in chapter 2 could still show a widening gap between the heavily and lightly unionized sectors.

Dichotomization of any form of social or economic behavior is risky. It can always be argued that rather than two types of unions—resistance and economic—there is a spectrum of kinds of behavior with the two models as extreme cases. Examples can be found of unions that sometimes exhibit characteristics of the resistance model and other times of the economic model. Statistical evidence on union earnings differentials of the type discussed below cannot distinguish between the types of union behavior that contributed to those differentials.

Are Union Wages Higher?

It is possible in theory for employer resistance to be so strong (for resistance unions) or the wage-employment trade-off to be considered so adverse (for economic unions) that unions would have no pay-raising impact. There could still be collective bargaining, and the bargaining process would make the casual observer believe that the unions had won something.[18] That is, employers would offer less than they really intended to pay and unions would demand more, making it appear that the final wage outcome was a movement in the union's direction. But the outcome might be the same as what the employer would have unilaterally determined without a union.

Even if the suggestion that the union strike threat has no effect whatsoever on the pay outcome seems implausible, it is conceivable that the unions only affect items that are not easily measured. These include work rules and working conditions and the establishment of industrial jurisprudence.[19] In such a world unions would simply be using their power to obtain real, but difficult-to-quantify, concessions. For obvious reasons, this section sticks to the measurable aspects of compensation.

The determination of whether union earnings are different from what earnings would be without unions is a matter of some complexity. But one easily observable characteristic of the American labor market is

18. This notion was a guiding principle in the "Boulware" approach at General Electric into the 1960s. The company took the position that it would have granted equitable wage adjustments even without union pressure and that the unions were simply trying to take credit for a predetermined outcome. Hence the company made a point of not deviating significantly from its initial offer. See Morris D. Forkosch, " 'Take It or Leave It' as a Bargaining Technique," *Labor Law Journal,* vol. 18 (November 1967), pp. 676–98.

19. Such effects on the work place may be quite important to workers, even though they cannot be easily quantified. See Richard B. Freeman, "Individual Mobility and Union Voice in the Labor Market," *American Economic Review,* vol. 66 (May 1976, *Papers and Proceedings, 1975*), pp. 361–68.

Table 3-1. *Hourly Earnings and Unionization, Selected Industries and Selected Years, 1953–76*

Earnings in dollars

Source of unionization data and year	Industries with above-average unionization rates (1)	Industries with below-average unionization rates (2)	Ratio, col. 1: col. 2 (3)
Contract file			
1976	6.15	4.83	1.27
1973	4.75	3.83	1.24
1971	4.08	3.39	1.20
1968	3.36	2.83	1.19
1964	2.84	2.37	1.20
1958	2.34	1.97	1.19
1958[a]	2.34	2.03	1.15
1953[a]	1.88	1.68	1.12
Compensation survey			
1976	5.76	4.66	1.24
1973	4.48	3.71	1.21
1971	3.89	3.28	1.19
1968	3.22	2.75	1.17
1964	2.73	2.28	1.20
1958	2.26	1.87	1.21
1958[a]	2.29	1.91	1.20
1953[a]	1.84	1.59	1.16
Current population survey			
1976	5.99	4.73	1.27
1973	4.63	3.78	1.22
1971	4.02	3.35	1.20
1968	3.31	2.78	1.19
1964	2.81	2.30	1.48
1958	2.31	1.90	1.22
1958[a]	2.36	1.99	1.19
1953[a]	1.89	1.66	1.14

Source: Appendix A.
a. Includes only industries for which 1953 earnings data were available.

that union earnings for broad groups of workers are usually higher than nonunion earnings. Among the production and nonsupervisory workers included in the employment and payroll surveys of the Bureau of Labor Statistics, higher paid workers tend to be in the more highly unionized industries.

Table 3-1 is based on hourly earnings data and the three series of

Table 3-2. *Annual Earnings and Unionization, by Demographic Group, 1972*
Earnings in dollars

Source of unionization data and demographic group	Industries with above-average unionization rates (1)	Industries with below-average unionization rates (2)	Ratio, col. 1: col. 2 (3)
Contract file			
White males	11,525	10,754	1.07
White females	6,670	5,718	1.17
Black males	8,453	7,355	1.15
Black females[a]	6,232	5,264	1.18
Compensation survey			
White males	11,387	10,551	1.08
White females	6,445	5,447	1.18
Black males	8,274	7,062	1.17
Black females[a]	6,139	5,061	1.21
Current population survey			
White males	11,507	10,563	1.09
White females	6,788	5,465	1.24
Black males	8,461	7,114	1.19
Black females[a]	6,143	5,055	1.22

Sources: See appendix B, descriptions of sources and analyses for *WMSOC, WFSOC, BMSOC, BFSOC.*
a. Includes only industries for which earnings data for black females were available.

unionization rates for the ninety-three industries used in chapter 2 and discussed in appendix A. It shows the association between unionization and earnings quite clearly. In 1976 average hourly earnings (including overtime pay) in industries with above-average unionization rates were 24 to 27 percent higher than in industries with below-average unionization rates, depending on which unionization series was used. The relative gap between the union and nonunion sectors widened after the Korean War until the late 1950s, remained about the same or even declined over the next decade, and then resumed widening.

Data taken from social security payroll tax records permit a demographic breakdown of the observed differential. Table 3-2 presents figures drawn from these records, which compare annual earnings by race and sex for workers in industries with above- and below-average rates of unionization in 1972. The table suggests that the gap between the earnings of women and blacks in the highly unionized industries and those of their counterparts in less unionized industries is wider than the gap between the earnings of white males in the highly unionized industries and the earnings of white males in the other industries, though white males earn more in general. This observation is consistent with census studies for the mid-1960s and with studies ascribing a more causal relationship between unionization and such differences than a tabular presentation such as that in table 3-2 permits.[20]

The breakdown between highly and lightly unionized industries is rather crude, since within highly unionized industries there are generally some nonunion establishments (and vice versa for the lightly unionized sector). Some understanding of union-nonunion differences in specific industries can be gained from the periodic "industry wage surveys" of the Bureau of Labor Statistics. These studies often present average straight-time hourly earnings in establishments, broken down by collective bargaining coverage *within* industries where there are significant numbers of both union and nonunion workers. From these data, an unadjusted union wage premium relative to nonunion establishments can be calculated. As table 3-3 shows (column 3), these intraindustry earnings premiums vary widely, but they always turn out to be positive. Thus the generalization that the earnings of union workers are higher (for whatever reasons) than those of nonunion workers appears to be true within industries as well as across industries.

Available data on wages often omit fringe benefit payments. This omission was of minor concern when average hourly earnings data first began to be collected and when the first industry wage surveys were conducted. But fringe benefits have steadily grown in importance as a com-

20. A census study for 1966 found the following union–nonunion ratios of full-time median earnings: white males, 1.06; black males, 1.52; white females, 1.12; black females, 1.52. Bureau of the Census, *Current Population Reports,* series D-20, no. 216, "Labor Union Membership in 1966" (GPO, 1971), table 2, pp. 10–11.

It has been argued that unionization in an industry tends to act as a barrier to black entry, although obviously the degree to which this tendency occurs may vary substantially. In particular, the climate for blacks is apparently better in industrial unions than in craft unions. Leonard A. Rapping, "Union-Induced Racial Entry Barriers," *Journal of Human Resources,* vol. 5 (Fall 1970), pp. 447–74; Orley C. Ashenfelter, "Racial Discrimination and Trade Unionism," *Journal of Political Economy,* vol. 80 (May–June 1972), pt. 1, pp. 435–64; and Orley C. Ashenfelter and Lamond I. Godwin, "Some Evidence on the Effect of Unionism on the Average Wage of Black Workers Relative to White Workers, 1900–1967," Industrial Relations Research Association, *Proceedings of the Seventy-fourth Annual Winter Meeting* (Madison, Wis.: IRRA, 1972), pp. 217–24. The Ashenfelter and Godwin estimates suggest a small positive union effect on the ratio of blacks' wages to whites' wages in the mid-1960s, which the authors expected to rise as a result of the increased participation of blacks in unionized sectors.

Table 3-3. *Selected Union-Nonunion Wage Differentials for Production Workers, by Industry*

Industry	Year of study (1)	Percentage of workers unionized[a] (2)	Gross union premium as percent of nonunion wage (3)	Adjusted union premium as percent of nonunion wage[b] (4)
Industrial chemicals	1976	77	3	1
Paints and varnishes	1976	68	17	8*
Textile dyeing	1976	37	14	5
Corrugated and solid fiber boxes	1976	87	21	...
Nonferrous foundries	1975	57	18	10*
Structural clay products	1975	68	27	6*
Candy and other confectionary products	1975	54	13	...
Fabricated structural steel	1974	71	32	...
Wood household furniture	1974	35	23	10*
Men's and boys' shirts and nightwear[c]	1974	39	17	11*
Miscellaneous plastics	1974	47	8	4*
Meat products	1974	83	60	...
Iron and steel foundries				
Gray iron except pipe and fittings	1973	88	35	⎫
Gray iron pipe and fittings	1973	71	8	⎬ 8*d
Steel	1973	88	19	⎭
Cigar manufacturing	1972	42	3	...
Bituminous coal				
Underground mines	1967	84	47	...
Surface mines	1967	54	61	...

Source: Bureau of Labor Statistics, *Industry Wage Survey*, bulletins 1583, 1796, 1894, 1896, 1901, 1914, 1921, 1930, 1935, 1939, 1942, 1952, 1967, 1973, 1978.

* Significant at 5 percent level.

a. Workers in establishments where the majority were covered by collective bargaining.

b. Union dummy coefficient from regression explaining straight-time earnings using size, region, urbanization, and other characteristics. This coefficient has been divided by nonunion wages.

c. Excludes work shirts.

d. Single regression used for three industry divisions. Regression coefficient divided by nonunion earnings for combined divisions where nonunion earnings have been calculated using nonunion employment weights.

ponent of the overall compensation package. And in general, despite some methodological problems, they can be quantified in dollars, unlike less tangible elements of work rules and industrial democracy. Although there were precedents for such items as pensions and health and welfare programs in the years before the surge in unionization (1930s and

Table 3-4. *Hourly Wages and Benefits and Unionization of Nonoffice Workers, 1974*

Amounts in dollars

Item	Union establishments[a] (1)	Nonunion establishments (2)	Ratio, col. 1: col. 2 (3)
All industries			
Pay for time worked	5.41	3.55	1.52
Straight-time pay	5.15	3.45	1.49
Private fringe benefits[b]	1.21	0.38	3.18
Total compensation	7.12	4.26	1.67
Manufacturing			
Pay for time worked	5.02	3.81	1.32
Straight-time pay	4.74	3.65	1.30
Private fringe benefits[b]	1.21	0.55	2.20
Total compensation	6.69	4.71	1.42
Nonmanufacturing			
Pay for time worked	5.96	3.46	1.72
Straight-time pay	5.73	3.38	1.70
Private fringe benefits[b]	1.19	0.32	3.72
Total compensation	7.73	4.10	1.89

Source: Bureau of Labor Statistics, *Employee Compensation in the Private Nonfarm Economy, 1974,* bulletin 1963 (GPO, 1977), p. 33.

a. Establishments where a majority of nonoffice workers were covered by union agreements.

b. Excludes payments for social security, unemployment insurance, and workers' compensation.

1940s), even the most casual reading of the historical record suggests a strong interest in, and a push for, fringe benefits in the union sector. Observed union-nonunion pay differentials might be expected to be wider if fringe benefits were included in the calculation.

Table 3-4 quickly confirms this expectation. The table is based on a survey of compensation conducted in 1974, which included benefits as well as wages. On a "pay for time worked" basis, which approximates the average hourly earnings data of table 3-1, the estimated union wage for nonoffice workers in all nonfarm industries exceeded the nonunion wage by 52 percent. But when total compensation, including all fringe benefits, is used for the calculation, the premium rises to 67 percent. The same pattern is found when the figures are disaggregated into manufacturing and nonmanufacturing. For the overall nonfarm sector, hourly expenditures in union establishments on private benefits such as pensions and health and welfare programs were over three times the level found in the nonunion sector. It therefore seems clear that any study that omits fringe benefits in estimating union pay effects understates those effects.

None of these observed differentials prove that unions make pay levels higher than they otherwise would be in the units in which they bargain. A number of characteristics of the union sector could conceivably explain at least some of the earnings gap. Demographic differences in the union and nonunion work forces might be part of the explanation. Table 3-5 shows that, when industries with above-average unionization are compared with industries with below-average unionization (using any of the three series on unionization), there is little difference in the proportion of nonwhites employed in the two sectors. The evidence does not suggest that the earnings gap is the result of a concentration of nonwhites (who typically receive below-average pay) in the nonunion work force. However, evidence at more disaggregated levels suggests a stronger association.[21]

Female employees constitute a larger proportion of the lightly unionized group of industries than of the heavily unionized group. On the average women receive lower pay than men (table 3-2). They also are more likely to work part-time and to be less strongly attached to the work force.[22] These characteristics suggest that they would be more likely than men to be employed in industries with "secondary" labor-market characteristics.[23] The costs of turnover in such industries are likely to be lower, and employers are less likely to pay workers a wage premium to reduce turnover. Table 3-5 shows, for example, that voluntary quit rates are higher in the lightly unionized sector than in the heavily unionized sector. Fringe benefits have a tendency to tie workers to the employer and reduce turnover. Table 3-4 demonstrated that unionization is associated with higher levels of fringes, an observation that table 3-5 confirms with different sources of data.

21. Note that table 3-2 shows that nonwhites earn less than whites in both the heavily unionized and the lightly unionized sectors. Regression analysis presented in appendix B shows a significant negative association between black representation in the work force and earnings in many of the estimated equations.

22. Women accounted for 74 percent of the adult (aged twenty and older) part-time civilian labor force in 1976. Their participation rate in the overall labor force was 47 percent; the male participation rate was 78 percent. Bureau of Labor Statistics, *Handbook of Labor Statistics, 1977* (GPO, 1977), pp. 21–22, 63–64.

23. On the secondary labor market, see Peter B. Doeringer and Michael J. Piore, *Internal Labor Markets and Manpower Analysis* (Heath, 1971), pp. 163–83; and Michael L. Wachter, "Primary and Secondary Labor Markets: A Critique of the Dual Approach," *Brookings Papers on Economic Activity, 3:1974*, pp. 637–80.

Table 3-5. Correlates of Unionization, Various Years, 1971–76

Characteristic	Contract file		Compensation survey		Current population survey	
	Industries with above-average unionization rates	Industries with below-average unionization rates	Industries with above-average unionization rates	Industries with below-average unionization rates	Industries with above-average unionization rates	Industries with below-average unionization rates
Percent of nonwhite workers, 1976 (BLK76)	12	11	12	10	11	10
Percent of female workers, 1976 (PFEM)	22	32	24	36	20	33
Median education (years), 1970 (ED)	12	12	12	12	12	12
Quit rate (percent), 1976[a] (QT76)	0.9	1.9	1.2	2.1	1.3	2.3
Workers per establishment, 1974 (ESSIZ)	326	65	257	54	323	43
Depreciation per employee (dollars), 1973[b] (KLDEP)	2,310	1,533	2,282	1,287	2,634	1,416
Depreciable assets per employee (dollars), 1973[b] (KLDEPA)	44,021	25,275	43,262	19,347	50,601	22,653
Private fringe benefits as percent of private compensation, 1971[c] (PFRIN)	9.9	6.7	8.9	6.2	9.2	5.9
Number of industries	34	59	49	39	34	35

Sources: Definitions of variables and source for each variable are given in appendix B.
a. Data available for 52 industries using contract file, 50 industries using compensation survey, and 36 industries using current population survey estimates of unionization.
b. Data available for 92 industries using contract file, 87 industries using compensation survey, and 68 industries using current population survey estimates of unionization.
c. Manufacturing only. Data available for 63 industries using contract file, 61 industries using compensation survey, and 41 industries using current population survey estimates of unionization.

An interesting question is whether employers in the unionized sector would be more likely to pay a premium to reduce turnover than other employers, apart from any direct impact of unionization itself. Two indexes in table 3-5 shed some light on this issue. Highly unionized industries tend to have larger establishments than other industries. In large work places direct supervision is more difficult (more costly), and employees who can work without constant supervision are especially valued.[24] Such valuation could result in a higher wage for these workers in the labor market generally. Table 3-5 also presents two measures of the degree of capitalization in the two sectors: the ratio of depreciation per employee and the ratio of depreciable assets per employee. These ratios, which are forms of capital-labor indexes, tend to be higher in industries with above-average unionization rates. High capitalization may require more skilled workers (capital and skilled workers may be complementary factors of production), and skilled workers are likely to be paid more than unskilled workers. Also, highly capitalized industries are often characterized by a small ratio of labor costs to total sales. The effect of labor costs on product pricing and sales would thus be less important to these industries.[25] In turn, management points of resistance to union wage demands in these industries would tend to be at higher absolute levels than in other industries.

Do Unions Cause Higher Wages?

It is clear that unionization and higher pay levels are associated statistically. But it is also clear that the unionized sector is characterized by other forces that might lead to above-average pay. Two problems are raised by these observations. First, a simple correlation between unionization and pay is likely to produce misleading results since the union

24. Richard Lester, "Pay Differentials by Size of Establishment," *Industrial Relations,* vol. 7 (October 1967), pp. 64–65; and Stanley H. Masters, "An Interindustry Analysis of Wages and Plant Size," *Review of Economics and Statistics,* vol. 51 (August 1969), p. 341.

25. The "importance of being unimportant" principle in the text does not always hold. It assumes that the elasticity of demand for the product is high relative to the elasticity of substitution. Normally it can be assumed that the firm is operating on the elastic portion of its product demand curve since only in that range will marginal revenue be positive. (Marginal revenue must be positive if marginal costs are positive.) So the critical issue is whether the elasticity of substitution is greater than unity. See Hicks, *The Theory of Wages,* pp. 245–46.

effect would be confused with the effect of these other forces. Related to this is the possibility that unionization may affect these other forces. Second, it is conceivable that unionization is not an exogenous influence on wage determination, but rather part of a larger system in which causal arrows could run from wages to unionization as well as the other way. Much of the existing literature attempts to deal with the first problem, but some recent contributions have been aimed at the second as well.

Union-Nonunion Pay Differentials: Conceptual Issues

Various approaches can be taken to measuring the union effect on pay, on the assumption that unionization is an exogenous influence. An important initial step is defining exactly what is meant by the union pay effect. If unions are hypothesized to have an indirect effect on nonunion pay, a conceptual problem arises. The most natural place to look for a union pay effect is in comparisons of union and nonunion situations. If, however, unions influence nonunion pay determination, the observed union-nonunion differential will not be an index of the degree to which unions raise the pay levels of their members relative to what those pay levels would have been without unions.

Unions can influence nonunion pay levels through several channels. If nonunion employers see a potential threat of unionization, they may react by raising the pay of nonunion workers—this is the so-called threat effect.[26] It is easy to find anecdotal evidence of such behavior, especially in partially unionized firms or industries.[27] In some instances, the threat effect may be a legislative mandate, such as the Davis-Bacon Act of 1931 covering the construction industry, which requires federal contractors—including nonunion contractors—to pay "prevailing" wages (which generally means union wages).[28]

26. H. G. Lewis, *Unionism and Relative Wages in the United States: An Empirical Inquiry* (University of Chicago Press, 1963), pp. 23–24.

27. For example, Segal examined a situation in which skilled union workers in textiles and unskilled nonunion workers were linked in a fixed wage differential. Martin Segal, "Interrelationship of Wages Under Joint Demand: The Case of the Fall River Textile Workers," *Quarterly Journal of Economics*, vol. 70 (August 1956), pp. 464–77. See also Eaton H. Conant, "Defenses of Nonunion Employers: A Study from Company Sources," *Labor Law Journal*, vol. 10 (February 1959), pp. 100–09, 132; and Nicholas S. Perna, "Wage Determination in a Nonunion Firm" (Ph.D. dissertation, Massachusetts Institute of Technology, 1970).

28. D. N. Gujarati, "The Economics of the Davis-Bacon Act," *Journal of Business*, vol. 40 (July 1967), pp. 303–16.

Normal market channels can also link union and nonunion pay levels. If nonunion workers can be substituted for union workers, a rise in the union rate of compensation should increase nonunion pay. Substitution can occur entirely within the internal labor market—as is the case when a partially unionized employer shifts work from union to nonunion plants —or through the product market. In the product-market case, the union pay increase, through its effect on costs and prices, tends to shift demand to firms in the nonunion sector. The added demand for nonunion output is translated into added demand for nonunion labor, which could have a pay-raising influence.

Union pay increases might have a negative effect on compensation in the nonunion sector. Although there is evidence that the demand for labor in unionized industries is more inelastic than in other industries,[29] there will still be some displacement of union workers (relative to what would have occurred) because of wage increases. These displaced workers (who may simply be workers who would otherwise have been employed in the unionized sector) must then seek jobs elsewhere.[30] The effect of this addition to the nonunion labor supply is to lower nonunion pay.

There may also be nonunion workers who are complements in production to union workers. Examples include nonunion clerical employees in firms with unionized blue-collar workers and nonunion production workers in firms that supply intermediate products for unionized firms. If union pay increases reduce the demand for output in the union sector (and the demand for union workers), the demand for these complementary nonunion workers may be reduced and their pay rates may be lowered.

Cross-Industry Historical Estimates: Methodological Problems

In recent years data sets that make possible direct observation of the union or nonunion status of individuals or establishments have become available. These data sources unfortunately cannot be used to trace the historical experience of union-nonunion pay differentials because direct

29. R. B. Freeman and J. L. Medoff, "Substitution Between Production Labor and Other Inputs in Unionized and Non-unionized Manufacturing," Discussion Paper 581 (Harvard University, Institute of Economic Research, 1977).

30. Lawrence M. Kahn, "Unions and the Employment Status of Nonunion Workers," *Industrial Relations,* vol. 17 (May 1978), pp. 238–44.

observation of such differentials before the 1960s was limited. However, even before the newer data sources were collected, a technique was developed for estimating union-nonunion pay differentials through the use of unionization rates and industry earnings statistics. Since this study is concerned with the period extending from the mid-1950s to the mid-1970s, the cross-industry technique will be used in this section. One question to be asked is whether the upward creep in earnings in the heavily unionized sector in relation to those in the lightly unionized sector (observed in the previous chapter) remains after standardization for other influences on earnings levels.

Industry data on hourly earnings represent an average of the earnings paid in union and nonunion establishments in the industry. An estimate can be made of the average union-nonunion earnings differential by running a regression—that is, fitting a line relating earnings in the industry to the unionization rate after standardizing for other factors (aside from unionization) that might affect earnings. What emerges is a line of the form $E = a + bU$, where E is the average earnings for the entire industry (union and nonunion components) and U is the unionization rate. The estimated slope of this line b can then be interpreted as reflecting a union effect on earnings.

Unfortunately, the union earnings effect may vary with circumstances, a possibility that complicates the interpretation of b. In particular, it is conceivable that the union effect on union wages will be greater if an industry is heavily unionized than if it is lightly unionized. In a heavily unionized industry the problem of nonunion competition in the product market is less likely to arise than in a lightly unionized industry, and this could intensify the effectiveness of the union. The same is true for nonunion earnings, which were seen to be potentially related (positively or negatively) to the union effect on union earnings. If the rate of unionization influences union strength, it might influence the indirect union effect on nonunion earnings.

The significance of these relationships can be demonstrated by the use of a simple numerical example. Consider two industries, one with 25 percent of the workers organized and the other with 75 percent organized, both of which would provide weekly earnings of $400 without unionization. It is useful to measure three indicators of the union earnings effect: the average union-nonunion earnings differential, the fitted coefficient b described above, and the average true union earnings effect on the union wage. The last indicator, since it measures the difference between

Table 3-6. *Hypothetical Numerical Examples Pertaining to Union Earnings Effect*

Dollars unless otherwise specified

Case	Unionization rate (U) (percent)	Nonunion earnings (W_n)	Union earnings (W_u)	Difference $= W_n - W_u$	Average weekly earnings (W) = $W_n(1 - U)$ $+ W_uU$	True union earnings effect on union earnings = $W_u - \$400$
I	25	400	440	40	410.00	40
	75	400	440	40	430.00	40
II	25	400	410	10	402.50	10
	75	400	430	30	422.50	30
III	25	410	410	0	410.00	10
	75	430	430	0	430.00	30
IV	25	405	410	5	406.25	10
	75	415	430	15	426.25	30
V	25	390	420	30	397.50	20
	75	350	440	90	417.50	40
VI	25	395	415	20	400.00	15
	75	265	445	180	400.00	45
VII	25	440	440	0	440.00	40
	75	440	440	0	444.00	40

Source: Numerical example described in the text.

the actual union wage and what union workers would receive without a union, is presumably the most interesting of the three, and also the most difficult to measure. And even it omits cross-industry effects of unionization.[31]

Table 3-6 presents seven cases based on the two hypothetical industries, each with different assumptions about the impact of the unioniza-

31. The true union earnings effect on the union wage defined in the text is the difference between what the industry pays union workers and what it would pay if there were no union in that industry. This is not the same as the union effect on the earnings of union workers relative to what would be paid without unions in all industries. That is, the nonunion earnings level in a particular industry could have been little affected by unionization in the industry (for instance, because of small displacement effects) but might have been affected by displacement from other unionized industries. In that case, what is called the "true union earnings effect" in the text would be greater than what could be called the *total* union effect on union earnings in the industry. The latter would measure the effect of all unionization—both inside and outside the industry—on the union earnings level in the industry relative to the earnings level that would prevail in the industry in a totally nonunion economy.

Table 3-7. *Alternative Indexes of Union Earnings Effect*

Case	Mean earnings differential	Fitted b coefficient	Mean true union earnings effect on union earnings level
I	$\dfrac{40 + 40}{2} = \$40$	$\dfrac{430 - 410}{.75 - .25} = \$40$	$\dfrac{40 + 40}{2} = \$40$
II	$\dfrac{10 + 30}{2} = \$20$	$\dfrac{422.50 - 402.50}{.75 - .25} = \$40$	$\dfrac{10 + 30}{2} = \$20$
III	$\dfrac{0 + 0}{2} = \$0$	$\dfrac{430 - 410}{.75 - .25} = \$40$	$\dfrac{10 + 30}{2} = \$20$
IV	$\dfrac{5 + 15}{2} = \$10$	$\dfrac{426.25 - 406.25}{.75 - .25} = \$40$	$\dfrac{10 + 30}{2} = \$20$
V	$\dfrac{30 + 90}{2} = \$60$	$\dfrac{417.50 - 397.50}{.75 - .25} = \$40$	$\dfrac{20 + 40}{2} = \$30$
VI	$\dfrac{20 + 180}{2} = \$100$	$\dfrac{400 - 400}{.75 - .25} = \$0$	$\dfrac{15 + 45}{2} = \$30$
VII	$\dfrac{0 + 0}{2} = \$0$	$\dfrac{440 - 440}{.75 - .25} = \$0$	$\dfrac{40 + 40}{2} = \$40$

Source: Based on the numerical examples in table 3-6.

tion rate on the union and nonunion earnings levels in each industry.[32] Since there are only two observations, regression analysis degenerates into simply fitting a line that runs through two points on a diagram with E on the Y-axis and U on the X-axis. The slope of this line is the b coefficient, dE/dU.

In case I it is assumed that unionization has no effect on the nonunion earnings level and a fixed effect on union earnings that is independent of the unionization rate. Nonunion weekly earnings in both industries remain at $400 but union earnings rise to $440, a $40 union difference. Table 3-7 shows that in this unique case the average union-nonunion earnings difference, the b coefficient, and the average true union effect on the union level of earnings are all equal to $40. However, as soon as the strict assumptions are dropped, the b coefficient will generally be either

32. The examples in the text generally follow the discussion in Lewis, *Unionism and Relative Wages,* pp. 31–40, but at a much simplified level.

an upward- or downward-biased estimate of either the mean union-nonunion differential or the mean true union earnings effect.[33]

In case II the assumption that the union wage is unrelated to the unionization rate is relaxed, and it is assumed that there is a positive relationship. However, it is still assumed that nonunion earnings are unaffected by the rate of unionization. Average weekly earnings are affected by two influences: the difference between the union and the nonunion earnings levels in the two industries (which is a function of the unionization rate) and the "weights" on union and nonunion earnings (the proportion of union and nonunion workers, respectively). Case I differs from case II because in the former example only the weights influenced the calculation of average weekly earnings. Table 3-7 shows that under the assumptions of case II the fitted coefficient lies above both the mean union-nonunion earnings differential and the mean true union earnings effect. Case II is often assumed to be an approximation of actual circumstances.

Case III is an extreme example of the effect of assuming that the nonunion earnings level is positively influenced by the rate of unionization. In this case it is assumed that union earnings are a positive function of the unionization rate and that the nonunion earnings are always set exactly equal to union earnings. Under the case III assumption, the union-nonunion earnings differential in each industry (and the mean differential for both) is zero by definition. Hence, any positive b coefficient will be an upward-biased measure of the differential. But as table 3-7 demonstrates, there will be a positive estimate of b because the wage in the more heavily unionized industry will be higher than the wage in the other industry. It can be seen that b exceeds both the mean union-nonunion earnings differential and the mean true union earnings effect. The latter effect occurs because, in case III, b is equivalent to the marginal effect of unionization on union earnings. In any increasing function, the marginal effect will exceed the average.

33. In the limited case in which a group of units is either virtually 100 percent unionized or totally nonunion (so that there is no union-nonunion differential *within* any group), the b coefficient will simply measure the difference in earnings between union units and nonunion units and will be unbiased. For example, municipal fire departments are generally either close to 100 percent unionized or almost entirely nonunion. In a study of the effect of unionization on fire department salaries, Ashenfelter was able to estimate the b coefficient without risking a bias. See Orley C. Ashenfelter, "The Effect of Unionization on Wages in the Public Sector: The Case of Fire Fighters," *Industrial and Labor Relations Review,* vol. 24 (January 1971), pp. 191–202.

Case III has some real world applications. One interpretation of it is a situation with "perfect" threat effects, where nonunion employers endeavor to match union earnings levels, thereby weakening the incentive for their employees to organize. Although examples of this behavior can be found, case III also can apply in other instances. Suppose data were gathered on wage determination units that were not covered by union shop clauses but that were all engaged in collective bargaining. (This is a common situation in government employment.) In any unit, union and nonunion workers would exhibit the same level of earnings (since the union would be the bargaining agent for the entire unit). Hence a correlation between the unionization rate (defined by membership) and earnings across units would simply measure the marginal effect of the unionization rate on the level of earnings.

It is not necessary to adopt the extreme assumptions of case III, however, to demonstrate the impact of assuming that nonunion earnings are positively associated with the unionization rate. Case IV makes this assumption but does not assume that the nonunion wage is pulled all the way up to the union wage. Even with this milder assumption, the b coefficient shown in table 3-7 exceeds both the mean difference between union and nonunion weekly earnings and the mean true union earnings effect on union earnings.

Case V reverses the assumption that nonunion earnings are boosted by the rate of unionization and assumes that the opposite is true. Since the gap between union and nonunion earnings widens with the unionization rate because of its effect on union earnings and on nonunion earnings, it is not surprising that the mean union-nonunion earnings differential now exceeds the b coefficient. As it happens, in case V the b coefficient also exceeds the mean true union earnings effect. But case VI demonstrates that this relationship need not hold. To emphasize the point, case VI represents a (rather implausible) situation in which the negative effect of the unionization rate on nonunion earnings exactly offsets the positive effect on union earnings in the calculation of average weekly earnings. Since in both industries average weekly earnings are $400, the correlation between unionization and average earnings is zero. This means that the b coefficient is zero, which makes it less than the mean true union earnings effect, the opposite of case VI.

Case VII is a cross between case I and case III. It assumes that there is no marginal effect of unionization on either union or nonunion earnings but that there is an average effect. It also assumes perfect threat

Table 3-8. *Summary of Union Earnings Effect*

Case	Marginal unionization effect		Average unionization effect on union earnings	Result
	Union earnings	Nonunion earnings		
I	Zero	Zero	Positive	Mean earnings differential = fitted b coefficient = mean true union earnings effect
II	Positive	Zero	Positive	Mean fitted b coefficient > mean earnings differential = mean true earnings effect
III and IV	Positive	Positive	Positive	Mean fitted b coefficient > mean true union earnings effect > mean earnings differential
V and VI	Positive	Negative	Positive	Mean earnings differential > fitted b coefficient Mean earnings differential > mean true union earnings effect Fitted b coefficient $\gtrless$ mean true union earnings effect
VII	Zero	Zero	Positive	Mean true union earnings differential > fitted b coefficient = mean earnings differential = 0

Source: Tables 3-6 and 3-7.

effects so that the level of union earnings and the level of nonunion earnings are identical. That is, the mere presence of unionization drives up earnings by $40 in both the union and nonunion sectors without regard to the unionization rate. In case VII the mean union-nonunion earnings differential is zero by definition. The fitted b coefficient is also zero since there is no observed variation across the two data points. But there is a definite true union earnings effect of $40 in both industries. Obviously, the assumptions of case VII are extreme. They might apply to special data sets but would be most unlikely to occur in a broad sample of industries.

Table 3-8 summarizes the results obtained from the numerical examples. If both the union and the nonunion earnings levels are unaffected by the rate of unionization, the b coefficient is an accurate measure of both the mean union-nonunion earnings differential and, in case I, the mean true union earnings effect. In all other cases, the coefficient differs from both these measures. Note, however, that only under two circumstances would the b coefficient turn out to be zero (or negative) in spite of an actual union influence on earnings. Such aberrations could occur either if there were no *marginal* unionization influence and perfect threat effects or if the union effect on nonunion earnings was strongly negative. In general, therefore, a positive b coefficient is a sufficient condition for a union effect on union earnings, but not a necessary condition.

Analysis of Hourly Data, 1953–76

The most readily available source of earnings data is the monthly establishment survey of the Bureau of Labor Statistics, on which tables 2-4 and 2-5 were based. These data are available in a detailed industry form over a relatively long period of time. But union and nonunion earnings are aggregated; no separate breakdown is available. Since the earnings series is the only broad measure that can be used to trace union-nonunion earnings differentials historically, it would be useful to have some measure of the bias introduced by using the unionization rate to estimate the differential.

For recent years, surveys are available from the Bureau of Labor Statistics that provide actual union and nonunion compensation rates for many of the industries included in the average hourly earnings series used in chapter 2. Hence, the union-nonunion pay differential can be observed directly and compared with the estimate obtained indirectly through the use of the various unionization rates. The outcomes give some indication of the severity of the bias created by correlations between unionization rates and union or nonunion earnings discussed in the previous section.

If the contract file is used as the source of the unionization rate, a sample of seventy-seven industries can be obtained for which union-nonunion earnings differentials are available. The corresponding numbers for the compensation survey and current population survey sources are seventy-three and sixty industries, respectively. From these samples, mean union-nonunion compensation differentials can be obtained for

Table 3-9. *Union Wage Effects in Selected Industries, by Source of Unionization Data, 1974*[a]

Percent

Source of unionization data and type of compensation	Mean union-nonunion compensation difference as percent of nonunion compensation (1)	Estimated b coefficient divided by nonunion compensation (2)	Estimated b coefficient divided by average compensation (3)
Contract file			
Straight-time hourly earnings	28	33	29
Private fringe benefits[b]	80	127	88
Total compensation[c]	33	41	35
Compensation survey			
Straight-time hourly earnings	28	27	24
Private fringe benefits[b]	83	128	88
Total compensation[c]	33	38	33
Current population survey			
Straight-time hourly earnings	31	25[d]	22[d]
Private fringe benefits[b]	100	164	107
Total compensation[c]	36	38	32

Source: Appendix tables B-15, B-16, and B-17.
a. Industries for which union and nonunion observations were available.
b. Excludes shift differentials and legally required fringe benefits such as social security taxes.
c. Includes shift differentials and legally required fringe benefits.
d. The *b* coefficient was not statistically significant.

straight-time earnings, private fringe benefits, and total compensation.[34] Table 3-9 converts these mean differentials into percentages by dividing them by mean nonunion compensation in each of these three categories. Column 1 of the table indicates that, for the seventy-seven-industry sample, the mean union-nonunion differential amounted to 28 percent of average nonunion straight-time pay. The differential for private fringe benefits was much larger: 80 percent. For total compensation, the differential was 33 percent. These differentials are standardized for global

34. The data were taken from a BLS computer tape containing the underlying data for the 1974 biennial establishment survey, which is described in Bureau of Labor Statistics, *BLS Measures of Compensation,* bulletin 1941 (GPO, 1977), chap. 4. A summary of the data from this survey can be found in BLS, *Employee Compensation in the Private Nonfarm Economy, 1974,* bulletin 1963 (GPO, 1977). However, the published data do not contain the detail on industries available from the tape. Industries for which data were available are listed in table A-1.

industry characteristics but not for individual establishment characteristics, and so are probably upwardly biased.

In an analysis in appendix B the unionization rate was found to be significantly correlated with union earnings and fringes only when the series derived from the contract file was used. Associations between the unionization rate and nonunion pay rates were generally insignificant, no matter which series was used. Of course, even insignificant relationships can affect indirectly estimated union-nonunion earnings differentials.[35]

The regressions presented in appendix B were used to calculate the b coefficient. In addition to the unionization rate, five variables—defined in appendix B—were used to standardize the wage or total compensation estimates. These were the proportion of nonwhite workers in the industry work force ($BLK76$), the proportion of women in the industry work force ($PFEM$), the average establishment size in the industry ($ESSIZ$), weighted median educational attainment (ED), and the ratio of depreciation to employment ($KLDEP$), the last being a representation of the industry capital–labor ratio. Blacks and women tend to receive lower wages because of labor-market discrimination[36] and lower average levels of skill. Earnings are thus likely to be lower in an industry with a large black or female labor force. Establishment size has been thought to exert a positive influence on wages, perhaps because large establishments require workers who need less supervision. The variable may also pick up

35. Regressions were run that included other explanatory variables, which are listed below in the text. See tables B-15, B-16, and B-17. It is possible that the relationship between the unionization rate and union or nonunion wages is of a complex, nonlinear form, which the simple regressions of appendix B fail to reflect. See S. Rosen, "Trade Union Power, Threat Effects and the Extent of Organization," *Review of Economic Studies*, vol. 36 (April 1969), pp. 185–96.

36. Studies of earnings have usually shown significant race and sex differentials after standardizing for other worker characteristics. As an example of a racial differential study, see James Gwartney, "Discrimination and Income Differentials," *American Economic Review*, vol. 60 (June 1970), pp. 396–408. A review of empirical studies of sex differentials can be found in Hilda Kahne, "Economic Perspectives on the Roles of Women in the American Economy," *Journal of Economic Literature*, vol. 13 (December 1975), especially pp. 1258–62. In the case of women, the occupational composition of employment "explains" a significant portion of the earnings residual. Hence, some observers have suggested that social discrimination (which steers women into sex-stereotyped careers) is a major element of the different earnings experience of men and women. Obviously, the use of the unexplained earnings residual as an index of discrimination has its problems. In particular, the residual will include the effect of all unmeasured characteristics. Nevertheless, even skeptics of the approach have found it difficult to explain away such differentials. As an example, see Robert H. Frank, "Why Women Earn Less: The Theory and Estimation of Differential Overqualification," *American Economic Review*, vol. 68 (June 1978), pp. 360–73.

the influence of firm size and possibly of oligopolistic product market conditions, which, especially in the presence of a union, might affect wage determination. Education represents accumulated human capital and may also reflect other industry characteristics such as technical sophistication. The proxy for the capital–labor ratio may pick up labor-force characteristics if skilled workers are more likely to be employed in capital-intensive industries; it may also be correlated with the ratio of total costs to labor costs, which could influence union power.[37]

It is worth noting that some of these industry characteristics could themselves be influenced by unionization. For example, if firms are forced by unions to pay higher compensation levels, they might respond by becoming more capital intensive or by employing a higher proportion of males. Thus controlling for capital intensity or a large proportion of female workers could bias downward the estimate of the union effect on compensation.

Table 3-9 presents an indirect estimate of the mean union-nonunion differential based on the b coefficients from the regression analysis. Column 2 divides the estimated b coefficients by the corresponding nonunion component of compensation. There are notable differences when the estimates are compared with the actual figures. However, the biases in the b coefficient vary depending on which unionization rate is used. There is an upward bias when the private fringe benefit component or total compensation is the dependent variable. For straight-time pay, the bias is positive in one case and negative in two.

In column 3 of table 3-9, the estimated b coefficient is divided by industry average compensation rather than nonunion compensation. Since average industry pay is higher than nonunion pay, the figures in column 3 are smaller than those in column 2. However, the column 3 estimates are the product of a truly indirect estimating technique, since no knowledge of union or nonunion pay was used in their preparation. Except in one instance—straight-time pay using the current population survey—the estimates turn out to be reasonable approximations of the directly

37. Detailed definitions of the variables and the actual regression results are presented in appendix B. The signs for BLK76 and PFEM are expected to be negative, and the signs for ED, ESSIZ, and KLDEP are expected to be positive. These expectations are fulfilled except in the case of ESSIZ. Studies of establishment size have usually been confined to manufacturing; if the regressions are confined to manufacturing, the expected positive coefficient results. Outside manufacturing, the concept of establishment changes. For example, the Bureau of Labor Statistics considers each railroad to be a single establishment. The lack of a significant coefficient for ESSIZ outside manufacturing may therefore simply reflect this conceptual problem. The variable ED often produces insignificant, though positive, coefficients.

Table 3-10. *Coefficient of Unionization Rate Divided by Average Hourly Earnings from Regression Analysis, Selected Years, 1953–76*[a]

Percent

Year	Contract file		Compensation survey		Current population survey	
	Industries from table 3-9 (1)	All available industries (2)	Industries from table 3-9 (3)	All available industries (4)	Industries from table 3-9 (5)	All available industries (6)
	Industries for which complete data are available, 1953–76[b]					
1953	25	19	13[c]	26	1[c]	5[c]
1976	43	24	33	36	18[c]	20[c]
	Industries for which complete data are available, 1958–76[d]					
1958	24	25	34	41	25	34
1964	28	26	31	37	26	34
1968	27	23	25	29	19[c]	25
1971	28	22	25	28	19[c]	24
1973	33	26	31	31	26	29
1974	33	26	34	34	29	33
1976	37	28	39	38	37	41

Source: Appendix tables A-1, B-1, B-2, B-3, B-6, B-7, and B-8.

a. The *b* coefficient was adjusted for percent nonwhite, percent female, establishment size, capital–labor index, and median education. See appendix B for details.

b. The number of industries represented in columns 1–6 are, respectively, 49, 58, 46, 55, 39, and 44. All estimates exclude ordnance.

c. Based on a *b* coefficient that was not statistically significant.

d. The number of industries represented in columns 1–6 are, respectively, 77, 92, 73, 87, 60, and 68. All estimates exclude ordnance.

observed figures of column 1. In that one instance, there is an underestimate. Moreover, the estimates based on straight-time pay in column 3 are always lower than the actual figures for total compensation. This suggests that even an upward-biased estimate of the hourly earnings effect such as in column 3, first row, is likely to be downward biased relative to an estimate of the total compensation effect because of the omission of fringe benefits. However, lack of control for establishment-level characteristics still makes an upward bias possible.

Table 3-10 provides a series of estimates based on hourly earnings data for various years, including 1974. Columns 1, 3, and 5 present estimates of the *b* coefficient divided by average hourly earnings, that is, computed in the same way as the figures in column 3, table 3-9. The 1974 estimates in these columns—33 percent, 34 percent, and 29 percent—can be compared with the direct estimates for straight-time pay of 28 percent, 28 percent, and 31 percent in table 3-9. Taken as a whole, the table suggests that estimates derived from regression analysis in the 25–40 percent range can be expected for data from the mid-1970s. Even if the estimates are upward biased, the magnitude of the figures in table 3-10 is striking, especially since fringe benefits are omitted. In a model that assumes unionization is exogenous, these results suggest there is a significant union influence on the earnings of production and nonsupervisory workers.

In a much-cited study, H. G. Lewis put the union-nonunion compensation differential at 10–15 percent in the 1950s.[38] Even with a healthy allowance for an upward bias, a higher estimate—say, a 20–30 percent estimate for production and nonsupervisory workers in the mid-1970s—seems reasonable. As was pointed out in chapter 2, raw data on heavily and lightly unionized industries suggested a faster pace of earnings growth in the former sector than in the latter. Table 3-10 suggests that the results obtained from the raw data are mirrored in the regression estimates. The top two rows of the table are applicable to the industries for which pre-1958 data were available. All show a widening of the estimated union-nonunion earnings differentials during 1953–76. However, the results vary greatly with the industry sample and the source of unionization data. Moreover, the results obtained when the unionization rates from the current population survey are used are below customary levels of statistical significance for the more limited sample.

In summary, unions do seem to have a marked influence on earnings. The size of this effect can be debated, but broad samples of industries produce rather large estimates. If unionization is accepted as an exogenous influence, it is difficult to argue that the entire observed earnings effect is a statistical illusion. There is evidence that the union impact on earnings increased during the 1953–76 period—any estimate of how much is sensitive to the industry sample chosen and the source of unionization data.[39]

38. *Unionism and Relative Wages*, p. 193. However, Lewis was apparently impressed by later direct estimates indicating larger differentials. See Albert Rees, "H. Gregg Lewis and the Development of Analytical Labor Economics," *Journal of Political Economy*, vol. 84 (August 1976), pt. 2, p. S5.

39. One possibility is that demographic changes in the work force are responsible for the different movement of earnings and the b coefficients. However, experiments using the proportion of women in the work force in 1953 for those industries for which such data could be obtained did not suggest that the increased participation of women in the work force could explain the results. The correlation between $PFEM$ in 1976 and in 1953 is quite high ($R = 0.97$), but the limited sample of industries for which 1953 data on women were available does not permit definite conclusions. Only manufacturing industries could be included. Although the change in the proportion of female workers is negatively related to the change in hourly earnings in 1953–76, the amount of influence is too small to have much effect.

Analysis of Demographic Data

Estimates of the *b* coefficient can be made to analyze the demographic effects of unions on earnings. Table 3-2 presented data indicating that women workers and black workers tended to have higher annual earnings in more highly unionized industries. But table 3-11 presents more ambiguous evidence. After standardization for other influences on earnings,

Table 3-11. *Coefficient of Unionization Rate Divided by Average Annua Earnings from Regression Analysis, 1972*[a]

Percent

Source of unionization data and demographic group	Estimated b coefficient as percent of mean annual earnings	Number of industries
Contract file		
White males[b]	16	92
White females[b]	16	92
Black males	22	92
Black females	20	85
Compensation survey		
White males[b]	22	87
White females[b]	23	87
Black males	54	87
Black females	33	81
Current population survey		
White males[b]	13[c]	68
White females[b]	31	68
Black males	45	68
Black females	41	64

Source: Appendix tables B-11, B-12, and B-13.
a. See table 3-10, footnote a, for regression variables.
b. "White" includes all nonblacks.
c. Based on a *b* coefficient that was not statistically significant.

the estimated union influence on the earnings of white females is the same as that for white males for two of the three sources of unionization data. It is less for black females than for black males no matter which source is used.[40] However, although the data of table 3-10 include a partial ad-

40. The same variables used to standardize the regressions on industry-average hourly earnings were used to estimate the annual earnings of the demographic groups. Note that one of these variables is *PFEM*, the proportion of women in the work force. When this variable is used in a regression on the wages of females, it has a somewhat different meaning than in a regression on industry-average earnings. In the

justment for part-time work, the estimates are more likely to be distorted for females (who are more apt to work part-time) than for males.[41]

Unions appear to have more effect on the earnings of blacks than of whites, even after controlling for industry characteristics. The results are consistent with earlier findings that the net effect of unions is to raise the black–white earnings ratio.[42] This does not imply that unions are free of discriminatory practices. Available statistical evidence suggests that racial discrimination is more prevalent in craft unions than in industrial unions.[43] Some unions may have limited entry of blacks into certain sectors, depressing the earnings of blacks except those who have broken through the barrier. But other unions have pushed up earnings, especially in certain industries that blacks are entering in greater numbers, which yields a net positive influence.

The general upward push unions have given wages for all groups helps explain the tendency for quit rates to be lower in the union sector. Table 3-5 showed that mean quit rates are notably lower in more highly unionized industries. To the extent that unions raise pay above market levels, thereby making other jobs appear less attractive, the quit rate should fall. Moreover, the higher earnings achieved by unions are likely to be accompanied by higher fringe benefits (some of which tend to bind workers to their jobs) and the provision of industrial jurisprudence services. Even after adjustment for other factors, unionization seems to exert a negative influence on the quit rate, although much of this probably comes through the compensation channel.[44]

---

latter type of regression, the variable mainly reflects the lower wages women receive on average. In a regression involving the earnings of women, the negative coefficients that are produced (see tables B-11, B-12, and B-13) may be picking up a crowding effect related to the tendency of women workers to gravitate to certain industries and occupations. See Elizabeth Waldman and Beverly J. McEaddy, "Where Women Work—An Analysis by Industry and Occupation," *Monthly Labor Review*, vol. 97 (May 1974), pp. 3–13.

41. The data of tables 3-2 and 3-11 partially correct for part-year work by considering only workers who worked in each of the four quarters in the year. However, part-time workers may work a full year, and part-year workers may work in each of the four quarters but have spells in one or more of the quarters when they are not employed.

42. Ashenfelter and Godwin, "Some Evidence on the Effect of Unionism," pp. 217–24.

43. Rapping, "Union-Induced Racial Entry Barriers."

44. Tables B-11, B-12, and B-13 present regression equations explaining the quit rate in selected industries by unionization and other variables. Unionization has the predicted negative impact on quits, no matter which of the three unionization indexes is used, although the unionization coefficient derived from the current population survey is not statistically significant.

Other Empirical Studies

Besides the Lewis study cited earlier, there have been numerous attempts to quantify union effects on compensation. Some studies have been aimed at particular industries, and hence generalizations from them to other sectors are risky.[45] Other studies have simply been aimed at showing that there is a significant union effect, without trying to pinpoint its magnitude.[46] Still others examined the effects on wage differentials of factors relating to "ability to pay" such as market concentration (in manufacturing), plant size, and profitability. Union effects enter these studies either incidentally—as an influence for which standardization is needed—or as a possible interaction with the ability-to-pay variable.[47]

Since the various studies differ in the workers and time periods covered, no precise agreement between their results can be expected. The empirical results presented above indicate that, for broad industry coverage, differences in the 20–30 percent range for production and nonsupervisory workers can be expected, with possibly a higher effect if fringe benefits as well as earnings are considered. This range is in line with several studies undertaken in the late 1960s and the 1970s, and greater precision cannot really be expected.[48]

45. For example, Rayack, "The Impact of Unionism on Wages in the Men's Clothing Industry"; Stephen P. Sobotka, "Union Influence on Wages: The Construction Industry," *Journal of Political Economy,* vol. 61 (April 1953), pp. 127–43; Walter Fogel, "Union Impact on Retail Food Wages in California," *Industrial Relations,* vol. 6 (October 1966), pp. 79–94; and Albert E. Schwenk, "Earnings Differences in Machinery Manufacturing," *Monthly Labor Review,* vol. 97 (July 1974), pp. 38–47.

46. As an example, Ozanne compares wage changes in the 1920s and the 1950s and attributes the differences in outcomes to unions. Such differences indicate a union presence in the wage determination process but do not provide an index of the absolute union-nonunion wage differential. Robert Ozanne, "Impact of Unions on Wage Levels and Income Distribution," *Quarterly Journal of Economics,* vol. 73 (May 1959), pp. 177–96.

47. Lester, "Pay Differentials"; Masters, "An Interindustry Analysis of Wages and Plant Size"; Leonard W. Weiss, "Concentration and Labor Earnings," *American Economic Review,* vol. 56 (March 1966), pp. 96–117; and Leonard A. Rapping, "Monopoly Rents, Wage Rates, and Union Wage Effectiveness," *Quarterly Review of Economics and Business,* vol. 7 (Spring 1967), pp. 31–47. For an attempt to explain some of the empirical findings on concentration and union effects on wages, see Harold M. Levinson, "Unionism, Concentration, and Wage Changes: Toward a Unified Theory," *Industrial and Labor Relations Review,* vol. 20 (January 1967), pp. 198–205.

48. For example, see Frank P. Stafford, "Concentration and Labor Earnings: A Comment," *American Economic Review,* vol. 58 (March 1968), pp. 174–81. Staf-

Because the literature is both large and diverse, a detailed summary of the individual studies cannot be undertaken here. However, a few generalizations from some recent Bureau of Labor Statistics reports are worth noting. First, if the unit of observation is the establishment or the individual, recent regression studies typically yield larger differentials associated with unionization than Lewis estimated for the 1950s, especially if the study is confined to production workers and those in similar occupations.[49]

Second, if differentials between union wages and nonunion wages are

---

ford, using data from the *1966 Survey of Consumer Finances*, finds differentials ranging from 18 to 52 percent for clerical and sales workers, laborers, craftsmen, and operatives. Rosen also reported estimates of the union wage impact higher than Lewis's levels, although his occupational breakdowns differ from Stafford's. Sherwin Rosen, "Unionism and the Occupational Wage Structure in the United States," *International Economic Review,* vol. 11 (June 1970), pp. 269–86. A second paper by Rosen using a demand-supply framework produced similar results. Sherwin Rosen, "On the Interindustry Wage and Hours Structure," *Journal of Political Economy,* vol. 77 (March–April 1969), pp. 249–73. Boskin, using data from the *1967 Survey of Economic Opportunity,* found a union-nonunion wage differential for craftsmen, operatives, and laborers in the 15–25 percent range. Michael J. Boskin, "Unions and Relative Real Wages," *American Economic Review,* vol. 62 (June 1972), p. 467. Throop, in a study dealing primarily with cyclical variations in the differential, found point estimates of 22 percent for 1950 and 26 percent for 1960, using cross-industry average hourly earnings data. Adrian W. Throop, "The Union-Nonunion Wage Differential and Cost-Push Inflation," *American Economic Review,* vol. 58 (March 1968), pp. 79–99.

49. For example, using data for the 1968 biennial establishment survey, Bailey and Schwenk estimate a union effect on hourly compensation of nonoffice workers ranging from $0.535 to $0.721 in manufacturing. Relative to nonunion hourly compensation in that year, these effects imply differentials ranging from 18 to 24 percent. William R. Bailey and Albert E. Schwenk, "Wage Differences Among Manufacturing Establishments," *Monthly Labor Review,* vol. 94 (May 1971), pp. 16–19. Bailey and Schwenk did not publish the nonunion average wage in their sample. The text assumes it to have been $3.03, the figure reported in the official Bureau of Labor Statistics publication of the survey, *Employee Compensation in the Private Nonfarm Economy, 1968,* bulletin 1722 (GPO, 1971), p. 20. A paper by Baldwin and Daski, based on establishments in a 1973–74 area wage survey, found union-nonunion differentials of 16 percent for skilled maintenance workers, 38 percent for unskilled plant workers, and 31 percent for clerical office workers. An insignificant coefficient was found for electronic data processing workers, but the estimate of unionization for these workers was considered unreliable by the authors. Stephen E. Baldwin and Robert S. Daski, "Occupational Pay Differences Among Metropolitan Areas," *Monthly Labor Review,* vol. 99 (May 1976), pp. 29–35. Union-nonunion wage differences for blue-collar workers ranging from 17 to 44 percent were found in an analysis of data from the May 1973 current population survey; Paul M. Ryscavage, "Measuring Union-Nonunion Earnings Differences," *Monthly Labor Review,* vol. 97 (December 1974), pp. 3–9.

studied within industries, the estimated union effect is usually more modest.[50] For example, column 4 of table 3-3 presented union-nonunion wage differentials adjusted by regression analysis for establishment characteristics. The union premiums estimated by the Bureau of Labor Statistics range from a high of 11 percent to a low of 1 percent. However, the BLS industry wage studies report union-nonunion differentials only for industries in which there are significant numbers of both kinds of workers and have usually been confined to manufacturing. The limited number of industries studied, the potential for threat effects, and the limited potential of the industries studied for substantial product differentiation across firms are all grounds for reluctance to generalize from these industry-specific studies to the overall economy. Moreover, the studies omit union wage effects in totally unionized industries such as automobile manufacturing.

Unionization as an Endogenous Influence

Given the persistence of large union-nonunion differentials in simple, cross-industry regression studies, the emergence of a new literature that criticizes the methodology rather than challenging the data is not surprising. Implicit in the simple regression studies of the type presented and cited in the last three sections is the assumption that unionization is an *exogenous* influence on earnings determination. If that assumption is not accepted, the regression results lose both their causal implications and their statistical accuracy.

In the regression studies, the variable to be explained is the level of earnings. For unionization to be exogenous, unionization should affect earnings, but earnings should not affect the degree of unionization. If a plausible case can be made that unionization is a function of earnings, finding a correlation between earnings and unionization might not indi-

50. For example, see Schwenk, "Earnings Differences in Machinery Manufacturing"; and Albert E. Schwenk and Martin E. Personick, "Analyzing Earnings Differentials in Industry Wage Surveys," *Monthly Labor Review*, vol. 97 (June 1974), pp. 56–59. These findings are reminiscent of earlier research by Maher, who, using industry wage survey data, found little evidence in the 1950s of a significant union-nonunion differential in wages. Although the Maher results were later criticized by Kaun, even Kaun's differentials were generally modest. John E. Maher, "Union, Nonunion Wage Differentials," *American Economic Review*, vol. 46 (June 1956), pp. 336–52; and David E. Kaun, "Union-Nonunion Wage Differentials Revisited," *Journal of Political Economy*, vol. 72 (August 1964), pp. 403–13.

cate that unionization causes earnings to be higher. Instead, it could indicate that highly paid workers are more likely to become unionized.[51]

Added to this interpretation problem is the statistical problem of simultaneous-equation bias. Suppose it is assumed that unionization, plus other variables, explains the level of earnings across industries and that the level of earnings, plus other variables, explains unionization. Then there are at least two equations in the system rather than one: an earnings-determination equation and a unionization-determination equation. When the earnings-determination equation is estimated by ordinary least squares regression analysis, it is implicitly assumed that the explanatory variables are uncorrelated with the *unexplained* variance in earnings. But in the two-equation system, this cannot be a valid assumption. If earnings in a given industry are higher than expected, the second equation says that the degree of unionization should be higher. Unionization (an explanatory variable in the first equation) must thus be correlated with the unexplained variance in that equation. In this particular example, the positive correlation would make the coefficient of unionization in the earnings-determination equation (the *b* coefficient) higher than the actual union-nonunion earnings differential.

The relatively few studies using the simultaneous-equation approach that have been undertaken sometimes have found unionization effects (*b* coefficients) of substantially smaller size and lesser statistical significance than were found in simple regression studies of the type presented above, although this is not always the case.[52] If the notion that higher earnings

51. George E. Johnson, "Economic Analysis of Trade Unionism," *American Economic Review*, vol. 65 (May 1975, *Papers and Proceedings, 1974*), p. 25. Johnson notes that his skepticism about the degree to which unionization can be viewed as an exogenous influence "is *not* widely shared by other labor economists" (emphasis in the original).

52. Studies that use a simultaneous approach and find a negligible union wage effect include Peter Schmidt and Robert P. Strauss, "The Effect of Unions on Earnings and Earnings on Unions: A Mixed Logit Approach," *International Economic Review*, vol. 17 (February 1976), pp. 204–12; Orley Ashenfelter and George E. Johnson, "Unionism, Relative Wages, and Labor Quality in U.S. Manufacturing Industries," *International Economic Review*, vol. 13 (October 1972), pp. 488–508; and Harlan David Platt, "A Simultaneous Equations Model of Wage Determination under Collective Bargaining" (Ph.D. dissertation, University of Michigan, 1976). But the findings of these studies are contradicted in John M. Abowd and Henry S. Farber, "An Analysis of Relative Wages and Union Membership: Econometric Evidence Based on Panel Data," paper presented at the December 1977 meeting of the Econometric Society; and Lung-Fei Lee, "Unionism and Wage Rates: A Simultaneous Equations Model with Qualitative and Limited Dependent Variables," *International Economic Review*, vol. 19 (June 1978), pp. 415–33. Lee found a union-

cause unionization is allowed to creep into the model, the result could be a lessening of the impact on earnings attributed to unionization. But the mere fact that a simultaneous approach is used does not necessarily produce this result.

Two issues are raised by the simultaneous methodology. First, and most obvious, is whether unionization is indeed an exogenous variable. If it is, the simultaneous approach is unnecessary. Second, if the notion that the unionization rate is endogenous rather than exogenous is accepted, the correct model to describe its relationship to earnings levels must be specified. Clearly, it is possible to accept the notion of an endogenous unionization rate without accepting a particular model that incorporates this notion.

The question of whether unionization is endogenous is really a special case of a whole family of problems in empirical economic analysis. In a world in which even weather conditions are said to be affected by economic activity, it is difficult to find truly exogenous variables. For example, recent literature on monetary policy has debated whether central bank decisions can be viewed as an "outside" influence.[53] (Monetary policy is made with reference to other economic variables such as inflation, unemployment, and interest rates, all of which are themselves endogenous.) In a very broad sense, the principle that unionization as a social phenomenon is not an extrasocietal force must be accepted. However, the issue is really whether currently observed wage rates can plausibly be thought to have a significant influence on currently observed unionization. This issue must be tackled before simultaneous equations are estimated.

One of the most impressive features of American unionization is the sudden growth of unions set off by the depression and accompanying changes in public policy. By the end of the 1940s the pattern of unionization had been largely established. Industries that were heavily unionized then remain heavily unionized today. If the pattern of unionization

---

nonunion wage differential effect for operatives of about 16 percent as of 1967. And a study by Schmidt published after the Schmidt-Strauss paper seemed to contradict the earlier results. In the later paper unionization had a positive effect on earnings but the union-nonunion earnings differential had no effect on unionization. Peter Schmidt, "Estimation of a Simultaneous Equations Model with Jointly Dependent Continuous and Qualitative Variables: The Union-Earnings Question Revisited," *International Economic Review,* vol. 19 (June 1978), pp. 453–65.

53. Frederic S. Mishkin, "Efficient-Markets Theory: Implications for Monetary Policy," *Brookings Papers on Economic Activity, 3:1978,* pp. 707–52.

was largely determined thirty or forty years ago, conceptual problems are raised by treating unionization as if it were a continuous function of today's wage rates.

Some econometric studies have attempted to capture the factors influencing union membership growth, the Ashenfelter-Pencavel study being the best known. Although the authors state at the outset that they have shown it to be unnecessary to resort—as labor historians have—to explanations of "social unrest" in the 1930s,[54] examination of their explanatory variables suggests that social unrest is a prominent behind-the-scenes force. Included are the percentage of Democrats in Congress, which was certainly affected by the social unrest of the depression. Indeed, the very meaning of Democrats in Congress takes on a different significance because of the political alliance forged at that time between the Democratic party and organized labor. Also included is the trough unemployment rate from the last depression or recession (with a decay factor). In the period studied (1904–60) the magnitude of the depression's trough unemployment rate was not approached except for a brief period in the 1920s.

The point is not the semantic issue of whether "social unrest" or economic factors should be viewed as the cause of the union upsurge in the 1930s; it is that what happened then conditions the current union situation. The Ashenfelter-Pencavel study predicts the change in union membership growth, not the absolute level of union membership. One of the variables used to predict changes is the change in employment in the union sector. Various explanations for the importance of this variable can be proffered, including the obvious one that union-security clauses often require new employees to become union members. What the Ashenfelter-Pencavel equation is really saying, then, is that once the 1930s and 1940s had produced huge membership growth unionization rates in particular industries could be expected to change relatively slowly unless there was another period of extreme values of the explanatory variables. So even if union membership growth can be explained econometrically, the fact remains that the pattern of unionization was determined by economic conditions many years ago. This conclusion suggests that it has become legitimate to treat a variable that was endogenous long ago as currently exogenous.

The same issue arises if the unit of observation is the individual rather

54. Orley Ashenfelter and John H. Pencavel, "American Trade Union Growth: 1900–1960," *Quarterly Journal of Economics*, vol. 83 (August 1969), p. 434.

than the industry. Most private sector workers who become union members today do not become unionized by organizing their employers but by going to work for already unionized employers. At the margin, some nonunion employers become unionized and some unionized employers go nonunion. This view is entirely in keeping with the Ashenfelter-Pencavel finding of support for the "saturationist" view: that there is a "unionizable" sector and that since the 1950s unions have been pressing against a diminishing-returns point in this sector.[55]

Individual choice in the union membership decision is therefore more limited than a simple function explaining that decision on the basis of the wage rate would imply.[56] A worker can choose to be nonunion by working for a nonunion employer. An automobile worker, if he no longer wants to be a union member, can quit his job, but he has little chance of mounting a successful campaign to unseat the United Auto Workers. Similarly, a bank employee who wants to be represented by a union can seek work in a unionized industry, but the probability of his successfully organizing his current employer is empirically quite small. Whether the unit is the individual or the industry, unionization is primarily a reflection of past events.

The model of unionization outline is similar to the "putty-clay" model of capital that is sometimes used in economic theory. In the latter model, capital is initially a malleable substance that can be employed in any industry. Once an investment in an industry is made, however, the capital is suited only to that industry. Unionization went through a "fluid" period in the 1930s and 1940s, when there was a great deal of uncertainty about which industries might be successfully unionized. Now that unions have been "put in place," the broad range of possibilities is no longer open.

A putty-clay model of unionization suggests that the simultaneous-equation approach ought to be applied if the object is to explain the relation between earnings and unionization in the 1930s and 1940s, but that it ought not be applied to data of the 1960s and 1970s. However, whether this criticism of the simultaneous approach is valid depends importantly on whether a putty-clay model of earnings structure is taken.

55. Ibid., p. 444.

56. Abowd and Farber, in "An Analysis of Relative Wages and Union Membership," stress this point. Their model explicitly allows for the formation of a queue for union jobs; that is, they recognize that not everyone who wants a union job can have one.

If earnings differentials were established in the 1940s and now remain relatively frozen in the earnings structure, data from the 1940s and the 1970s are inherently equivalent and hence the simultaneous approach should be applied even to current data.

It is known that the earnings structure changes slowly.[57] However, what matters is not the overall earnings structure but the portion of the earnings structure that is not explained by factors other than unionization. The observation, discussed earlier, that the union-nonunion earnings differential has changed in certain subperiods since the mid-1950s suggests that the union earnings effect is at least somewhat malleable. Whether a simultaneous approach should be used comes down to a matter of assumptions about the malleability of earnings differentials compared with that of unionization differentials. If in the past unionization was effectively frozen but earnings differentials were not, the simple regression approach treating unionization as exogenous is appropriate. If both unionization and earnings differentials were frozen in the past, current data require a simultaneous (endogenous) approach since the past and present are identical by assumption. Finally, if both unionization and earnings differentials are regarded as malleable today, the simultaneous approach is also needed. I believe the first view is the closest to current reality, but the issue is one about which reasonable observers can disagree.

If a researcher believes that unionization is an endogenous variable, he or she cannot estimate the b coefficient without specifying the precise nature of the model. At the least, an earnings function containing unionization and other variables must be estimated along with a unionization function, which must contain earnings and other variables. The task becomes much more demanding since the results now depend on precise notions of how the variables interact and which variables belong in each function. In contrast, the exogenous case involves a "reduced-form" equation in which precise views on structure are not necessary.[58]

57. Donald E. Cullen, "The Interindustry Wage Structure," *American Economic Review*, vol. 46 (June 1956), pp. 353–69.

58. A reduced-form equation is one in which all the explanatory variables are exogenous. Although there may be a complex set of interactions between the exogenous variables and other variables that ultimately influences the dependent variable, a reduced-form equation shows the net effect of the exogenous variables on the dependent variable. It produces unbiased coefficients and can be estimated by ordinary least squares.

It has been known for some time that simultaneous-equation estimates can be sensitive to the specification assumptions, data errors, and
intercorrelations of the exogenous variables.[59] For this reason, a believer
in the endogenous nature of the unionization rate must still be cautious
about accepting as accurate any particular simultaneous-equation estimate of the *b* coefficient. It could turn out that, despite the inherent bias
in the simple regression approach, the *b* coefficient resulting from ordinary least squares was closer to the true value than a corresponding
coefficient estimated from a simultaneous system.

Experiments with the industry hourly earnings data used to construct
table 3-10 produced widely divergent results when alternative simultaneous structures were used. Estimated *b* coefficients varied from impossibly
large positive union effects on earnings to negative effects. The results
were extremely sensitive to the inclusion or exclusion of an explanatory
variable in the earnings function.[60] It appears that unless a researcher
firmly believes in a particular specification of the model little confidence
can be placed in the outcome.

The difficulty of choosing a particular specification of the variables in
the earnings and unionization functions is apparent in the literature
using the simultaneous approach. For example, Ashenfelter and Johnson put the proportion of female workers in the earnings function.[61] But
could it not be argued that women, who typically have a looser attachment to their employers than men, would have less interest in forming
unions to deal with those employers? If this seems reasonable, a case
can be made for putting the percentage of females in the unionization
function. Ashenfelter and Johnson do provide alternative specifications
in their paper, but all the possible combinations of variables are not presented. Despite their finding of an insignificant effect of unionization on
earnings, Ashenfelter and Johnson wisely pull back from accepting this
estimate as gospel.[62] In a later study Schmidt and Strauss are somewhat
bolder, but still cautious.[63] And Platt is willing to say only that the hy-

59. J. Johnston, *Econometric Methods,* 2d ed. (McGraw-Hill, 1972), pp. 408–20.

60. Two-stage least squares analysis was employed in these experiments.

61. "Unionism, Relative Wages, and Labor Quality."

62. They state: "Given the qualitative and quantitative limitations of the data,
we are prepared to say only that we are uncertain of the magnitude of the effect
of unions on interindustry wage differences." Ibid., p. 505.

63. They conclude that their findings "may suggest that the common statement
that unions raise wages may suffer from an incomplete notion of causation." "The
Effect of Unions on Earnings and Earnings on Unions," p. 211.

pothesis that high earnings cause unions rather than that unions cause high earnings cannot be rejected.[64]

The real issue, however, is not the estimation techniques used by various authors, the adjectives they use to describe their findings, or even whether in some sense of the word unionization is endogenous to the economic system. Instead, it is the assumptions that are made before any statistical results are obtained. Since the basic pattern for unionization was established a long time ago and since workers cannot choose between being unionized and not being unionized as easily as they choose whether or not to buy apples, unionization should not be viewed as currently endogenous for purposes of statistical analysis. That is, to me the observed correlation between wages and unionization—given these assumptions—cannot be due to a contemporary tendency of higher-paid workers to "purchase" union services. It is due, rather, to the tendency of unions to raise wages.

Summary

The theory of the union wage effect is inherently imprecise. For most unions, the establishment of pay goals is not a matter of a simple maximization process analogous to the model of the firm in price theory. It is important to include management resistance in any model of collective bargaining since unions do not set wages unilaterally. Within such a model, the costs to both sides of an impasse will most often outweigh considerations of demand elasticities and the wage-employment trade-off that many economists stress.

It would be surprising if statistical evidence suggested that unions had no effect on pay levels. Unions are in a position to impose costs on management and presumably must deliver some service to their members. Conceivably, these services could all be in areas other then compensation, but this seems unlikely as a general rule. The statistical evidence does suggest a simple association between unionization and pay. Unions are apt to be in higher-paying industries. The association is particularly striking in the case of fringe benefits.

64. Platt, however, is willing to treat the propensity to strike as an exogenous variable even though unionization is viewed as endogenous. Moreover, the strike variable is said to be included because "work stoppages are expected to be inversely related to the union's ability to provide job security." Why this should be expected is a mystery. "A Simultaneous Equations Model of Wage Determination," p. 77.

Even after standardization by regression analysis for other factors that might influence pay, an association between unionization rates and industry average earnings persists. The interpretation of the regression coefficients is complicated by various biases, which may affect the results. Moreover, the absolute results will vary depending on the source of data. No single estimate of *the* union impact on earnings is above reproach. However, if Lewis's estimate of 10–15 percent for the union-nonunion pay difference in the 1950s is accepted, a larger estimate seems appropriate for the 1970s. Earnings have risen more rapidly in the union sector than in the nonunion sector, a phenomenon that appears in both raw data and regression estimates. For production and nonsupervisory workers an estimate of 20–30 percent for the differential in the mid-1970s is reasonably consistent with that of a number of recent studies and allows for a margin of upward bias in the regression results presented in this chapter. The unions' effect on earnings appears to be stronger for black workers than for others.

The evidence presented above strengthens the case for considering the role of collective bargaining in the inflation process. If unions can raise wages, they may also influence the response of wage adjustments to macroeconomic policy. And they may add a discretionary element to wage determination that might otherwise not exist.

IV

Determinants of Wage Change

THE DYNAMICS of wage determination, both union and nonunion, have been of special interest to makers of macroeconomic policy during the past three decades. Few professional economists would espouse the view that wage setting, or collective bargaining in particular, is the principal cause of inflation, although many observers have the uneasy sense that the wage-determination process contributes to the difficulty of stopping inflation once it has begun. Experience in the early 1960s showed that collective bargaining was compatible with relative price stability. And few would attribute the buildup of price inflation in the late 1960s to cost-push in the labor market. Demand pressure stemming from the monetary and fiscal policy that accompanied the Vietnam War and the Great Society was the spark.

An important question is whether the collective bargaining sector has characteristics that perpetuate inflation. Such perpetuation can occur if today's wage settlements and wage adjustments reflect current and past price inflation. If they do, the inflationary problems of the past will be automatically transmitted to the present and current inflationary pressures will be reinforced. When inflation continues, the traditional government response is monetary and fiscal restraint, which is supposed to slow the pace of economic activity and help moderate both wage and price inflation. Another question is how sensitive wage behavior is to deliberately induced economic slack. Lack of sensitivity would make inflation fighting by conventional economic policy difficult. In short, to the extent that unionization increases sensitivity to lagged and current price inflation or reduces sensitivity to economic slack, it can impede anti-inflation efforts.

Two qualifications should be noted. First, if unionization is associated with characteristics that impede inflation-limiting policies, it is also associated with characteristics that can help stimulate real economic activity. That is, in a period when the rate of inflation was low and the object of public policy was reducing unemployment, stimulatory policy would not result at first in substantial wage increases. Stimulation would not increase the rate of wage inflation in the short run.

Second, although the emphasis in this chapter is on wage determination, this does not imply that there are no elements of price determination that contribute to the rate of inflation. Indeed, the rate of inflation is usually defined in terms of price change rather than wage change. But when guideposts or wage-price controls have been implemented in the past, wages have been subject to an absolute standard (3.2 percent, 5.5 percent, or 7 percent in the Kennedy-Johnson, Nixon, and Carter administration programs) and price controls have been based on markups.[1]

Programs with absolute standards for wages and markup standards for prices implicitly rely on the wage side to bring the inflation rate down. No programs have set an absolute standard for prices and geared wages to "markups" above the cost of living. Policymakers believe—with good reason—that wage controls are easier to administer than price controls. The definition of "wage" is easier to specify than the definition of "price." Moreover, the product market is more likely to suffer from shortages and distortions if tampered with than the labor market. In choosing whether to attack the wage-price spiral from the price or wage side, therefore, policymakers, when implementing guidelines or controls, chose the wage side in the 1960s and 1970s as being more feasible administratively. Given this predilection, an understanding of the dynamics of wage determination is especially relevant to the inflation issue.

Discussions of wage determination and inflation often center on the unionized sector of the labor force. There are several reasons for this. First, union wage bargains, especially the visible ones, cover large numbers of workers and sometimes lead to dramatic labor-management confrontations. During a period of formal controls or voluntary guidelines, there is always concern about whether big labor will cooperate with the program. Second, it is often held that union wage negotiations spill over into the nonunion sector. To the extent that there is spillover (an issue taken up in chapter 5), the importance of the union sector is enhanced. Even with the declining trend in relative unionization, the union sector still retained a weight of about 35 percent in the Bureau of Labor Statistics' employment cost index in 1977. With spillover, the effective weight would be somewhat higher.

A third reason that attention focuses on the union sector is the possibility that the union sector is less responsive to economic slack than the

1. The program begun by the Carter administration in October 1978 set a "deceleration" standard for price increases. However, if the deceleration rule resulted in a profit squeeze, an alternative markup standard was available.

nonunion sector. In a period of rising unemployment, nonunion employers might be expected to react to the growing labor surplus in making their wage decisions. Retirement and retention problems are eased by high unemployment, reducing the incentive for nonunion firms to raise wages. For the union sector—where wages are typically set above market rates—the impact of an increased number of job seekers is likely to be attenuated. The employer generally has a queue of potential workers who want jobs, so the lengthening of the queue is of small importance. For employees, the above-market rate of pay—combined with fringe benefits, which inhibit mobility—tends to diminish the incentive to quit, even in a relatively tight labor market.[2] A rise in unemployment might be correlated with decreased ability to pay (and greater resistance) on the part of employers and with diminished union bargaining power. For example, in the event of a strike, union members might have trouble finding temporary jobs, and secondary workers in union households might be less likely to obtain or retain employment. But this shift in the strategic balance is a different mechanism from what would be expected in the nonunion sector.

Finally, the union sector, unlike the nonunion sector, is characterized by long-term agreements.[3] In any given year, large numbers of union workers do not negotiate but instead receive wage adjustments pursuant to contracts signed one or two years before. Wages under such agreements cannot reflect contemporary economic conditions unless those conditions were forecast correctly at the time of the negotiations or unless there is a contingency clause in the contract. The most common form of contingency clause is the cost-of-living escalator, which gears wage adjustments to movements in prices by some formula. Wages under existing contracts will at most reflect current inflation rates; they will not reflect other economic circumstances such as the level of real economic activity. By way of contrast, in the nonunion sector, even where formalized personnel practices are used, the decision period for wage adjustments is seldom more than one year. (The decision in a given year may be to give no general wage increase, but what is at issue is not the size of the adjustment but the frequency of decisions.)

2. A tight labor market is one in which unemployment is low and job opportunities are plentiful. Unfortunately, in recent years a period of high unemployment has been misleadingly described in the press as a tight job market. When unemployment is high and vacancies are few, the labor market should be described as "loose."

3. Bureau of Labor Statistics, *Characteristics of Major Collective Bargaining Agreements, July 1, 1976*, bulletin 2013 (Government Printing Office, 1979), p. 6.

Industrial Relations and Real Economic Activity

Industrial relations practices in the union sector are affected by real economic influences. Researchers who have looked at such questions as the frequency of strikes or the "ebb and flow" of union membership have generally related these elements of industrial relations to economic variables.[4] Of course, other variables, such as the political and legislative climate, may also play a part. But it would be incorrect to characterize the union sector as being immune to the general state of the economy.

For example, unions, employers, and individual workers representing over 70 percent of payroll employment in the private nonfarm sector have access to the facilities of the National Labor Relations Board.[5] Both unions and employers are subject to the prohibitions of section 8 of the amended Wagner Act. Charges may be filed against employers by unions or workers under section 8(a) on the ground that the employer has violated one of these strictures and thus committed an "unfair labor practice." Similarly, employers or workers may file unfair labor practice charges under section 8(b) against unions that have allegedly committed prohibited acts. Charges filed often arise from strikes or union organization drives. The number of unfair labor practice charges filed in a given year may reflect labor-management conflict.

A simple regression analysis, in appendix table C-1, suggests that the filing of unfair labor practice charges is cyclically sensitive. The number of charges filed against both unions and employers shows a significant upward trend reflecting the increasing legalism of industrial relations. But when controlling for this trend, the number of charges filed is usually lower during periods of economic prosperity (when real GNP is above its trend) than in periods of economic slack. This suggests that prosperity reduces labor-management tension, perhaps because the economic "pot" is bigger for both parties. On the other hand, a rise in the level of economic activity tends to increase the number of charges filed, at least

4. Orley Ashenfelter and John H. Pencavel, "American Trade Union Growth: 1900–1960," *Quarterly Journal of Economics,* vol. 83 (August 1969), pp. 434–38; Farouk Elsheikh and George Sayers Bain, "American Trade Union Growth: An Alternative Model," *Industrial Relations,* vol. 17 (February 1978), pp. 75–79.

5. The NLRB was estimated to cover 44.1 million workers in 1975. About 62.3 million workers were reported to be on private nonfarm payrolls. *Daily Labor Report* (May 17, 1978), p. A-11; and Bureau of Labor Statistics, *Handbook of Labor Statistics, 1977,* bulletin 1966 (GPO, 1977), p. 88.

against employers, and a fall in economic activity tends to reduce them. It may be that unions increase their pressure on management (in organization drives and in bargaining) as economic conditions improve and that management is slow to believe in the improvement. A similar union lead in adjusting behavior toward management could account for a reverse reaction in downswings.

Regression analysis of NLRB representation elections supports this view.[6] When the fact that more elections are held now than in the past is taken into account, an increase (decrease) in real economic activity is associated with an increase (decrease) in the number of elections. There is weaker evidence that the number of elections is higher in periods of relative prosperity (see appendix table C-2, columns 1–3). But union success in these elections is not significantly greater during upswings, which suggests that management resistance to unionization drives offsets the union propensity to call for more elections. In periods of relative prosperity, however, union success is significantly greater than in other periods, suggesting that management resistance declines when it is clear that economic gains are available for sharing (see table C-2, columns 4–6).

The number of workers involved in strikes, after adjustment for the number of workers covered by expiring contracts and the effects of wage controls, also shows cyclical sensitivity.[7] The change in the number of workers involved in work stoppages becomes larger in periods of prosperity but smaller as the level of economic activity improves. The propensity to strike evidently is generated by a different mechanism than union organization drives. Taken literally, the strike regression equations presented in appendix C imply that in steady-state economic conditions the number of workers involved in strikes would increase indefinitely. This implausible result suggests that a more elaborate model of strike generation is needed. However, the principle that strike activity is influenced by the business cycle is supported.[8]

6. Two studies relating NLRB election results to the business cycle are Joseph Krislov, "Union Organizing of New Units, 1955–1966," *Industrial and Labor Relations Review*, vol. 21 (October 1967), pp. 31–39; and Joseph Krislov and Virgil L. Christian, Jr., "Union Organizing and the Business Cycle, 1949–1966," *Southern Economic Journal*, vol. 36 (October 1969), pp. 185–88.

7. Table C-3 presents three equations that are extensions of strike regressions that appeared in Arnold R. Weber and Daniel J. B. Mitchell, *The Pay Board's Progress: Wage Controls in Phase II* (Brookings Institution, 1978), p. 443.

8. See also Orley Ashenfelter and George E. Johnson, "Bargaining Theory, Trade Unions, and Industrial Strike Activity," *American Economic Review*, vol. 59 (March 1969), pp. 35–49; and Albert Rees, "Industrial Conflict and Business Fluctuations," *Journal of Political Economy*, vol. 60 (October 1952), pp. 371–82.

Table 4-1. *Impact of Business Cycle on Selected Industrial-Relations Measures*

Industrial-relations measure	Impact of relative prosperity	Impact of improving economic conditions
Number of charges of NLRB unfair labor practices filed		
Against employers	Negative	Positive
Against unions	Negative	n.s.
Number of NLRB representation elections held		
All sectors	n.s.	Positive
Manufacturing	Positive	Positive
Involving only one union	n.s.	Positive
Success rates of unions in NLRB representation elections		
All sectors	Positive	n.s.
Manufacturing	Positive	n.s.
Involving only one union	Positive	n.s.
Annual change in number of workers involved in work stoppages		
Over wage issues	Positive	Negative
Over contract renegotiations	Positive	Negative
All stoppages	Positive	Negative

Source: Regression equations in appendix tables C-1, C-2, and C-3.
n.s. No significant effect.

Table 4-1, which summarizes the findings just discussed, emphasizes the fact that various industrial relations measures are influenced by the state or the direction of the economy, or both. It would thus be wrong to view the union sector as being oblivious to the economic climate or to rule out, in particular, the possibility that union wages are influenced by economic conditions. Evidence presented in the next section suggests that an influence—though an attenuated one—is felt but that its degree depends on which components of union contracts are studied.

Determinants of Wage Change

It is important to recognize from the outset that a distinction must be made between the determinants of wage change over time and the determinants across industries. All industries are subject to general forces in the economy. For example, the rate of inflation as observed by wage setters across industries at any one time is the same.[9] Individual industries will experience different fluctuations in demand, but the demand for most products will be closely associated with the overall state of the economy. Similarly, the availability of labor will vary across industries, depending on their location and the types of workers they employ, but all labor markets will reflect the general condition of the labor market as indicated by some aggregate measure such as the overall unemployment rate.[10]

Relative versus General Wage Movements

The explanation of *relative* wage changes across industries is inherently a much more difficult task than the explanation of wage changes in a particular sector or in the whole economy. General economic indicators, though they may explain why wages change, cannot be used to explain why wages in, say, the steel industry rose faster or more slowly than wages in retail food stores. For example, the rate of consumer price inflation might help explain wage movements in both industries. But since the rate of consumer price inflation was the same for steelworkers and food-store workers, it cannot be used to explain the difference in wage movements in the two industries.

In principle, the explanation of why some industries pull ahead in wage changes while others fall behind is to be found at the industry level. As an empirical matter, the most readily available measures of industry economic conditions are not well correlated with relative industry wage movements. For example, table 4-2 presents the simple correlation coefficient (R) between the change in the number of production and nonsupervisory workers and the change in hourly earnings

9. There are, of course, regional variations in the rate of inflation that this statement overlooks. However, only about 10 percent of escalated contracts are linked to the consumer price index for a particular city rather than to the national index. See Robert H. Ferguson, *Cost-of-Living Adjustments in Union-Management Agreements* (Cornell University, New York State School of Industrial and Labor Relations, 1976), p. 29.

10. For example, in the 1975 recession employment fell in each of the two-digit classifications of manufacturing as well as in construction, wholesale trade, transportation-communications-utilities, and finance-insurance-real estate. See Bureau of Economic Analysis, *Business Statistics, 1977* (GPO, 1978), pp. 73–75.

Table 4-2. *Simple Correlation Coefficient (R) of Percentage Change in Hourly Earnings and Percentage Change in Production and Nonsupervisory Employment across Industries, 1953–76*

	Industries with above-average unionization rates			Industries with below-average unionization rates			
Period	Contract file (1)	Compensation survey (2)	Current population survey (3)	Contract file (4)	Compensation survey (5)	Current population survey (6)	All industries in sample (7)
1953–58[a]	−0.03	−0.03	−0.35	−0.10	0.04	0.24	−0.07
1958–64	0.02	0.12	0.10	0.06	−0.25	0.12	0.03
1964–71	−0.17	0.20	−0.07	0.32	−0.00	0.13	0.15
1971–76	0.20	0.16	0.22	0.04	−0.26	−0.16	−0.00
1953–76[a]	−0.02	−0.04	−0.23	−0.03	−0.29	−0.15	−0.14

Source: Earnings and employment data drawn from Bureau of Labor Statistics, *Employment and Earnings, United States, 1909–75,* bulletin 1312-10 (Government Printing Office, 1976), pp. 1–675; and *Employment and Earnings,* vol. 24 (March 1977), tables B-2 and C-2.

a. Based only on industries for which 1953 earnings data were available.

across the sample of industries used in tables 2-4 and 2-5.[11] One conceivable explanation for earnings change might be that industries with rapidly expanding employment would have to outbid other industries for labor by raising wages faster. Similarly, industries experiencing a decline in employment would be relatively unconcerned about employee retention and recruitment. Hence such an industry might exhibit a relatively slow rate of earnings change.

Plausible though this theory may seem, it receives no empirical support from table 4-2. The correlation between change in employment and change in wages is low and is often negative.[12] This suggests that the specific factors which influence differential wage adjustments in particular industries are not likely to be captured in simple models. It also suggests that, while aggregate business conditions may help explain aggregate earnings change, relative business conditions do not necessarily contribute much to an understanding of relative wage change.

11. The industries are those listed in table A-1.
12. This result is similar to evidence obtained from various countries, including the United States, in Organization for Economic Cooperation and Development, *Wages and Labor Mobility* (OECD, 1965), chap. 6.

Union versus Nonunion Wage Changes: Initial Results

In the early 1960s the "Phillips curve" took the economics profession by storm. The original article by A. W. Phillips postulated a relationship between the rate of wage change and the level of unemployment.[13] Successive articles by other observers added to the list of variables besides the unemployment rate that might be used to explain wage change. These included price change, productivity, and profits.[14] In general, the aggregate wage equations that were estimated have proved to be unstable, suggesting that the search for new and better variables may have been pushed too far. What remains is a general consensus that in a wage equation it is useful to have some measure of the rate of price inflation (because price changes affect the purchasing power of wages and because prices may also indicate employers' ability to pay) and some measure of real economic conditions (because real demand for labor should play some role in wage determination).

A series of simple regression equations were run explaining the annual change in hourly earnings for each of the ninety-three industries listed in table A-1. Earnings changes were explained by the rate of change of consumer prices during the previous year and the current official unemployment rate (in inverted form).[15] The ninety-three industries could then be grouped according to whether they exhibited above-

13. A. W. Phillips, "The Relation Between Unemployment and the Rate of Change of Money Wage Rates in the United Kingdom, 1861–1957," *Economica,* vol. 25 (November 1958), pp. 283–99.

14. For a sample of such studies, see George L. Perry, "The Determinants of Wage Rate Changes and the Inflation-Unemployment Trade-off for the United States," *Review of Economic Studies,* vol. 3 (October 1964), pp. 287–308; E. Kuh, "A Productivity Theory of Wage Levels—An Alternative to the Phillips Curve," *Review of Economic Studies,* vol. 34 (October 1967), pp. 333–60; Sara Behman, "Wage-Determination Process in U.S. Manufacturing," *Quarterly Journal of Economics,* vol. 82 (February 1968), pp. 117–42; Kenneth M. McCaffree, "A Further Consideration of Wages, Unemployment, and Prices in the United States, 1948–1958," *Industrial and Labor Relations Review,* vol. 17 (October 1973), pp. 60–74; Sara Behman, "Labor Mobility, Increasing Labor Demand, and Money Wage-Rate Increases in United States Manufacturing," *Review of Economic Studies,* vol. 31 (October 1964), pp. 253–66; and Robert J. Flanagan, "The U.S. Phillips Curve and International Unemployment Rate Differentials," *American Economic Review,* vol. 63 (March 1973), pp. 114–31.

15. For the industries on which earnings data were not available until 1958, the regressions were run for the period 1959–76. For all other industries, the observation period was 1954–76.

Table 4-3. *Comparative Industry Characteristics by Sensitivity of Hourly-Earnings Change to Unemployment and Lagged Price Change*

Characteristic	Unemployment-sensitive industries[a] (1)	Unemployment-insensitive industries[a] (2)	Price-sensitive industries[b] (3)	Price-insensitive industries[b] (4)
Unionization rate (percent)				
Contract file	23.9	38.3	35.4	28.5
Compensation survey	41.5	56.4	56.9	43.8
Current population survey	27.9	44.1	42.8	31.6
Employees per establishment, 1974	64.0	240.6	248.5	82.2
Private fringe benefits as percent of private compensation, 1971[c]	5.9	9.1	9.2	6.5
Percent of female employees, 1976	36.8	21.5	22.2	34.0
Depreciation per employee (dollars), 1973[d]	908	2,587	2,085	1,578
Average hourly earnings (dollars), 1976	4.65	5.86	5.67	4.99
Average monthly quit rate (percent), 1976[e]	2.3	1.0	1.1	2.0

Source: See appendix B.
a. Sensitive (insensitive) industries are those whose unemployment coefficient is above (below) the all-industry mean.
b. Sensitive (insensitive) industries are those whose price-change coefficient is above (below) the all-industry mean.
c. Sixty-three manufacturing industries.
d. Excludes ordnance.
e. Fifty-six industries.

or below-average direct sensitivity to unemployment or above- or below-average sensitivity to price inflation.[16]

Table 4-3 shows unemployment-sensitive and -insensitive industries and price-sensitive and -insensitive industries classified by various characteristics. The table suggests that unemployment-sensitive industries are less highly unionized than unemployment-insensitive industries, regardless of which of the three measures of unionization is used. They are also characterized by smaller establishments, a smaller proportion of compensation in the form of fringe benefits, a larger proportion of female employees, a lower degree of capital intensity (measured by depreciation per employee), lower hourly earnings, and higher quit rates. There is a similar, though less pronounced, tendency for price-insensitive industries to exhibit the same sort of characteristics as unemployment-sensitive industries. Both, for example, have lower average rates of unionization.

These differences in average characteristics not only are themselves interrelated but also can be related to what has been called the "dual labor market" approach, which postulates that the labor market can usefully be divided into two segments for purposes of analysis. In the primary sector are found good jobs with high pay, comprehensive fringe benefits, employees with good work habits, low rates of turnover, and so forth. In the secondary sector are found low-wage jobs without much opportunity for occupational advancement, few fringe benefits, workers with poor work habits, and high rates of turnover. The industries identified as unemployment-insensitive and price-sensitive have primary-market characteristics.[17]

16. The mean coefficient for the inverse of the unemployment rate was 11.96. Industries with coefficients above (below) 11.96 were classified as exhibiting above (below) average unemployment sensitivity. Of the ninety-three industries, forty-two had unemployment coefficients above the mean. The mean price change coefficient was 0.67. Industries with price-change coefficients above (below) 0.67 were classified as exhibiting above (below) average price sensitivity. Of the ninety-three industries, forty-four had price change coefficients above the mean. It should be noted that long-run sensitivity to monetary and fiscal policy is not synonymous with sensitivity t unemployment, since some aggregate-demand effects can be passed into wages indirectly through the lagged price-change coefficient. See Michael L. Wachter, "The Changing Cyclical Responsiveness of Wage Inflation," *Brookings Papers on Economic Activity*, 1:1976, pp. 115–59.

17. On the dual labor market approach, see Peter B. Doeringer and Michael J. Piore, *Internal Labor Markets and Manpower Analysis* (Heath, 1971), pp. 163–83; and Michael L. Wachter, "Primary and Secondary Labor Markets: A Critique of the

The primary market is supposed to be more highly unionized, with the formality in industrial relations and personnel practices a contractual relationship implies. Workers are usually tied to their employers by their above-market wage rates and their fringe benefits, which may be contingent on continued employment. This employer-employee connection could be expected to lower the rate of voluntary quits. Establishments and firms in the primary market tend to be large, another reason for formality in personnel policy. Large establishments, it has been argued, require workers who can work responsibly without detailed supervision.[18] Thus better work habits might well characterize such employees. Higher capital intensity could be associated with newer technology, embodied in capital, and accompanying demands for employee skills. It may also be a proxy for barriers to entry into the industry, and therefore oligopolistic market structures, which could be exploited by a union to achieve higher compensation levels. The proportion of female employees in the primary market would presumably be lower than elsewhere, since women tend to have less strong attachments to their employers than men and are more likely to seek part-time employment.

Two lessons can be drawn from table 4-3. First, since unionization seems to be associated with different sensitivity to both price inflation and unemployment, it would be fruitful to disaggregate the labor market into union and nonunion segments. Second, the table points out that divisions such as union and nonunion will not capture all sources of difference in interindustry wage determination. There are union workers in both the unemployment-sensitive and -insensitive sectors, for example, although there is a higher unionization rate in the latter. Some union industries behave as if they were nonunion, and vice versa.

A relationship between unionization and price sensitivity is shown in table 4-3. However, a more detailed analysis in appendix C produces a statistically significant association between unionization and price sensi-

---

Dual Approach," *Brookings Papers on Economic Activity, 3:1974,* pp. 637–80. A major disagreement between dual theorists and their critics is over why firms and industries in the primary sector have extensive internal labor markets. The explanation is less important for the purposes of this study than the observation that they do.

18. Stanley H. Masters, "An Interindustry Analysis of Wages and Plant Size," *Review of Economics and Statistics,* vol. 51 (August 1969), p. 341; and Richard Lester, "Pay Differentials by Size of Establishment," *Industrial Relations,* vol. 7 (October 1967), pp. 64–65.

tivity only when the compensation survey index of unionization is used.[19] In general, the Phillips-curve view seems less applicable to the union sector than to the nonunion sector. For this reason wage equations containing some index of real business conditions are less likely to perform well for the union sector than for the nonunion sector unless further account is taken of institutional forms (which are discussed below).

Another note of caution must be included. There was relatively little unionization in the labor force before the mid-1930s. The number of union members began to fall after 1920, a period of strong employer opposition to unionization. In the early 1930s, as the economy descended into the depression, unionization of the labor force fell still further.[20] It might appear, therefore, that in the 1920s and early 1930s the free market reigned supreme in determining wages and that wages should have been far more sensitive to real economic conditions than at present. Fragmentary evidence suggests that the labor market was more fluid in the earlier part of this century than it is today.[21] But table 4-4, which presents estimates of the responsiveness of wage change to unemployment in various periods, suggests that the differences, at least in manufacturing, were less dramatic than might be expected.

The estimates in the table were derived from earnings equations reported in appendix C. In general, an increase from 6 percent to 7 percent unemployment in the early period seems to have had much the same effect on wage change as in the later period—that is, a slowing of the rate of wage change of about 0.5 percentage point. The estimates are sensitive to the precise periods chosen for analysis. Moreover, questions could be raised about the comparability and reliability of data in the two pe-

19. Table C-4 relates the unemployment coefficient (column 1), the lagged price-change coefficient (column 2), and the coefficient of determination (column 3) to six types of indexes of industry characteristics: the three indexes of the unionization rate, the proportion of nonwhites in the work force, the average establishment size, the proportion of women in the work force, the ratio of depreciation to employment, and weighted median education.

20. Data on union membership during this period can be found in Bureau of the Census, *Historical Statistics of the United States: Colonial Times to 1970* (GPO, 1975), pt. 1, p. 178.

21. Daniel J. B. Mitchell, Introduction, in Mrs. John Van Vorst and Marie Van Vorst, *The Woman Who Toils: Being the Experiences of Two Ladies as Factory Girls* (UCLA Institute of Industrial Relations, 1974 [1903]), pp. I–XXXII.

Table 4-4. *Wage-Change Determinants in Manufacturing, Selected Periods, 1920–76*

Worker group	Period of observation (1)	Estimated effect on wage change of a 1 percentage point increase in unemployment rate at 6 percent unemployment (2)	Estimated effect on wage change of a 1 percentage point increase in rate of price inflation[a] (3)
All workers	1920–32	−0.6	*
Females	1922–32	−0.5	*
Males	1922–32	−0.5	*
Skilled	1922–32	*	*
Unskilled	1922–32	−0.5	*
All workers[b]	1954–76	−0.5	0.6

Source: Appendix table C-5.
* Not significant.
a. Wage change one year after price-inflation increase.
b. Straight-time hourly earnings.

riods.[22] But even when all those complications are taken into account, the estimates for the early period make it hard to argue that the labor market was once characterized by textbook perfect competition, which was somehow lost in the later period. Table 4-4 suggests that the labor market never met the condition of perfect competition, that is, that wages would fall indefinitely as long as there was excess labor supply.[23]

The most interesting difference between the early and recent periods in table 4-4 is the reaction to lagged price change. Although the underlying equations for the early period generally indicate some responsiveness of wage change to lagged price change, the relation is not strong enough to develop statistical significance. In the later period the relationship is quite strong.

22. For example, unemployment was not surveyed regularly by government agencies during the early period, and the historical unemployment data now available had to be assembled from fragmentary sources. The equations underlying table 4-4 can be found in table C-5.

23. Economists have become so accustomed to the empirical fact that wages do not plummet indefinitely once excess supply appears in the labor market that the notions of wage rigidity and wage insensitivity to unemployment are often treated as though they were synonymous. Wages do respond to unemployment, but they do not respond as flexibly as a textbook model with perfect competition and homogeneous labor would predict. An example of a study that uses insensitivity and rigidity synonymously is Clarence D. Long, "The Illusion of Wage Rigidity: Long and Short Cycles in Wages and Labor," *Review of Economics and Statistics,* vol. 42 (May 1960), pp. 140–51.

Table 4-5. *Annual Hourly-Earnings-Change Determinants in the Private Nonfarm Sector, 1960–76*

Industry group and source of data	Estimated effect on hourly-earnings change of a 1 percentage point increase in unemployment rate at 6 percent unemployment (1)	Estimated effect on hourly-earnings change of a 1 percentage point increase in consumer price inflation rate[a] (2)
All industries[b]	−0.3	0.5
93 industries[c]	−0.3	0.5
Heavily unionized industries[c]		
Contract file	*	0.6
Compensation survey	*	0.5
Current population survey	*	0.5
Lightly unionized industries[c]		
Contract file	−0.3	0.6
Compensation survey	−0.3	0.6
Current population survey	−0.4	0.6

Source: Appendix table C-6.
* Not significant.
a. Earnings change one year after price-inflation increase.
b. Based on hourly earnings index adjusted for overtime in manufacturing and interindustry employment shift.
c. Annual percentage change in hourly earnings in each industry weighted by production and nonsupervisory employment in 1976.

Price movements were also different in the two periods. Consumer prices fell in the early 1920s, then stabilized. The onset of the depression brought substantial new price reductions. In contrast, except for a brief episode in the mid-1950s, consumer prices rose during the later period. Sometimes they crept up and sometimes they leapt up, but the direction was almost always upward. Conceivably, the difference between the trends of prices in the two periods led to greater sensitization to price movements by wage setters in the later period. Unions may have contributed to the price sensitivity in the later period, partly through the use of escalator clauses. But, as has been noted, price sensitivity has not been the exclusive property of the union sector in recent years. An argument that unions have caused or created the price sensitivity would probably have to involve some sort of spillover effects from the union to nonunion sector. (Spillover is discussed in chapter 5.)

If industries are grouped by unionization rates, typical behavior in the heavily and lightly unionized sectors can be compared. Table 4-5 presents the results of such a grouping. The ninety-three industries used previously were separated into those with above-average and those with below-average unionization rates. Equations explaining the annual change in hourly earnings in the two sectors by price changes of the previous year and the current unemployment rate were estimated (see table C-6). The results suggest that (1) observed aggregate earnings behavior is dominated by the nonunion sector, and (2) the union sector is less sensitive to real economic conditions than the nonunion sector. The first conclusion is not surprising, given the large majority of nonunion workers in the U.S. labor force. The second is in keeping with analysis earlier in this chapter.[24]

Both the union and the nonunion sectors appear equally sensitive to changes in the rate of consumer price inflation. Whatever differences there may be between the two sectors cannot be derived from the simple equations upon which the estimates of table 4-5 are based. However, it will be shown below that within the union sector negotiators who demonstrate their concern about price inflation by installing escalator clauses do exhibit stronger price sensitivity than their counterparts who do not use such clauses.

Wage Changes in Manufacturing

The estimates obtained so far are suggestive, but the method used to divide the economy into union and nonunion sectors is not totally satisfactory. Since there are union workers in the lightly unionized sector—however defined—and nonunion workers in the heavily unionized sector, the division between the two is not "clean." An alternative approach is to classify the work force according to its employment in union or nonunion establishments rather than by employment in lightly or heavily organized

24. Similar conclusions have been reached with other data sources or methods of analysis. See David E. Kaun and Michael H. Spiro, "The Relation Between Wages and Unemployment in U.S. Cities, 1955–1965," *Manchester School of Economic and Social Studies,* vol. 38 (March 1970), p. 10; O. C. Ashenfelter, G. E. Johnson, and J. H. Pencavel, "Trade Unions and the Rate of Change of Money Wages in United States Manufacturing Industry," *Review of Economic Studies,* vol. 39 (January 1972), pp. 33–34; and Robert R. France, "Wages, Unemployment, and Prices in the United States, 1890–1932, 1947–1957," *Industrial and Labor Relations Review,* vol. 15 (January 1962), pp. 171–90. A recent investigation revealed that collective bargainers rarely refer to official employment and unemployment statistics during negotiations but do refer to the consumer price index. See Daniel Quinn Mills, *Employment and Unemployment Statistics in Collective Bargaining,* National Commission on Employment and Unemployment Statistics, background paper 10 (GPO, 1979).

sectors. Such establishment data are not generally available on an economywide basis, but they have been published by the Bureau of Labor Statistics since 1959 for manufacturing industries.[25] Virtually all workers listed as union in these surveys have their wages determined by collective bargaining, and virtually all workers listed as nonunion are not covered by collective bargaining.

One advantage of the manufacturing wage-change series is that it permits a breakdown of the wage changes taking place in the union sector by type of change. For example, some union wage changes come about through first-year adjustments; others occur pursuant to escalator clauses or scheduled increments in the later years of union contracts. Because these changes come about through different mechanisms, lumping them all together, as was done in the previous section, may obscure the wage-determination process.

A second advantage of the manufacturing series is that a distinction can be made between the major-union sector (agreements covering 1,000 or more workers) and the minor-union sector (with smaller agreements). Published data on union wage developments are usually confined to the major-union sector. Since the major sector is made up of roughly half of the union portion of the labor force, many union workers are not included. Without statistical estimates, it is difficult to determine whether workers in the minor-union sector are subject to the same processes of wage determination as their major-union-sector counterparts.

Unfortunately, the breakdowns between the type of wage increase and major- versus minor-union sector cannot be made directly from the published data. Instead, to estimate all the desired components a number of approximations must be made. The actual published data provide estimates for both first-year and total effective wage changes in the major-union sector of manufacturing and in the whole union sector (major and minor). Effective wage changes include first-year, deferred, and escalated adjustments so that, if the first-year changes could be factored out, a distinction could be made between first-year and deferred-plus-escalated adjustments. Similarly, if the major-union sector could be factored out of

25. The data are published in *Current Wage Developments*. They apply to establishments that make general wage adjustments—adjustments affecting 10 percent of the work force at any one time or all the workers in an occupation. Fringe benefits are not included. For a technical description of the series, see Bureau of Labor Statistics, *BLS Handbook of Methods*, bulletin 1910 (GPO, 1976), pp. 154–60.

the overall union sector, the residual would be wage changes in the minor-union sector.[26]

For much of the period covered by the manufacturing wage series, the data were published in the form of median wage changes. Only in the late 1960s did mean changes become available. To obtain a consistent time series, the median data must be used, but they must nevertheless be treated as means in order to factor out the implicit components of the series. This is not a serious problem since the medians and the means did not differ much in the years for which both are available.

A more difficult problem is determining the appropriate weights for first-year versus deferred and escalator increases. The Bureau of Labor Statistics provides data on the number of workers receiving first-year increases and the total number receiving effective adjustments. An approximation for the number receiving deferred and escalator adjustments can be obtained by subtracting the first-year workers from the effective workers. However, this method of estimation (the only one available) results in an undercount of the number receiving deferred-plus-escalator adjustments because some workers receive both first-year and deferred-plus-escalator adjustments. This contingency can arise if a contract providing some deferred increments expires partway through the calendar year and is then followed by a first-year increment under a new contract. Or it can arise if workers receiving a first-year adjustment are also covered by an escalator clause that provides further adjustments during the calendar year. The latter problem is particularly severe because it intensifies whenever escalators become more popular or provide more money, as in periods of high inflation. Hence the degree of upward bias in the deferred-plus-escalator adjustment estimate is correlated with an explanatory variable and will produce biased regression coefficients.[27]

26. Wayne Vroman published a study in 1970 that used a union wage-change series for manufacturing as the dependent variable in several wage equations. The series he used was obtained from the Bureau of National Affairs, which conducts a survey of union wage settlements. However, Vroman treats the BNA series as if it measured all union wage changes (he compares it with results obtained from equations using hourly earnings changes) when it actually measures only first-year adjustments. This probably accounts for the fact that his unemployment coefficients for the union sector (the BNA series) are not substantially less than the unemployment coefficient for the hourly earnings series. Wayne Vroman, "Manufacturing Wage Behavior with Special Reference to the Period 1962–1966," *Review of Economics and Statistics,* vol. 52 (May 1970), pp. 160–67.

27. This problem is distinct from the one discussed in the next section of this chapter (on evidence from union contract data), in which deferred adjustments in escalated contracts from the union contract file are underestimated.

There are also problems with the nonunion wage-change data. The series includes only general changes in wage rates. Increases that accrue through merit plans or to individuals are excluded. This omission appears to bias the nonunion estimates downward, since individualized compensation rewards are more common in the nonunion sector.[28]

Despite these difficulties, it seems reasonable to estimate the unknown components of the union wage series with the available data, and then to interpret the results with the data limitations in mind. At least some of the potential problems can be alleviated by referring to the alternative contract data set discussed in the next section. Six data series were taken or estimated from the BLS manufacturing data:

(1) first-year adjustments (excluding escalator adjustments) in the major-union sector;

(2) first-year adjustments in the minor-union sector;

(3) deferred and escalator adjustments (called "deferred" hereafter) in the major-union sector;

(4) deferred adjustments in the minor-union sector;

(5) nonunion effective wage changes; and

(6) effective wage changes for the combined union and nonunion sectors.[29]

Wage changes for 1960–76 were regressed in annual equations against year-to-year changes in the consumer price index ($\dot{P}$) and the inverse of the unemployment rate (U^{-1}). Two versions of the unemployment rate were tried: the official (published) rate and the weighted Perry rate.[30] The weighted unemployment rate is a conceptual improvement over the

28. There is no way of confirming the nonunion bias directly. However, the manufacturing wage-change series for both the union and nonunion sectors generally runs below other estimates of manufacturing wage change. For example, in 1977 the manufacturing series reported a mean wage adjustment of 7.2 percent, and the employment cost index indicated an increase of 7.8 percent. *Current Wage Developments,* vol. 30 (April 1978), p. 67, and vol. 30 (August 1978), p. 49.

29. Data were available directly for effective and first-year adjustments (including zero and negative adjustments) for major-union situations and all union situations. With the use of employment weights, the implicit minor-union first-year adjustments were calculated. Available data on major-union effective wage adjustments and first-year adjustments were used to calculate the implicit major-union deferred adjustment (including escalator adjustments). Available data for all unions on effective and first-year adjustments were used to calculate minor-union effective adjustments and these were combined with the estimates of minor-union first-year adjustments to calculate the implicit minor-union deferred adjustments.

30. George L. Perry, "Changing Labor Markets and Inflation," *Brookings Papers on Economic Activity, 3:1970,* pp. 411–41.

Table 4-6. *Annual Wage-Adjustment Equations for Manufacturing*

Dependent variable	Constant	Explanatory variable					$\bar{R}^2$	Standard error	Durbin-Watson	rho 1	rho 2
		$\dot{P}_0$	$\dot{P}_{-1}$	$\dot{P}_{-2}$	U_0^{-1}	U_{-2}^{-1}					
First-year wage adjustments											
1. Major union	(−1.52)	...	0.88*	...	19.30*	...	0.83	1.07	1.96	0.14	...
2. Minor union	(−0.22)	...	0.58*	...	15.75*	...	0.91	0.62	2.04	0.66	...
Deferred wage adjustments											
3. Major union	5.38*	1.01*	...	(0.14)	...	−24.72*	0.93	0.85	2.03	0.25	−0.38
	(0.74)	(0.07)									
4. Minor union		...	...	0.55*	...	5.25*	0.89	0.56	2.10	−0.76	−0.05
Effective wage adjustments											
5. Nonunion	(−1.24)	...	0.58*	...	16.82*	...	0.74	0.96	2.07	0.19	...
6. Union and nonunion	(−2.40)	...	0.29	...	(6.87)	...	0.84	0.76	2.42	0.83	...

All variables are expressed in percentage points. Coefficients in parentheses are not significant at the 10 percent level. The rho coefficients result from first- and second-order autocorrelation corrections. Periods of observation are adjusted for these corrections. Lines 1, 2, 5, and 6 are for 1960–76. Lines 3 and 4 are for 1961–76.
* Significant at the 5 percent level or better.

official rate, since it adjusts for changes in labor-force composition that have affected the relation between observed unemployment and the "looseness" or "tightness" of the labor market. However, the two rates are highly intercorrelated ($R = 0.9$) over the observation period, and the autoregressive correction used in the estimation of the equations tends to eliminate the impact of the trend divergence of the two series. Also, the two rates have different average levels and therefore produce different coefficients of U^{-1}. This makes the equations run with weighted unemployment somewhat cumbersome if a translation for policy purposes into official rate terms is desired. For this reason, only the equations using the official unemployment rate will be discussed.[31]

Various lag structures were used as appropriate for the price and unemployment variables. As noted, escalator coverage in the union sector is concentrated in the larger settlements. Symptoms of escalator influence should thus be expected in equations based on the series of deferred adjustments in the major-union sector.

Table 4-6 provides a summary of the regression results. Note first that the nonunion sector in line 5 exhibits the expected sensitivity to real business conditions. At 6 percent official unemployment, line 5 suggests that a 1 percentage point increase in the unemployment rate would slow nonunion wage rate increases by 0.5 percentage point. The coefficient for $\dot{P}_{-1}$ indicates that a 1 percentage point rise in the inflation rate translates roughly into a 0.6 percentage point increase in nonunion wage inflation.

The most interesting features of the table are in the union sector. First-year adjustments in both the major- and minor-union components show roughly the same sensitivity to unemployment as the nonunion sector. One inviting interpretation of this finding might be that the initial

31. It might be noted that the use of the official and the Perry unemployment rates was simply intended as a proxy for real business conditions. The following alternative indicators were tried with similar results: the manufacturing quit rate, the inverse of the unemployment rate for white males aged thirty-five to forty-four, and the ratio of real GNP to its logarithmic trend. Experiments inserting the year-to-year change in the unemployment rate generally produced insignificant coefficients. A lagged manufacturing profit-to-sales variable added to the equations tended to produce negative coefficients. Since wage increases potentially reduce profits and since both profits and wage changes are highly correlated with their lagged values, this result is understandable. It is possible—indeed, probable—that profits as an index of ability to pay do influence wage movements but that these simple equations do not pick up the effect. Experiments using lagged money-supply changes instead of price changes produced insignificant money-supply coefficients.

wage increase in long-term agreements reflects real business conditions at the time of negotiations. However, the next section presents evidence that the apparent sensitivity comes not from long-term agreements but from short agreements in which the first-year increment constitutes most or all of the life-of-contract wage change. Still, the concentration of un-employment sensitivity in short agreements need not mean that parties to long-term contracts are always insensitive. In some cases, they may react to what they perceive as temporary aberrations in economic circum-stances by adopting a short (temporary) agreement, presumably to be followed by a reversion to long agreements when the economic climate changes.

Both the major- and minor-union sectors show sensitivity to lagged price change $(\dot{P}_{-1})$, although the major-union coefficients are larger than the minor-union and the nonunion coefficients and are also close to unity. Given the crudeness of the data and equations, there seems little differ-ence, however, between the short-term pattern in nonunion and first-year union wage adjustments.

It is in the deferred components of the union sector that important dif-ferences between the union and nonunion sectors can be seen. Before exploring these, it is essential to note that the deferred wage adjustment estimates are dominated by past wage decisions, including past decisions to use contingency arrangements. Since union contracts average two to three years in length, explanatory variables employed to explain deferred adjustments must be lagged. The equations in the table assume that the appropriate lag is two years (year $t - 2$). However, an exception must be made for escalator contingency clauses geared to the consumer price index. For contracts with such clauses, the current rate of price change $(\dot{P}_0)$ is clearly a needed explanatory influence.[32]

The major-union sector is associated with cost-of-living escalation, so it is not surprising that contemporary price inflation shows up as a sig-nificant explanatory variable in line 3. (The magnitude of the coefficient is discussed below.) On the other hand, escalation is much rarer in the minor-union sector so that contemporary price change should not be

32. Escalator clauses usually include some lag. However, for purposes of the regression the current rate of price change was defined as the percentage increase in the annual consumer price index divided by the index for the previous year. Use of annual averages to produce $\dot{P}_0$ effectively incorporates a short lag since sudden accelerations or decelerations appear in the data gradually.

expected to have much influence on the deferred portion of the contract. And in fact the coefficient of $\dot{P}_0$ in line 4 is essentially zero. Apart from escalator effects, deferred wage changes might reflect price inflation at roughly the original contract negotiation date: $\dot{P}_{-2}$. The minor-union sector, where escalation is less common, does exhibit a significant coefficient for $\dot{P}_{-2}$ with a magnitude approximately equal to the coefficient for $\dot{P}_0$ in the first-year equation. Line 4 implies that wage rates in the nonescalated sector in all years of the contract react similarly to the price inflation existing when the agreement was originally signed. One interpretation is that nonescalated contracts carry inflation assumptions from the past into the future. Another is that they catch up with price inflation gradually. The escalated major-union sector shows virtually no sensitivity to lagged inflation in the deferred element of the contract. Evidently negotiators are willing to rely mainly on escalators to handle future inflation.

What is puzzling about the major-union sector's deferred performance is the magnitude of the coefficient of $\dot{P}_0$. The unitary coefficient is higher than studies of actual union escalator clauses suggest it should be. One study, for example, found that escalators typically provided a 0.57 percent wage increase for each 1 percent of consumer price index inflation.[33] From an institutional viewpoint, this less-than-proportional relationship results from the formulas that are applied and from special limitations placed on the actual operation of the formulas.

The question of why the estimated coefficient of $\dot{P}_0$ is so large in line 3 remains. Its magnitude appears to stem primarily from the method of estimation of deferred wage adjustments rather than from any true structural relationship. It was noted earlier that the deferred wage estimate would be overstated by more in periods when escalators became more important in the total deferred wage adjustment because the number of workers receiving such increases would be understated by more in such periods. Escalators become more important as sources of wage increases when more workers are covered by escalators and when escalators pay larger amounts. Both these circumstances tend to exist during periods of rapid inflation, and their effect is to bias the coefficient upward. If the

33. See Victor J. Sheifer, "Collective Bargaining and the CPI: Escalation vs. Catch-Up," in Industrial Relations Research Association, *Proceedings of the Thirty-first Annual Meeting* (Madison, Wis.: IRRA, 1979), p. 261.

period 1973–76 is dropped from the equation in line 3, for example, the coefficient falls to 0.5.[34]

The reaction of deferred wage changes to lagged unemployment (U_{-2}^{-1})—that is, to unemployment at the time of negotiations—raises some interesting issues. In the minor-union sector the unemployment coefficient retains its correct sign and remains significant. But its size is substantially reduced. If the coefficient for the life-of-contract wage change of a two-year agreement in the minor-union sector consists of an average of the first-year and deferred-reaction coefficients (in this case, 10.5), a 1 percentage point increase in the official unemployment rate from a 6 percent level would cut the life-of-contract wage increase by only one-fourth of 1 percent. For a three-year contract, the reaction would be even smaller. For the major-union sector, the deferred unemployment coefficient actually exhibits the wrong sign. Taken literally, the deferred coefficient would outweigh the first-year coefficient in a two- to three-year contract. The perverse reaction to unemployment appears again to be due to the method of calculating deferred increases rather than to any true behavorial relationship. Starting in 1973, estimated deferred increases become quite large while at the same time unemployment rises. Of course, escalator clauses, mirroring the inflation in prices, would have substantially raised the deferred component of the major-union sector. But, as noted, the calculation method tends to exaggerate deferred wage increases as escalators become more significant. And this exaggeration coincides with a period of high unemployment. Omitting the 1973–76 period causes a drop in the unemployment coefficient in both size and significance.[35]

If the true coefficient of U_{-2}^{-1} in line 3 is taken to be zero, the effect of unemployment on the overall life-of-contract wage change would be quite small, roughly comparable to the life-of-contract estimate for the minor-

---

34. The established equation (in which boldface coefficients are significant at the 5 percent level or above) is:

$$MDEF = \mathbf{3.73} + \mathbf{.51}\dot{P}_0 + \mathbf{.36}\dot{P}_{-2} - \mathbf{12.55}U_{-2}^{-1},$$

$\bar{R}^2 = .81$; standard error $= .43$; Durbin-Watson $= 2.27$; rho 1 $= .07$; rho 2 $= -.01$

where $MDEF$ is estimated deferred adjustments in the major-union sector. Note that the lagged price coefficient picks up in size and significance, presumably reflecting the fact that the major-union sector was less extensively escalated in the earlier period.

35. The coefficient of U_{-2}^{-1} in the equation of the previous footnote falls just below significance at the 10 percent level.

union sector. In any given year, substantial numbers of workers in the major- and minor-union sectors would receive only deferred adjustments, which could not react to current unemployment and which apparently would not reflect past unemployment either. This result is in sharp contrast to the nonunion sector, where the option to change wages in response to current circumstances is always open.

A final point in the manufacturing wage equations is worth noting. Line 6 of table 4-6 presents an aggregate equation that attempts to explain effective wage change in manufacturing. Represented in the dependent variable are both the union and the nonunion sectors and, within the union sector, both first-year and deferred adjustments. The result of running an equation in aggregate form is a regression with an implausibly low (and barely significant) price coefficient, a regression that depends mainly on the autoregressive properties of wage data for its explanatory power. It therefore appears that aggregate equations that take no account of labor-market institutions are likely to miss important elements of the wage-determination process.[36]

Evidence from Union Contract Data

In recent years a number of empirical studies of union wage determination based on observations of samples of individual agreements rather than general wage indexes have been conducted.[37] Using contract data has many advantages. It permits explicit division of the sample into long-term, short-term, escalated, and nonescalated agreements. Even the manu-

36. Aggregate earnings equations, such as those in table C-6, generally produce somewhat better results. This may be because they include earnings changes caused by factors other than general wage increases.

37. See Daniel S. Hamermesh, "Wage Bargains, Threshold Effects, and the Phillips Curve," *Quarterly Journal of Economics,* vol. 84 (August 1970), pp. 501–17; Daniel S. Hamermesh, "Market Power and Wage Inflation," *Southern Economic Journal,* vol. 39 (October 1972), pp. 204–12; Gordon R. Sparks and David A. Wilton, "Determinants of Negotiated Wage Increases: An Empirical Analysis," *Econometrica,* vol. 39 (September 1971), pp. 739–50; and L. N. Christofides, R. Swidinsky, and D. A. Wilton, "A Micro Econometric Analysis of the Canadian Wage Determination Process, 1966–75" (Guelph, Ont.: University of Guelph, April 1978). Contract data have also been used to analyze nonwage outcomes. See Thomas A. Kochan and Richard N. Block, "An Interindustry Analysis of Bargaining Outcomes: Preliminary Evidence from Two-Digit Industries," *Quarterly Journal of Economics,* vol. 91 (August 1977), pp. 431–52.

facturing wage data presented in the previous section could not be disaggregated directly at such a detailed level. Knowledge of the timing of
negotiations permits the design of explanatory variables more closely
related to this timing.

The chief problem in using contract data lies in assembling such information. Although the Bureau of Labor Statistics maintains a file of contracts for its own costing purposes, the cost information contained therein
is confidential and not available to the public for individual agreements.
But the BLS does make available the *Wage Chronology* series for a number of important collective bargaining situations, and its monthly periodi-
cal *Current Wage Developments* provides data on reported wage increases in individual union situations. These two sources, however, most
frequently report wage increments in cents per hour. Moreover, the
limited information on fringe benefits they include does not allow valuation of the benefits. Finally, although the chronologies provide information on some occupational categories, no information is available on the
average base wage before the start of the contract.

Despite this lack of precise information, the advantages of using contracts (rather than time periods) as observations suggest that it is worth
attempting to estimate the wage costs involved, partly as a check on the
results obtained in the preceding section. Consequently, estimates of the
wage-rate increments involved in 172 union contracts negotiated by
seventeen major employers or employer associations during 1954–76
were made, primarily from wage-chronology information. The 172 contracts covered manufacturing, mining, and transportation; they are listed
in appendix C. The following measures of wage change were computed
and converted into annualized percentage rates based on average hourly
earnings data for the relevant industry classification.

FIRST is the percentage wage-rate change resulting from general wage
increases during the first twelve months of the contract. These estimates
generally exclude "inequity" adjustments made for particular subgroups
of workers and exclude escalator increases.

LIFE is the annualized percentage wage-rate change resulting from
general wage increases and escalator payments over the entire life of the
contract. Inequity adjustments are generally excluded.

DEFERRED is the annualized percentage wage-rate change resulting
from general wage increases and escalator payments over the life of the

contract, excluding increments reported in *FIRST*. Since escalator payments often occur during the first year, the annualization period for escalated contracts is the full life of the contract. For nonescalated contracts, the annualization period is the life of the contract minus twelve months. *DEFERRED* was not computed for contracts of less than eighteen months' duration (none of which were escalated in the sample).[38]

The BLS wage chronologies also provide some information on wage rates paid to particular occupational groups. Thanks to special inequity adjustments, certain groups of workers may experience different rates of percentage wage changes. An interesting question is whether the forces that explain general wage changes have a different effect on skill classes.

38. In the preceding section, estimating deferred adjustments involved a statistical problem concerning inaccurate estimates of the number of workers affected. In this section, a different problem of annualization arises because escalator clauses may be activated during the first twelve months of the contract. It is evident that for nonescalated contracts the deferred portion of the contract should be annualized over the contract's duration minus twelve months. Because escalators can be effective in the first year, the deferred portion of escalated contracts is annualized over the full contract. It might be argued, however, that this procedure understates the percentage rate of change of the deferred component of an escalated contract relative to that of a nonescalated contract. Imagine two twenty-four-month agreements, one escalated and the other nonescalated. Suppose that both called for semiannual adjustments starting with the first day of the contract and that both ended up increasing wages by 3 percent every six months. But suppose that the escalated contract called for a 1 percent fixed wage increase in each six-month period and the rest came from the escalator. Both would have a value of *LIFE* = 6.1 percent. The escalated contract would have a value of *FIRST* = 2.0 percent since no escalator increases were assigned to *FIRST*, and the nonescalated contract would show that *FIRST* = 6.1 percent. The escalated contract would provide for deferred increases of 2 percent, 2 percent, 3 percent, and 3 percent over twenty-four months, producing a value of *DEFERRED* = 5.1 percent. For the nonescalated contract, the final two 3 percent increases would be spread over twelve months, producing a value of *DEFERRED* = 6.1 percent. In short, because of the treatment of the escalator increase, a first-year increase of 2.0 percent and a deferred increase of 5.1 percent are associated with a life-of-contract annualized increase averaging 6.1 percent. The alternative procedure of annualizing the deferred component of the escalated contract over only the last twelve months of the contract would overstate the rate of increase during that period. Another possibility would have been simply to allocate escalated increments during the first year to *FIRST*, although this procedure is not in keeping with the methodology used by the Bureau of Labor Statistics in preparing the manufacturing estimates in table 4-6. The problem posed for the estimates of *FIRST* is lessened by the fact that a substantial fraction of the first-year adjustments in escalated contracts is often in the form of a fixed (rather than escalator) adjustment. The problem disappears entirely when *LIFE* is used as the dependent variable.

A narrowing of skill differences, for example, might cause dissatisfaction among skilled workers, a continuing problem in certain industrial unions. Such dissension can complicate the bargaining process and hinder contract ratification, as happened at Ford in 1973.[39]

To deal with the wage structure issue, three more wage change measures were computed for contracts for which the necessary data were available.

LOW is the annualized percentage increase in wage rates over the life of the contract for an occupation at the bottom of the wage structure, generally corresponding to janitors.

MEDIUM is the annualized percentage increase in wage rates over the life of the contract for an occupation in the middle of the wage structure.

HIGH is the annualized percentage increase in wage rates over the life of the contract for an occupation toward the top of the wage structure.

Four independent variables were initially used to explain wage changes according to these various measures for all contracts of at least eleven months.[40] Three of the variables correspond to the variables used in the preceding section.

First, $\dot{P}_{-1}$ is the year-to-year percentage increase in the consumer price index, lagged one year before the effective date of the contract.

Second, U_0^{-1} is the inverse of the official unemployment rate in the year the contract became effective.[41]

Third, *COLA* is the annualized percentage rate of change of the consumer price index over the life of the contract if the contract had an escalator; zero if it had no escalator.

Fourth, *REL* is an index of the relative earnings status of the industry under contract before the effective date of the contract. It was computed by dividing the base hourly-earnings figure (used to compute *FIRST,*

39. A number of industrial unions have had skilled trades problems. For background, see Arnold R. Weber, "The Craft-Industrial Issue Revisited: A Study of Union Government," *Industrial and Labor Relations Review,* vol. 16 (April 1963), pp. 381–404. The issue at Ford in 1973 involved voluntary overtime rather than wage differentials per se.

40. "Contracts" of less than eleven months were excluded because they often represented interim adjustments granted while negotiations were in progress.

41. As with the manufacturing equations, estimation of the equations was performed with both the official rate of unemployment and the Perry weighted rate of unemployment. Again, the two rates are so highly correlated that virtually the same results are obtained with both. The equations presented below include only the results from using the official rate.

LIFE, and *DEFERRED*) by average hourly earnings for the private non-farm economy in the year before the effective date of the contract, and then standardizing the ratio by dividing it by its mean value for all contracts of the same employer represented in the sample.

The use of the first three independent variables is straightforward and requires no special explanation. However, the *REL* variable had no counterpart in the preceding section and requires some discussion. Various strands in the literature on wage determination suggest that wages in different industries are linked. Wage imitation processes are sometimes said to tie wage settlements together (see chapter 5).[42] Often references are made to "catch-up" pressure affecting wage settlements,[43] although it is not always clear whether the references involve relative wages or absolute real wages. There is also some evidence that industries whose earnings surge ahead (fall behind) in relation to either the rate of price inflation or the national average rate of wage inflation experience less (more) industrial conflict. That is, a tendency can be observed for workers' involvement in work stoppages to increase when catch-up pressure of either the relative or the absolute type develops.[44]

It is important to emphasize that a tendency of earnings to stay in line could be consistent with a variety of hypotheses about the earnings-determination process. Wage imitation could be part of the explanation, but other models are available. In particular, the possibility of substitu-

42. Otto Eckstein and Thomas A. Wilson, "The Determination of Money Wages in American Industry," *Quarterly Journal of Economics,* vol. 76 (August 1962), pp. 379–414; John E. Maher, "The Wage Pattern in the United States, 1946–57," *Industrial and Labor Relations Review,* vol. 15 (October 1961), pp. 3–20.

43. Marvin Kosters, Kenneth Fedor, and Albert Eckstein, "Collective Bargaining Settlements and the Wage Structure," *Labor Law Journal,* vol. 24 (August 1973), pp. 517–25.

44. Table C-7 presents a series of pooled cross-sectional work stoppage equations, some of which contain real wage and relative wage movements as explanatory variables. Details of these regressions are presented in appendix C. However, the table shows that an interaction term involving the number of workers under expiring contracts and the real wage or relative wage movement experienced by such workers in the recent past affects the number of workers participating in stoppages resulting from contract renegotiations. Specifically, workers who experienced real or relative wage gains in twenty-seven private nonfarm industries in 1968–75 were less likely to be involved in work stoppages than other workers. Equations 3 and 5 in table C-7 suggest that, if an industry had experienced a 2 percent real wage gain in a year when 10,000 workers under major contracts had to renegotiate, 150–250 fewer workers would be involved in strikes than in an industry with no real wage gain. The relative wage hypothesis receives support from equations 4 and 6 in table C-7.

tion in the labor and product markets might limit wage demands of certain unions (see chapter 3) if their wage levels rose faster than wages in other industries. Employers' resistance might also intensify if wage demands threatened to push up wages at an unusually high rate.

In short, for many reasons an industry that had fallen behind its normal standing in the interindustry wage structure could be expected to speed up its rate of wage increase, all other things being equal. Similarly, an industry that had pulled ahead would slow down.[45] The coefficient of *REL* would thus be expected to be negative. A finding of a negative response to *REL* would simply indicate a tendency for wages to stay together. It would not differentiate between competing explanations for such a tendency, nor would it preclude changes in wage differentials across industries over long periods.

Analysis of the earlier regressions from the manufacturing sector suggested that wage change in major-union contracts would be sensitive to lagged price change and that sensitivity to a business conditions indicator such as unemployment would be found in first-year adjustments but would not be characteristic over the life of the contract. Table 4-7 presents regression results from the contract sample against which the earlier conclusions can be checked.

Equation 1 in the table presents the overall results for *FIRST* on all contracts in the sample. The coefficients for $\dot{P}_{-1}$ and U_0^{-1} are almost identical to those appearing in line 1 of table 4-6. Also, table 4-7 permits examination of the relative earnings variable, which has a negative sign and is statistically significant. Taken literally, the coefficient of *REL* suggests that, if earnings in the industry of a unit are 10 percent above "normal" before negotiations ($REL = 1.10$), wage rates would increase about 2 percentage points more slowly in the first year than if relative

45. This hypothesis should be distinguished from a seemingly related proposition sometimes found in the literature, which states that a "distortion" of the wage structure leads to a generalized increase in the rate of wage change. See Arnold H. Packer and Seong H. Park, "Distortions in Relative Wages and Shifts in the Phillips Curve," *Review of Economics and Statistics*, vol. 55 (February 1973), pp. 16–22. It must also be differentiated from the proposition that distortions in the rate of wage increase contribute generally to faster wage increases, through a competitive, leapfrogging process. See D. Q. Mills, "Explaining Pay Increases in Construction: 1953–72," *Industrial Relations*, vol. 13 (May 1974), pp. 196–201. The discussion in the text applies only to a particular industry whose earnings level has deviated from its traditional position in the earnings structure.

earnings were normal ($REL = 1.00$).[46] More generally, it suggests that forces arise which tend to preserve the earnings structure. These forces are consistent with a wage imitation model but could reflect other influences, too. It should be noted that a tendency is not the same as an iron law. A negative REL coefficient does not imply that the status of relative earnings cannot change.

Table 4-6 did not provide a direct measure of the variable $LIFE$, but it did suggest that the deferred portion of the package for major-union contracts was not sensitive to price change at the time of negotiation and that the reaction to unemployment was, if anything, perverse. Equation 3 of table 4-7 suggests that, over the life of the contract, sensitivity to price change before negotiation is a characteristic of labor contracts and that sensitivity to unemployment can also be found. These findings are not really contradictory to those of table 4-6. If $\dot{P}_{-1}$ affects only the first year of short contracts, it will still have an influence on $LIFE$. The wage increase over the life of the contract in short agreements includes the first-year adjustment as a major element.

The unemployment-sensitivity issue can be clarified by explicitly dividing the sample into short contracts (eleven to seventeen months) and long contracts (eighteen months and more). Equations 5 and 7 indicate that the short contracts show extremely high sensitivity to unemployment. For example, equation 7 suggests that a 1 percentage point increase in the official unemployment rate from a 6 percent level would slow life-of-contract wage change by 1.2 percentage points. In contrast, none of the equations for long contracts show statistically significant reactions to unemployment in wage changes in either the first year or the contract life.

There are two possible interpretations of the apparent relationship between contract duration and unemployment sensitivity. The short contracts tend to be concentrated in the earlier part of the period. Of the sixty-three short contracts, forty-seven were negotiated before 1965. Moreover, several of the later short contracts resulted from interruptions

46. Note that the relative wage variable was entered in the regressions in ratio form rather than as a wage premium. That is, for an industry with wages 1 percent above normal, REL is 1.01 rather than 0.01. Since REL averages unity in value, it receives a large coefficient, which is "counteracted" by a constant term of opposite sign and similar absolute magnitude. This in no way changes the interpretation of the REL coefficient as the derivative of wage change with respect to REL. The effect of a 1 percent increase in relative wage status is simply 0.01 times the coefficient of REL.

Table 4-7. Regression Results from Union Contract File

Dependent variable	Constant	Independent variable					Summary statistics		Number of observations	
		$\dot{P}_{-1}$	U_0^{-1}	COLA	REL	D7376[b]	$\bar{R}^2$	Standard error	1954–76	1973–76
All contracts										
1. FIRST	19.11*	0.84*	19.08*	...	−19.79*	...	0.34	2.70	172	...
2. FIRST	18.27*	0.88*	19.45*	...	−19.06*	(−0.40)	0.33	2.70	172	22
3. LIFE	13.31*	0.64*	16.09*	0.45*	−13.77*	...	0.49	2.06	172	...
4. LIFE	17.54*	0.44*	14.54*	0.40*	−17.44*	2.37*	0.53	1.97	172	22
Short-term contracts[c]										
5. FIRST	20.29*	0.67*	43.21*	...	−25.99*	...	0.38	1.98	61	...
6. FIRST	21.56*	0.40	37.46*	...	−25.85*	(1.86)	0.43	1.96	61	7
7. LIFE	17.40	0.77*	49.18	...	−24.24*	...	0.32	2.42	61	...
8. LIFE	20.71*	(0.06)	34.13	...	−23.87	4.87*	0.44	2.20	61	7

Long-term escalated contracts[d]

9. FIRST	28.03*	1.12*	(4.86)	...	−26.68*	...	0.57	2.17	48	..
10. FIRST	25.65*	1.17*	(6.09)	...	−24.58*	(−0.59)	0.56	2.18	48	10
11. LIFE	10.84	0.55*	(4.93)	0.53*	−9.24	...	0.67	1.61	48	..
12. LIFE	12.83*	0.58*	(6.41)	0.42*	−11.32*	(0.92)	0.67	1.62	48	10
13. DEFERRED[e]	(1.45)	0.37	(8.20)	0.49	(−1.38)	...	0.56	1.57	48	..
14. DEFERRED[e]	(4.86)	(0.40)	(10.75)	(0.30)	(−4.94)	1.57	0.58	1.53	48	10
15. LOW	(12.08)		(4.26)	0.84*	(−10.02)	...	0.70	1.89	37	..
16. MEDIUM	13.08	0.47*	(−0.17)	0.74*	(−10.68)	...	0.76	1.57	35	..
17. HIGH	(9.03)	(0.46)	(4.75)	0.51*	(−7.17)	...	0.53	2.02	35	..

Long-term nonescalated contracts[d]

18. FIRST	(17.19)	0.75*	(9.04)	...	(−15.16)	...	0.24	3.31	63	..
19. FIRST	(16.31)	0.80*	(8.88)	...	(−14.32)	(−0.76)	0.23	3.33	63	5
20. LIFE	14.49*	0.69*	(5.53)	...	−13.28*	...	0.53	1.68	63	..
21. LIFE	16.17*	0.58*	(5.83)	...	−14.87*	(1.45)	0.54	1.66	63	5
22. DEFERRED[f]	(8.99)	0.80*	(6.78)	...	(−9.20)	...	0.46	2.08	63	..
23. DEFERRED[f]	(11.81)	0.62*	(7.28)	...	−11.86	2.44*	0.49	2.02	63	5

Coefficients in parentheses are not significant at the 10 percent level. Data for price change, wage change, and unemployment rate are expressed in percentage points.

* Significant at the 5 percent level.

a. The variables are defined in the text.

b. Dummy variable, equal to 1 for contracts beginning in 1973–76, equal to zero otherwise.

c. Contracts of eleven to seventeen months' duration.

d. Contracts of eighteen or more months' duration.

e. Wage adjustments other than first-year annualized over contract life.

f. Wage adjustments other than first-year annualized over contract life minus twelve months.

of long contracts that occurred when the parties reopened existing agreements. For whatever reason, it seems that in the early part of the period the parties were more likely to be under pressure to adjust to real business conditions. Apparently they reacted by using short contracts as the vehicle for adaptation.[47]

A second possibility involves running the causal arrows in the other direction. Long-term contracts represent a procedure for minimizing transaction costs. The most obvious cost reduced is the threat of a strike. When being locked into a long arrangement in which wages may deviate from the desired path is not seen as especially perilous, the transaction-cost reduction is attractive. Once the decision is made to take a long view, it is natural to expect that wages will not reflect transitory business conditions that happened to exist at the moment of negotiations. Instead, the parties would take an "averaging" perspective.

One of the debates in the literature on the Phillips curve is the degree to which wage determination is characterized by "money illusion." Money illusion refers to a failure to take account of price inflation in making decisions. The early Phillips-curve literature suggested that it was possible to raise employment levels by increasing the rate of price inflation.[48] One explanation of this phenomenon is that workers do not fully realize that inflation is eroding their real wages. As a result, they accept a lower wage level relative to the prices of the products they produce as price inflation increases, thereby providing employers with an incentive to expand production and hire more workers. If workers eventually recognize that their real wage has declined as a result of inflation and if they take steps to restore the old parity (adjusted for any increases in productivity that have accrued in the meantime), the employment effect will be

47. Although the short contracts in the sample are concentrated in the earlier part of the period, there is evidence that a contract-duration response to adverse conditions is still found in the unionized labor market. For example, when American Motors found itself in financial difficulties, the United Auto Workers granted the company certain concessions under short contracts. After the economic outlook for AMC brightened, the parties concluded a two-year agreement in 1978 that eliminated some of these concessions. The wage-price controls initiated in 1971 were apparently viewed by the unionized sector as a temporary change in economic circumstances, and a notable shift to shorter contracts occurred. See Weber and Mitchell, *The Pay Board's Progress*, pp. 363–65.

48. Paul A. Samuelson and Robert M. Solow, "Analytical Aspects of Anti-Inflation Policy," *American Economic Review*, vol. 50 (May 1960, *Papers and Proceedings, 1959*), pp. 177–94. However, Samuelson and Solow were careful to note that the shape of the price inflation–unemployment trade-off could change (p. 193).

reversed. Thus if the money-illusion approach is used to explain the existence of the Phillips curve, an absence of money illusion suggests that the curve is a temporary phenomenon. In turn, this view suggests that there is a "natural rate of unemployment," which the rate of inflation cannot alter.[49]

An indication of an absence of money illusion can be found for the long-term escalated contracts represented in equation 11 in table 4-7. In a steady-state inflation, $\dot{P}_{-1}$ would be equal to $COLA$ for the sample of escalated contracts. The sum of the coefficients for these two variables (0.55 and 0.53) is approximately unity. A unitary price effect is sometimes taken as a signal that there is no money illusion in the wage-setting process, since every change in the rate of price inflation—when other influences are held constant—is matched by an equal change in wage inflation.[50]

In short, equation 11 suggests that units expressing an overt interest in prices by mechanically tying their wages to the consumer price index do make real wages immune from price inflation. On the other hand, units that do not openly express an interest in pricing (the short contracts and the long nonescalated contracts) have price coefficients that fall short of unity. Still, it might be argued that the spread of escalation in recent years shows that previously nonescalated groups, when they become sufficiently concerned about inflation, will change their price orientation. That is, they move themselves from the groups represented by equations 7 and 20, in which real wages are vulnerable to price inflation, to the group represented by equation 11, which is protected.

In principle, there is no reason why over long periods of time negotiators of nonescalated agreements should provide for smaller life-of-contract wage increases than negotiators of escalated agreements. During short periods, of course, unanticipated changes in the rate of inflation might not be reflected in nonescalated contracts. But table 4-8 indicates that the escalated contracts in the sample provided larger wage adjust-

49. Edmund S. Phelps, *Inflation Policy and Unemployment Theory: The Cost-Benefit Approach to Monetary Planning* (Norton, 1972), pp. 35–57; and Milton Friedman, "The Role of Monetary Policy," *American Economic Review*, vol. 58 (March 1968), pp. 8–11.

50. Aggregate wage equations often produce price coefficients below unity. Friedman, however, argues that the observed coefficient could be biased below unity because of an "errors-in-variable" effect. Specifically, lagged price change may not be a perfect indicator of expectations. Milton Friedman, *Unemployment versus Inflation? An Evaluation of the Phillips Curve* (Institute of Economic Affairs, 1975), p. 28.

Table 4-8. *Comparison of Wage Adjustments under Escalated and Nonescalated Agreements*

Percent

	Mean value		BLS mean estimate for major agreements expiring in 1976–79[b] (3)
Type of agreement	Unadjusted for time period (1)	Adjusted for time period[a] (2)	
Escalated	6.5	5.6	8.3
Nonescalated			
All	4.1	4.4	7.4
Long-term[c]	4.1	4.1	...

Sources: Columns 1 and 2 from data file described in the text; col. 3 from *Monthly Labor Review*, vol. 98 (December 1975), p. 12; vol. 99 (December 1976), p. 16; vol. 100 (December 1977), p. 35; and vol. 101 (December 1978), p. 15.

a. Simple average of mean rates of wage adjustments for contracts beginning in 1956, 1958–62, 1964–68, 1970, 1971, 1973, and 1974. These are the fifteen years in which observations were available for each of the three types of contracts shown in the table.

b. Simple average of values for each year, 1976–79.

c. Contracts of eighteen months' duration or more.

ments than the nonescalated contracts. Column 1 shows that the mean rate of wage adjustment under escalated contracts was 6.5 percent and under nonescalated contracts, 4.1 percent. However, this comparison is misleading since escalated agreements are usually negotiated during periods of high inflation when wage changes under all types of contracts would be expected to be relatively large. A more meaningful comparison is made in column 2, where an adjustment is made for the time period in which the contracts began. Column 2 shows the simple average of the mean rates of wage adjustment for each of the fifteen years in which contracts were included in the sample of the three types in the table. As expected, the gap between the life-of-contract wage adjustments under escalated contracts and those under nonescalated contracts narrows, though it is still large.[51]

In the mid-1970s the Bureau of Labor Statistics began publishing data on life-of-contract wage-rate adjustments for major agreements expiring in each year. As column 3 of table 4-8 indicates, the gap between wage adjustments under escalated contracts and adjustments under nonesca-

51. Footnote a of table 4-8 indicates the years for which the values of column 2 were calculated. There were no long nonescalated contracts in the sample in 1955, but there were some short ones. If 1955 is added to the period, the average for *LIFE* of the escalated contracts is still 5.6 percent and the average for all nonescalated contracts is still 4.4 percent.

lated agreements apparently continued into the late 1970s. Some of this gap in the late 1970s is due to the inclusion of the rarely escalated construction industry in the BLS sample. (No construction contracts are included in columns 1 and 2.) Most construction contracts during the late 1970s provided for wage increases that were modest compared with those of other industries. Even so, the difference under escalated and nonescalated contracts over a long period of time is puzzling.

It is possible, of course, that the negotiators of nonescalated contracts often underestimated the rate of price inflation from the mid-1950s to the late 1970s. The trend in inflation was generally up, so that if expectations were formed from projections of the past, consistent underestimates could be made. However, the ability of a union to obtain an escalator may be correlated with its relative bargaining power. Escalators make employers uncertain about future wage developments, and employers might be expected to resist. Unions that succeed in obtaining escalators may also be more successful in overcoming employers' resistance to wage increases generally than unions that do not.

Inflation and Wage Differentials

Equations 15, 16, and 17 of table 4-7 provide an interesting look at the impact of escalation on internal wage differentials. In long-term escalated contracts, the coefficients of *COLA* are apt to be higher for low-wage occupations than for high-wage occupations, reflecting the tendency of escalator formulas to provide flat cents-per-hour increases (rather than percentage increases) across the entire wage structure. Thus in periods when escalator increments are important, they squeeze the wage structure. This tendency does not necessarily mean that high-wage workers are losing real purchasing power as a result of inadequate escalation, since nonescalator increments and special inequity adjustments may also be provided. Taken literally, the sum of the coefficients of $\dot{P}_{-1}$ and *COLA* in equation 17 suggests that high-wage workers are fully compensated for steady-state inflation by the whole of the wage package. (Low- and medium-wage workers are overcompensated if the coefficients of equations 16 and 17 are accepted at face value.) But relative wage compression could provide grounds for dissatisfaction, placing strain on the union political structure and internal incentives.

Table 4-9 presents a breakdown of the 106 contracts for which data for *LOW, MEDIUM,* and *HIGH* were available. The tendency for wage

Table 4-9. *Mean Annualized Rate of Wage Increase at Selected Wage Levels, 1954–76*

Percent

Variable	Contracts with complete data		
	All	*Escalated*	*Nonescalated*
LOW	6.0	7.8	5.2
MEDIUM	5.6	7.1	4.9
HIGH	5.4	6.5	4.8
LIFE	5.3	6.7	4.7
Number of observations	106	35	71

Source: See appendix C.

differentials to narrow is apparent in both escalated and nonescalated contracts. (Wages can rise faster for the occupational groups than for *LIFE* as a result of periodic inequity adjustments.) But the gap between the rates of wage change for high- and low-wage workers is substantially wider in the escalated group of contracts than in the nonescalated group. Over a ten-year period, the 0.4 percentage point gap shown in the table under nonescalated contracts would result in an increase in the ratio of low wages to high wages of a little over 4 percent. The 1.3 percentage point gap under the escalated contracts would result in an increase in the ratio of about 14 percent.

Over the very long run, there has been a gradual narrowing of skill differences throughout the economy.[52] Apparently the escalator mechanism aggravates this trend and inequity adjustments given to high-wage workers do not fully offset the escalator effect. Perhaps, if inflation continues at a rapid rate, either escalator formulas will be modified to provide percentage increases—some escalators already have this feature—or inequity adjustments for high-wage workers will become more routine.[53] In

52. See Harry Ober, "Occupational Wage Differentials, 1907–1947," *Monthly Labor Review*, vol. 67 (August 1948), pp. 127–34; and Paul G. Keat, "Long-Run Changes in Occupational Wage Structure, 1900–1956," *Journal of Political Economy*, vol. 68 (December 1960), pp. 584–600.

53. A recent major agreement covering telephone workers contains an escalator combining percentage and flat adjustments. See "Wage Highlights," *Current Wage Developments*, vol. 29 (September 1977), p. 1. Deere and Company has departed from the practice of other farm machinery manufacturers by using a percentage escalator. See "Wage Highlights," *Current Wage Developments*, vol. 28 (December 1976), p. 1.

the short run, however, unrest may result and become yet another cost of adapting to an inflationary environment.

Profits and Wage Determination

Several studies have used profit variables in wage equations as an explanatory variable. In principle, a profit index might be an indicator of employers' ability to pay so that high or improving profits might be expected to be associated with higher wage gains.[54] A finding that wage change is highly sensitive to profits would suggest an additional channel by which monetary and fiscal policy could influence inflation rates. Profits are sensitive to business-cycle developments and could pass those developments into the wage-determination process.

These are conceptual problems in including a profit variable in the regressions on contract wage changes presented above. For example, in several cases the contracts involve firms that bargain in coordination with other firms in the same industry. This makes it unclear whether firm profits or industry profits would be the appropriate choice of explanatory variable. There are also problems of data availability.

Experiments were tried with data on both industry profits and firm profits for contracts for which such information could be obtained. In both cases, an index was created using the profit–sales ratio for the industry or firm in the year before the effective starting date of the contract. A standardization procedure was applied to adjust the index to reflect the "normal" (average) ratio of profits to sales for all observations of the particular employer. When added to the regression equations previously discussed, the industry-profit variable was never significant.[55] However,

54. Examples of studies using profit variables are Eckstein and Wilson, "The Determination of Money Wages in American Industry," pp. 379–414; Pawan K. Sawhney and Irwin L. Herrnstadt, "Interindustry Wage Structure Variation in Manufacturing," *Industrial and Labor Relations Review,* vol. 24 (April 1971), pp. 407–19; William A. Howard, "Wage Adjustment and Profit Rates: An Error-Learning Approach to Collective Bargaining," *Industrial and Labor Relations Review,* vol. 22 (April 1969), pp. 416–21; and Perry, "The Determinants of Wage Rate Changes," pp. 287–308.

55. The industry-profit variable was created from data appearing regularly in the *Monthly Economic Letter* of the First National City Bank of New York. Contracts were matched with industries appearing there. Where no match was possible, the contracts were omitted from analysis. The *Monthly Economic Letter* provided data on the percentage change in after-tax profits and in sales, from which an index of the profit–sales ratio in each industry could be derived. This index was then further standardized by dividing all observations for a given employer by their mean. Data were available for 146 of the 172 contracts in the sample.

the firm-profit index did produce a significant coefficient for long-term contracts.

The firm-profit index (*FPROS*) was based on profit-to-sales data appearing in the *Fortune* 500 listings and individual company annual reports. After-tax profit–sales ratio data for each firm were standardized by subtracting from them the mean of the observations for that firm used in the sample. Thus if the mean observation for a firm was 6.5 percent but in a particular year preceding a contract the ratio was 7.5 percent, the index would have a value of 1.0.

Data on *FPROS* could be obtained for 134 of the 172 contracts in the sample. In regressions involving all available contracts, *FPROS* did not take on a statistically significant coefficient. However, for the available subsample of 85 contracts with a duration of eighteen months or more (long contracts), the following equation (in which boldface coefficients are significant at the 5 percent level or above) was produced:

$$LIFE = \mathbf{11.71} + \mathbf{0.59}\dot{P}_{-1} + 5.13U^{-1} + \mathbf{0.60}COLA$$
$$- \mathbf{10.61}REL + \mathbf{0.22}FPROS.$$

$\bar{R}^2 = 0.75$; standard error $= 1.42$

Taken literally, this equation suggests that, for each percentage point by which a firm exceeded its average profit–sales ratio in the year before a negotiation, its contractual wage adjustment could be expected to be about 0.2 percentage point higher. Most of the significance of the *FPROS* coefficient arises from the long-term contracts that were not escalated.[56]

It is tempting to weave theories interpreting these results. For example, the significance of *FPROS* for wage adjustments in long-term contracts only might be taken to mean that negotiators who took a long view decided to share the ups and downs of firms' prosperity with their workers. That is, workers in such firms developed a partial equity interest in their employers' surpluses. But the evidence for a profits role in the sample is tenuous, and questions could be raised about the particular profit index chosen. All that can really be said is that there is limited evidence supporting a role for profits in wage determination based on the contract sample, but nothing definite.

56. No significant relation was found between *FIRST* and *FPROS*, even in long contracts. When the 85 contracts of the equation are separated into escalated and nonescalated groups, only a regression for the nonescalated contracts produces a significant coefficient of *FPROS* on *LIFE* (at the 10 percent level).

Developments in the Mid-1970s

Table 4-7 permits a limited analysis of the possibility of a structural shift in wage determination in the 1970s. A dummy variable, *D7376*, which is equal to 1 for contracts beginning in the period 1973–76 and equal to zero otherwise,[57] has been added to some of the equations. The period 1973–76 begins with a remarkable food price surge in 1973, which was reinforced by OPEC oil price increases later in the year. It includes actual shortages of meat and gasoline associated with price controls and the oil embargo as well as a substantial increase in the unemployment rate. The period has also been associated by some observers with a break in the cyclically adjusted trend rate of productivity improvement.[58] It is

57. Although it might seem desirable to include a dummy for the effect of the controls program that began in 1971, the 1971 contracts in the sample were either concluded before controls or based on precontrol conditions and permitted to operate that way by the Pay Board. The aerospace contracts were cut back, but the effect was simply to delay payment from the first to the second year of the contract (and even the lost money was eventually restored by a court decision). The longshore contracts were also cut, but the money was recovered when controls expired in 1974. Only two contracts in the sample—both in textiles—were negotiated in 1972, when Phase II controls were fully effective. A dummy for 1972, when added to equations 1 and 3 in table 4-7, produces a negative coefficient for *FIRST* (significant at the 10 percent level) and a nonsignificant negative coefficient for *LIFE*. But it may simply be picking up other influences, such as imports, of special significance to wage setting in the textile industry. Apart from these considerations, it has been argued elsewhere that the purpose of the controls was not to create subnormal wage increases (negative dummy coefficients), but rather to pull wage determination back to what was considered to be normal at the time. Thus negative coefficients should not be expected. See Weber and Mitchell, *The Pay Board's Progress*, pp. 306–15. In any case, the onslaught of price increases in early 1973 and the loosening of controls in Phases III and IV tended to dissipate the impact of wage controls, although as noted below, the expiration of controls in April 1974 triggered some wage reopenings.

If equation 3 is estimated with annual dummies for 1972–76, the following pattern of coefficients for the dummies is obtained:

Year	Coefficient of dummy	Number of observations
1972	−0.78	2
1973	2.98	8
1974	1.86	11
1975	1.63	2
1976	0.34	1

Only the dummies for 1973 and 1974 are statistically significant. The lack of significance in the later years may be due to the extreme thinness of the sample after 1974.

58. Edward F. Denison, "Where Has Productivity Gone?" *Basis Point*, vol. 3 (1:1978), pp. 11–13.

thus natural to wonder if the structure of union wage determination might have been altered by these dramatic events.

If the structure of wage determination was in fact turned in an inflationary direction during this period, a further question arises. It is possible that the effect was permanent so that wage determination after 1973–76 was still affected by a structural shift that had occurred several years before. Another possibility, however, is that there was a temporary structural shift in wage determination in the mid-1970s, which later disappeared. Unfortunately, since the contract file ends with the mid-1970s, there is no way of differentiating statistically between these alternatives.

Also, the dummy technique is crude and raises methodological problems. A period such as 1973–76, where explanatory variables take on extreme values, is of obvious statistical interest. If the underlying parameters do not shift during such periods, the extreme observations should help establish proper estimates. When such periods are explained away by dummy variables, parameter estimates are weakened and may be distorted. However, the risk of this distortion is somewhat reduced in a contract file (compared with time-series data of the type used for table 4-6) because of the large number of observations.

On the assumption that $D7376$ is not simply stealing significance from other variables, the dummy coefficient does suggest that wage increases were abnormally high during 1973–76. Equation 4 in table 4-7 suggests that, for the overall sample, wage changes averaged 2.4 percentage points above what would have been expected over the life of the contract. None of this effect appeared to stem from the first-year increment.

An obvious question is whether escalator increases were the source of the shift. Although the *COLA* coefficient should capture the escalator effect, it is conceivable that when inflation became severe escalator formulas were sufficiently liberalized to cause an underestimate of the direct impact of inflation on escalated contracts. The deferred portion of escalated contracts does show a 1.6 dummy coefficient, but this is not enough to make the dummy coefficient significant over the contract life (equation 12 in table 4-7). However, the dummy for long-term *nonescalated* deferred increases is positive and significant (equation 23), suggesting that the unexplained shift is not merely an escalator phenomenon.

The coefficient for $D7376$ is largest for the life-of-contract increases under short contracts (equation 8 in table 4-7). Seven of the short contracts began in 1973–76. All but one of these were associated with scheduled or unscheduled reopenings of existing agreements brought on by the sudden jump in inflation or the end of controls, or both.

The reopener phenomenon has three important effects on the data file. First, under the rules adopted in constructing the data, a contract was deemed to end either at its official expiration date or at a wage reopening, whichever came first. Reopeners turn long contracts into short ones and any structural shifts associated with reopening will thereby be associated with the short contract equations. Second, reopeners can make what were originally front-loaded contracts (*FIRST > LIFE*) into de facto back-loaded contracts (*FIRST < LIFE*). Consider a two-year agreement negotiated in 1973 providing a 5 percent increase in the first year and a 4 percent increase in the second year. The annual rate of increase over the life of the contract is about 4.5 percent, so the agreement is front-loaded. If the contract is interrupted by a reopener after fourteen months, the overall 9.2 percent increase ($1.05 \times 1.04 = 1.092$) is spread over a shorter period than planned and produces an annual increase of 7.8 percent. Since *FIRST* is now less than *LIFE*, the agreement has become back-loaded. Third, although the timing of the reopening in the example just described suggests a disturbance that arose in 1974, that disturbance becomes associated with a 1973 contract. Hence the reopener phenomenon moves the evidence of disturbance to a period preceding the disturbance.

None of the interrupted contracts were escalated. The sudden burst of inflation had almost certainly not been anticipated by the parties, who presumably were using $\dot{P}_{-1}$ or some related index as a guide to the future rate of inflation at the time of negotiations. When it became evident that their anticipation was incorrect, the contract was interrupted, arithmetically raising its *LIFE* value and thereby producing a significant and positive dummy coefficient.[59]

Implications

Labor economists have studied wage determination for many years, and the results presented above suggest that the analysis of union wage processes can be furthered by incorporating institutional features (such

59. The arithmetic explanation in the text is not meant to imply that the wage increases recorded were not "real." The point is simply that the costing methodology caused the real effect to be reflected in *LIFE* or *DEFERRED* estimates rather than the first year and that the impact shows up in the contract terminated by the reopener rather than in the new contract.

as contract length) into econometric analysis. However, the results also have implications for public policy, particularly for anti-inflation policy.

Sensitivity to Real Economic Conditions

Both the union and the nonunion sectors exhibit some direct sensitivity to real business conditions as represented by the unemployment rate. Their indirect sensitivity is greater, since prolonged high unemployment lowers the rate of price inflation (partially as a reflection of lower wage inflation), which in turn affects wage inflation through the price channel. But even with an allowance for indirect effects, the sensitivity of wage change to real business conditions should not be exaggerated.

The first-round effect of an increase in unemployment from 6 percent to 7 percent on the rate of wage change seems to be no more than -0.5 percentage point. If this reduction were fully passed into price inflation, so that the consumer price index slowed by 0.5 percentage point, there would be an additional effect on wages. If the price coefficient was 0.6 (a 1 percentage point reduction in price inflation produced a 0.6 percentage point reduction in wage change), the second-round effect would be -0.5×0.6, which must be added to the first-round effect. After all rounds were complete, the effect would be only 1.25 percentage points of reduction in wage inflation (and a corresponding reduction in price inflation).[60] The equations presented earlier in this chapter (tables 4-6 and 4-7) had a very simple lag structure, so the speed with which successive rounds would take place cannot be estimated. However, it is clear that the time involved for the process to work itself out would be measured in years.

One objection to this pessimistic analysis might be that it is too dependent on the magnitude of the price coefficient. A unitary price coefficient would suggest that eventually, as the rounds continued, an increase in the rate of unemployment would bring the rate of wage and price inflation down to any desired target level. However, the results in table 4-7 suggest that, in the union sector, only the long-term escalated contracts exhibit a unitary price reaction. As high rates of inflation persist, more bargainers adopt escalators, effectively raising the mean price coefficient for

---

60. The formula for the total impact on prices and wages is $I \times (1 + z + z^2 + z^3 + \ldots)$, where I is the initial effect (-0.5 in the example in the text) and z is the price effect (0.6). This formula is equivalent to $I/(1 - z)$.

the union sector. But this feature of the union sector does not lead to a happy conclusion. It suggests that if the price inflation rate is run up high enough, the moderating effect of a less-than-unitary price coefficient will gradually be lost, and inflation will accelerate. On the down side, it means that the closer policymakers wish to come to price stability, the less the indirect effect of the price coefficient will help them. That is, as price inflation begins to moderate, escalator clauses are likely to be dropped from union contracts, lowering the effective price coefficient and its accompanying indirect downtrend benefits.

A second possible objection relates to the magnitude of the direct unemployment effect. It could be argued that if government policymakers convincingly announced that they were prepared to engineer a recession and keep the economy depressed for as long as it took to control inflation, wage setters would not react the way typical wage equations suggest.[61] The recessions reflected in the wage equations were seen as transitory events by wage setters, this argument might run, because policymakers did not have sufficient backbone to maintain a depressed economy.

Two points can be made on this score. The first is essentially political. When the economy goes into recession policymakers are under great pressure to bring about a recovery. If this pressure was decisive in the past, there is every reason to suppose that it will be decisive in the future—that prolonged recession is not a feasible policy under the American political system. Wage setters are aware of this feature of political decision-making, and their behavior—as shown in estimated wage equations—reflects this knowledge.

There is also an economic point to be made. It is true that estimated regression coefficients do not include episodes of prolonged and determined recession engineering because none have occurred in recent memory. But it is also true that no one knows what such hypothetical regression coefficients would turn out to be. At the onset of the Great Depression, wages did fall in nominal terms. However, what is remarkable is the resistance of wages to the decline in real business activity. An hour of manufacturing labor in real terms cost almost 14 percent more in 1933—the trough of the depression—than it did in 1929. Compensation per full-

61. For example, see William Fellner, "Criteria for Demand Management Policy in View of Past Failures," in William Fellner, ed., *AEI Studies on Contemporary Economic Problems, 1976* (American Enterprise Institute for Public Policy Research, 1976), p. 106.

time employee in the entire domestic economy fell in real terms by less than 1 percent in 1929–33.[62]

The years of the Eisenhower administration might be cited as partial evidence for the determined recession approach. Policymakers then seemed more willing to accept a "soft" economy than was the case later, but they never committed themselves to fighting inflation no matter what the cost in unemployment and economic slack. The recession following the Korean War was accompanied by an absolute decline in the consumer price index. Yet there were special circumstances in the period. To some extent, the memory of the Great Depression still lingered and the possibility that the post–Korean War recession could snowball must have seemed real to some wage setters. Many observers expected a return to the depression after World War II. The postwar liquidity and the Korean War boom may have appeared to be temporary factors that had merely delayed the inevitable. Prices also rose sharply when the Korean War broke out in anticipation of excess demand and wage-price controls.[63] By the time controls were imposed, the price pressure had been relieved.[64] In fact, some prices may have overshot their optimum levels in an effort to beat the imposition of controls. Hourly earnings growth did slow during the post–Korean War recession, although some of the slowdown occurred after a wage bulge following the end of wage controls.

In short, wage equations do not suggest that earnings in either the union or the nonunion sector are sufficiently sensitive to real business

62. Bureau of the Census, *Handbook of Labor Statistics, 1975—Reference Edition* (GPO, 1975), pp. 248, 313; Bureau of Economic Analysis, *The National Income and Product Accounts of the United States, 1929–74* (GPO, 1977), p. 194.

63. When the Korean War started, President Truman was reluctant to impose measures suggesting the full-scale mobilization that had accompanied World War II. However, many people remembered the shortages of World War II and embarked on a buying-and-hoarding spree that pushed prices up. Eventually, as the war intensified, the President was forced to adopt mandatory controls. The consumer price index rose by 7.8 percent between June 1950, when the war broke out, and February 1951, when a price freeze was imposed. (The freeze was actually imposed at the end of January but would not have affected the consumer price index until February.) For details, see Craufurd D. Goodwin and R. Stanley Herren, "The Truman Administration: Problems and Policies Unfold," in Craufurd D. Goodwin, ed., *Exhortation and Controls: The Search for a Wage-Price Policy, 1945–1971* (Brookings Institution, 1975), pp. 69–78. Price data from Bureau of Economic Analysis, *Business Statistics, 1977* (GPO, 1978), p. 229.

64. The Eisenhower administration came into office and terminated the controls. From January 1953 to January 1954, the consumer price index rose only 1.1 percent, and thereafter prices declined. It does not seem that the controls were holding back much repressed price inflation.

conditions to allow a quick cure for inflation through demand restraint. A recession will have some effect on wage inflation, more so in the non-union than in the union sector. But miracles cannot be expected from aggregate demand restraint of the type practiced in recent years. Whether a different approach to demand policy would have a much different effect cannot be answered from the wage equation evidence. Any assertion that it would be different must be based on assumption rather than on observation.

Contract Duration and Escalator Clauses

The union sector appears to be less responsive to short-run changes in real economic conditions than the nonunion sector. Some of this insensitivity seems to be associated with long-term contracts, which have become commonplace. The question is whether the union sector could be made more responsive to demand policy if negotiators were forced to adopt contracts of short duration or to abandon the escalator clauses that help make long contracts possible.

Currently there are few public policies in this area, although the development of the long-term contract is generally viewed with favor by industrial relations specialists. The National Labor Relations Board has a "contract bar rule," which gives mild encouragement to such agreements. Under this rule, petitions to decertify a union or to replace it with a rival union will not be accepted by the NLRB during the life of an existing contract for up to two years.[65] The fact that existing contracts are usually given preferential treatment when controls or similar programs are imposed may also be a mild incentive to negotiating a two- or three-year contract.[66]

Two issues in contract duration must be considered. First, use of long-term contracts helps the parties reduce negotiating costs, including the chance of strikes. Evidence presented in appendix C suggests that, for every hundred workers covered under a major expiring contract in a

65. See A. Howard Myers and David P. Twomey, *Labor Law and Legislation*, 5th ed. (Cincinnati: South-Western Publishing, 1975), p. 171.

66. For the experience of the Pay Board in the deferred area, see Weber and Mitchell, *The Pay Board's Progress*, pp. 31–33, 57–63, 420–22. See also Daniel Quinn Mills, *Government, Labor, and Inflation: Wage Stabilization in the United States* (University of Chicago Press, 1975), pp. 137–40. The Carter administration exempted existing agreements from the 7 percent wage guidelines announced in October 1978.

given year, between twenty and forty are observed to be involved in a work stoppage.[67] This relationship overstates the proportion substantially, since workers in the major-union sector constitute roughly half of all union workers. However, even if the estimate is halved—to ten to twenty workers involved in stoppages per hundred workers under expiring contracts—the risk of a strike is still not negligible. And there is an automatic incentive to adopt procedures that reduce exposure to this risk. An official policy of discouraging long-term contracts would lead to more strikes. Not only would this impose costs on the parties, but it would also increase the potential for public inconvenience and, in certain industries, national emergency disputes. When national emergency disputes occur, government officials are under strong pressure to arrange a settlement, even if the rules of an anti-inflation program must be bent.

A second, more fundamental question concerns how parties who were forced to adopt short-duration contracts would behave. A voluntary adoption of a short contract is a symptom of strong pressure to adapt to some short-term circumstance—recession, controls, a severe financial crisis of the employer—that cannot be handled if commitments of two or three years must be negotiated. If the parties do not find themselves under this pressure, a proscription of long-term contracts could not preclude informal understandings about the course of wage change over two or three years. Obviously an informal arrangement would be more complicated for either party to enforce. But there is much to suggest that economic relationships are imbued with tacit understandings, not only in the labor market but elsewhere as well.[68] In other words, *forced* short-duration con-

---

67. Table C-7 presents a series of regressions covering twenty-seven industries for the period 1968–75. Each equation relates the number of workers involved in work stoppages resulting from contract renegotiation to the number of workers under major expiring agreements in the same year and industry (EXP). The coefficient of EXP varies between 0.22 and 0.36. Table C-3 relates the annual change in the number of workers involved in work stoppages resulting from wage disputes ($\Delta WAGWK$), from renegotiations ($\Delta RENWK$), and from all sources ($\Delta ALLWK$) to the annual change in the number of workers under expirations (ΔEXP). The coefficient of ΔEXP varies between 0.31 and 0.36 over the periods covered. For further details, see appendix C.

68. Michael L. Wachter and Oliver E. Williamson, "Obligational Markets and the Mechanics of Inflation," discussion paper 7 (University of Pennsylvania, Center for the Study of Organizational Innovation, November 1977). In the labor market the degree of workers' attachment to an employer (and whether this attachment was secularly increasing) began to be discussed in the late 1950s. See Arthur M. Ross, "Do We Have a New Industrial Feudalism?" *American Economic Review*, vol. 48 (December 1958), pp. 903–20. The notion of a quasi-fixed component of labor was

tracts might not prove to be more sensitive to real economic conditions than voluntary long ones.

Direct Intervention

The difficulty of making wages respond to aggregate demand policy has led to a search for alternative or supplementary policies. During World War II and the Korean War formal mandatory wage and price controls were used to contain the effects of excess demand. Although these episodes have been periodically reviewed in connection with more recent direct interventions in the process of wage and price determination, they were addressed to different circumstances. The wage-price guideposts of the Kennedy and Johnson administrations were aimed at prolonging the period during which the economy could be expanded without serious inflationary consequences. By 1966 demand pressure associated with the Vietnam War, an event not anticipated by the framers of the original guideposts, forced abandonment of the 3.2 percent wage standard and associated pricing rules.[69]

Formal wage and price controls were imposed in 1971, also during a period of recovery from recession. Again, the goal seemed to be insurance against the risk that inflation would rekindle before the economy was actually in a situation of insufficient capacity and labor supply. In retrospect, demand stimulation seems to have been pushed too far in 1972, eliminating economic slack faster than had been anticipated. Demand pressure, combined with the exogenous shocks of worldwide crop shortages, dollar devaluation, and the crystallization of an international oil cartel, destroyed the program in 1973, although controls lingered on through various phases.

Since these efforts at direct control have been discussed elsewhere, it would be inappropriate to attempt a thorough review here. But it is worth noting that both the Kennedy-Johnson guideposts and the 1971–74 controls program were initially aimed at prolonging an economic expansion.

---

developed in Walter Y. Oi, "Labor as a Quasi-Fixed Factor," *Journal of Political Economy,* vol. 70 (December 1962), pp. 538–55. The concept has since been incorporated into a number of empirical papers, such as Ronald G. Ehrenberg, "Heterogeneous Labor, the Internal Labor Market, and the Dynamics of the Employment-Hours Decision," *Journal of Economic Theory,* vol. 3 (March 1971), pp. 85–104. Related empirical work is cited in the Ehrenberg article.

69. John Sheahan, *The Wage-Price Guideposts* (Brookings Institution, 1967), pp. 44–61.

Another approach would be direct intervention in wage and price setting to shorten a recession. Such a program, by definition, would not be faced with rising demand pressure. The "voluntary" wage-price program announced by President Carter in October 1978, when many forecasters were predicting a recession or at least a general economic slowdown, may have been formulated with such a goal in mind.

A recession-oriented program of direct intervention can be viewed as an attempt to reinforce the impact of demand restraint, that is, to encourage the development of a larger-than-normal response of wage change to unemployment. To the extent that such a policy succeeded, the severity of the recession could be lessened. Government officials naturally are hesitant to admit that they use recession to deal with inflation, and they are loath to appear to be putting the burden on labor in an anti-inflation program. But the Kennedy-Johnson program, the Nixon program, and the Carter program centered on the labor market, the collective-bargaining sector in particular.

Apart from appearances, whether the burden falls on labor depends on how heavily unemployment is weighted in the calculation. Popular discussion of direct intervention efforts usually focuses exclusively on the rate of wage change relative to price change. But clearly the additional unemployment that would have been created in the absence of direct intervention is also a burden on labor. A program of direct intervention that reduces this burden cannot be wholly evaluated by its impact on the ratio of wages to prices.

V

Wage Imitation and Inflation

A CONTINUING ELEMENT of controversy in labor economics is the degree to which wage adjustments are linked through some sort of imitative mechanism. The literature abounds with discussions of wage "spillovers" and "patterns." The implications of this controversy extend beyond the range of labor economics to general questions of inflation and to public policies such as wage-price controls and guidelines.

Even from a purely theoretical viewpoint, the concept of wage imitation is important. The standard economic model postulates an isolated economic man maximizing his own utility. Some models are willing to let the family rather than the individual be the decisionmaking unit. However, simple economic models, whether based on individuals or on families, usually ignore the interdependence of utility functions. In these models such commonplace social activities as charitable donations are difficult to understand except as a form of enlightened self-interest.[1] Although some economists are willing to entertain the notion of interdependent utility functions,[2] use of the concept is discouraged by the potential complications entailed. A world in which events might feed back on themselves is bound to be more difficult to describe. And stable equilibria, which are often central to economic theorizing, could easily be more difficult to achieve.

1. There has been much recent discussion on self-serving cooperation in biological systems. For a discussion and references, see J. Hirshleifer, "Competition, Cooperation, and Conflict in Economics and Biology," *American Economic Review,* vol. 68 (May 1978), pp. 238–43.

2. For example, Thurow attributes rigidity in wage structures—wage interrelations—to interdependent preferences. Lester C. Thurow, "Psychic Income: Useful or Useless?" *American Economic Review,* vol. 68 (May 1978), pp. 145–48. Annable develops a theory of wage rigidity, essentially a rationalization of the standard Keynesian assumption about wages, based on utility functions that are partially dependent on wages paid to external reference groups. James E. Annable, Jr., "A Theory of Downward-Rigid Wages and Cyclical Unemployment," *Economic Inquiry,* vol. 15 (July 1977), p. 335.

Early Literature

Interrelationships in wage structure are compatible with a variety of explanations of which direct wage imitation is only one. In particular, labor markets are subject to pressure resulting from the state of the economy and the rate of inflation. The more closely wage determination units are related to each other in skill mix, region, common product markets, or input-output relationships, the more closely correlated their wage decisions can be expected to be. No special theories are necessary to explain such intercorrelations. Even the textbook economic model would predict them. All that is needed is correlation of movements in industry or firm demand and supply curves to produce intercorrelation in wage movements within the classical framework.

An important question is whether the predictions of wage-imitation models can be distinguished from simple correlations of the wage movements that economic forces could be expected to produce. That is, do wage-imitation models contain elements that seemingly override such forces? Put another way, would economists improve their predictive ability in the labor market by building wage-imitation models? There are approaches that suggest such an overriding influence, both leading to similar conclusions. One approach involves information costs and rules of thumb. For example, unit A might imitate wage developments in unit B if A had found in the past that B usually reacted "correctly" to economic circumstances. That is, A uses B as a proxy because B usually does what A would have wanted to do anyway. The common employer practice of surveying wages at other closely related firms as part of the wage-determination process could be an example of this type of behavior. But unless B starts doing the "wrong" thing and unless information costs are very high, such behavior would not differ substantially from independent wage determination at A and B.[3] Theories that stress wage imitation based on past economic relationships can be interpreted in the context of rules of thumb and high information costs. Behavior that once had an economic rationale continues because of tradition after the initial justification has disappeared.

3. If B starts doing the wrong thing and information costs are not high, A will perceive the problem and stop following B. The relation between A and B is thus ephemeral in that it is quickly terminated when subjected to strain.

A second approach to wage-imitation models is based directly on the concept of equity. It is simply assumed that interdependent utility functions are involved. That is, unit A follows unit B because this is the "fair" thing to do. Workers in unit A are disappointed if their wages lag behind those of B.[4] The wage of B is then an argument in the utility functions of unit A workers, since the B wage influences the satisfaction that A workers derive from their own wages. Behavior based on tradition can easily be put in the equity framework. It need only be assumed that people find the old way of doing things the equitable way. The equity framework can also encompass other forms of behavior. Workers in unit A might suddenly discover that unit C was paying a higher wage and seek to emulate that unit. Such behavior could not be justified by tradition but would easily fit into social norms such as "equal pay for equal work." However, if units frequently change their comparison groups, wage-imitation models would not have much predictive power.

Apart from the appeal of a particular rationalization of wage imitation is the question of precisely what form the imitation takes. Models in which what is imitated is the absolute wage can be imagined; that is, wage setters may seek to maintain wage differentials at some target level and may make adjustments when the actual result differs from the target. Alternatively wage setters may simply imitate wage movements and ignore wage differentials. These two approaches are clearly related; if the adjustment to departures from target wage differentials takes place quickly, wage movements will be almost identical across units. Because of the close interrelationships of these approaches, this chapter generally lumps the various models together under the heading "wage imitation."

Much of the early work on wage imitation was written in the 1940s, when pattern bargaining seemed to be a new and powerful feature of wage determination. Ross defined the concept of "orbits of coercive comparison" at that time as follows:

The buyer and seller of labor do meet within some fixed geographic area, but the price at which the exchange takes place is often determined by other agencies hundreds of miles away, without necessary knowledge or concern for each of the particular markets affected by the bargain. Locality, an essential char-

---

4. For example, craftsmen in manufacturing were said to resent the higher wages paid construction craftsmen in the early 1970s. Joel Seidman, "Bargaining Structure: Some Problems of Complexity and Dislocation," *Labor Law Journal,* vol. 24 (June 1973), pp. 341–42.

acteristic of the labor market so far as supply and demand are concerned, is of limited relevance for wage determination.[5]

Ross believed that classical demand and supply considerations could be overridden both within a single union's jurisdiction or bargaining unit and across industry and union lines. He emphasized equity considerations that determined the scope of the orbit.

In the mid-1950s Dunlop elaborated on imitative wage behavior in his well-known description of a "wage contour," which consisted of a stable group of firms linked together by their wage determination practices.[6] He emphasized "economic" factors that created the linkage, such as similar product markets or sources of labor. His view seemed to be in line with the rules-of-thumb–information-costs–tradition approach. Dunlop emphasized "key" wage rates, on which intrafirm wage structure was based, and "key" wage bargains, which set larger interfirm patterns.

The Importance of the Wage-Imitation Concept

The wage-imitation concept could be important for macroeconomic policy in two ways. As was pointed out in chapter 2, the union sector as a proportion of total employment has been declining since the mid-1950s. Even at its peak, the union movement never came close to representing a majority of wage and salary earners. However, if certain union wage decisions spill over into the nonunion sector, the number of union members could be a misleading indicator of union influence. Policymakers might thus need to give much greater weight to such settlements, particularly in the context of wage controls or wage guidelines, than appearances would suggest.[7] Certain major union settlements could have a multiplier effect extending to nonunion units.

A second possible effect is more subtle and depends critically on the assumed structure of wage imitation. Under certain assumptions, changes

5. Arthur M. Ross, *Trade Union Wage Policy* (University of California Press, 1948), p. 53.

6. John T. Dunlop, "The Task of Contemporary Wage Theory," in Dunlop, ed., *The Theory of Wage Determination* (St. Martin's, 1957), p. 17. Dunlop had earlier discussed wage imitation, though in a less formalized framework, in *Wage Determination Under Trade Unions* (Macmillan, 1944), pp. 126–30.

7. Obviously, the spillover effect could run in the other direction. In principle, some union wages might be set with reference to nonunion wages, making the effective economic size of the union sector smaller than it appears to be when measured by membership.

in wage structure, sparked by some initial cause, could continue to produce wage inflation long after the spark had flickered out. A simple numerical example illustrates this. Suppose unit A sets its wage change equal to last period's wage change in unit B, plus or minus a factor reflecting the degree to which the wage in A was a desired proportion of the wage in B. In each period, when the ratio $R(a)$ is not at the desired level, unit A makes up a fraction of the gap. For instance, if unit A wants its wage to be 80 percent of the unit B wage but in the preceding period the ratio was only 70 percent, it will try to make up some of the difference, as well as to match the preceding wage change in unit B. The fraction of catching up will be assumed to be an arbitrary percentage, $c(a)$, say, 50 percent. Hence, unit A would match the increase in unit B from the previous period, plus taking an added 5 percent to make up the gap (5 percent being one-half of 80 percent minus 70 percent). Assume further that unit B sets its wage with reference to unit A in exactly the same fashion.[8]

In this example, A watches B and B watches A. No other factors for wage determination have been introduced, and the example is a pure case of wage imitation. If both units have a common view of what their relative wage relationship should be, their wages will remain at the desired ratio and will rise at an unchanging rate. If wages initially rise, both units will experience the same rate of wage inflation.[9]

The numerical example in table 5-1 illustrates this stable relationship. In the upper half of the table, it is assumed that both units believe the

8. These relations can be described by the following equations:

$$(1) \qquad \%w(a) = c(a)\left(R(a) - \frac{w(a)_{-1}}{w(b)_{-1}} \right) + \%w(b)_{-1},$$

and

$$(2) \qquad \%w(b) = c(b)\left(\frac{w(a)_{-1}}{w(b)_{-1}} - R(b) \right) + \%w(a)_{-1},$$

where $\%w(a)$ and $\%w(b)$ are the percentage changes in wages in units A and B; $c(a)$ and $c(b)$ are the adjustment factors for units A and B; $R(a)$ and $R(b)$ are the desired ratios of the unit A wage to the unit B wage as seen by units A and B, respectively; $w(a)$ and $w(b)$ are the current wages in units A and B; and the subscript -1 indicates the prior period. It would make little difference if the model were formulated on the basis of absolute cents-per-hour differences rather than percentage differences.

9. Only if $R(a) = R(b)$ can both the terms in brackets on the right-hand sides of equations 1 and 2 be equal to zero. When they are, $\%w(a) = \%w(b)_{-1} = \%w(a)_{-2} = \%w(b)_{-3}$, and so forth. This is a steady-state solution under which wage inflation occurs at an unchanging rate and the ratio of wages in the two units is equal to the value desired by both units. A somewhat different formulation of this problem can be found in Daniel J. B. Mitchell, "Wage Determination," *Labor Law Journal*, vol. 28 (August 1977), pp. 484–85.

Table 5-1. *Numerical Example of Wage Imitation*

Percent unless otherwise specified

Period	Wage in unit A, W(a) (dollars)	Wage in unit B, W(b) (dollars)	$\dfrac{W(a)}{W(b)}$	$\dfrac{\Delta W(a)}{W(a)_{-1}}$	$\dfrac{\Delta W(b)}{W(b)_{-1}}$
		$R(a) = R(b) = 0.80; c(a) = c(b) = 0.50$			
1	4.00	5.00	0.80	0.05	0.05
2	4.20	5.25	0.80	0.05	0.05
3	4.41	5.51	0.80	0.05	0.05
4	4.63	5.79	0.80	0.05	0.05
5	4.86	6.08	0.80	0.05	0.05
6	5.11	6.38	0.80	0.05	0.05
		$R(a) = 0.90; R(b) = 0.80; c(a) = c(b) = 0.50$			
1	4.00	5.00	0.80	0.05	0.05
2	4.40	5.25	0.84	0.10	0.05
3	4.76	5.88	0.81	0.08	0.12
4	5.54	6.38	0.87	0.16	0.09
5	6.12	7.61	0.80	0.10	0.19
6	7.58	8.39	0.90	0.24	0.10

Source: See the text, pp. 167–70, for derivation of this example.

wage in unit A should be 80 percent of the wage in unit B and that both units have been experiencing wage inflation of 5 percent in each period. Starting from an assumed wage of $4.00 an hour in A and $5.00 in B, the table shows that the wages in both units will simply continue upward at a compound rate of 5 percent indefinitely, maintaining the 80 percent relationship.

Suppose unit A becomes dissatisfied with the 80 percent relationship and wants to increase its wage to 90 percent of the unit B level. Suppose further that unit B continues to feel that the old 80 percent ratio is the appropriate relationship. Clearly, these conflicting views will be reflected in wage developments in the two units.

The bottom section of the table shows the effect of this shift in the goals of unit A.[10] The two units begin at their old 80 percent relationship with unit A earning $4.00 an hour and unit B earning $5.00. But in period 2, unit A surges ahead as it decides to make up 50 percent of the gap be-

10. The numbers shown in the table were derived by starting at the values shown for period 1 and applying equations 1 and 2 (footnote 8) to obtain values in subsequent periods.

tween the old 80 percent relationship it has and the new 90 percent relationship it now desires. Unit A receives a wage increase of 10 percent, of which half stems from the 5 percent increase that B received in the previous period and half from making up 50 percent of the 10 percent wage gap. Meanwhile, unit B receives its normal 5 percent increase since it was happy with the previous period's 80 percent relationship and since A received a 5 percent increase in the previous period. The result of the two adjustments in period 2 is that unit A achieves an 84 percent wage relationship with B. This new ratio is not the desired one but from A's viewpoint is a definite improvement.

However, what is an improvement for A is a deterioration in the traditional wage differential for B. In period 3, it is unit B's turn to try and restore the old 80 percent relationship by making up some of the wage gap it perceives, plus taking last period's increase in unit A. Unit B now receives a 12 percent wage increase and A receives only 8 percent, since it had made up some of the gap in the previous period. The result of the two increases brings the wage relationship between A and B down to 81 percent. But this makes unit A more dissatisfied, so in period 4 a large increase in the unit A wage brings the relationship up to 87 percent. This process will be repeated indefinitely. Neither unit can achieve its goals because of their incompatible viewpoints, but the rate of wage inflation is accelerated by the attempt.

A critical element in the numerical example is that units watch each other. Unless they agree on what both of them ought to be doing, instability results. A model can be imagined in which B looked at A but A did not look at B. Then, the decisions of wage setters for unit A would simply have spillover effects on B. Unit A would set a pattern for unit B. Although both are models of wage imitative behavior, the conclusions for public policy could be very different depending on which structure was accepted.

Under wage controls, for example, a model in which there is substantial mutual interaction (A looks at B and B looks at A) suggests a program of manipulating wage differentials and trying to restore mutual agreement by the units involved. The diagnosis of the wage explosion in construction in the late 1960s and early 1970s was of this character.[11] And the solution imposed during 1971–74 was a system of wage controls

11. In 1970 first-year wage changes in major union settlements outside construction averaged 10.9 percent. In construction, they averaged 17.6 percent. *Current Wage Developments*, vol. 24 (February 1972), p. 35.

for construction based on wage relativities and the restoration of stable relationships.[12]

An alternative leader-follower model of simple pattern bargaining (B looks at A but A does not look at B) suggests a program of manipulating the wage decisions of a few key wage units in the hope that, through spillovers, many other units will be affected. Later in this chapter some observations are made about these two approaches: mutual interaction and pattern bargaining. Difficulties are inherent in either one.

Initial Empirical Observations

Raw data on earnings can be cited as supporting wage imitation or alternative hypotheses, depending on the bias of the observer. It is well known that the interindustry earnings structure changes slowly.[13] Table 5-2 shows the correlation coefficients (R) obtained by correlating hourly earnings across fifty-nine industries listed in appendix A over various periods from 1953 to 1976. As can be seen, the correlations of earnings structures between years are quite high although they decline as the period lengthens. For example, industry earnings in 1953 explain almost all of the cross-industry variation in earnings in 1958 but only about three-fourths of the variation in 1976.[14] The high correlations are certainly consistent with the presence of wage imitation, but they can also be explained by persistent differences between industries in such characteristics as skill, demography, and unionization.

When emphasis is placed on change in earnings rather than absolute earnings, a somewhat different picture emerges. Column 3 of table 5-3 presents the coefficient of variation of earnings change over the same fifty-nine industries for selected periods, all beginning in 1953. As can be seen, the industries experienced quite different rates of earnings increase in the various periods, despite the tendency of earnings changes to be intercorrelated.[15] The standard deviation of earnings change over the

12. For empirical evidence on this approach to construction wage controls, see Clark G. Ross, "The Construction Wage Stabilization Program," *Industrial Relations,* vol. 17 (October 1978), pp. 308–14; and D. Q. Mills, "Explaining Pay Increases in Construction, 1953–1972," *Industrial Relations,* vol. 13 (May 1974), pp. 196–201.

13. Donald E. Cullen, "The Interindustry Wage Structure, 1899–1950," *American Economic Review,* vol. 46 (June 1956), pp. 353–69.

14. The square of 0.87 is 0.76, the value of R^2.

15. Mitchell, "Wage Determination," pp. 485–87.

Table 5-2. *Interindustry Hourly Earnings Structure Correlation Coefficients, Selected Years, 1953–76*[a]

Hourly earnings in	Hourly earnings in						
	1953	1958	1964	1968	1971	1973	1976
1953	1.00	...	...	...	...	...	...
1958	0.98	1.00	...	...	...	...	...
1964	0.96	0.99	1.00	...	...	...	...
1968	0.91	0.96	0.99	1.00	...	...	...
1971	0.90	0.94	0.97	0.99	1.00	...	...
1973	0.87	0.93	0.96	0.98	0.99	1.00	...
1976	0.87	0.93	0.95	0.95	0.96	0.98	1.00

Source: See appendix A.
a. Based on the fifty-nine industries for which 1953 data were available.

Table 5-3. *Variation in Earnings Change, 1953–76*[a]

Percent

Period	Mean change in earnings (1)	Standard deviation of mean earnings change (2)	Coefficient of variation of earnings change[b] (3)
1953–58	22.3	5.7	25.6
1953–64	47.2	9.7	20.5
1953–68	75.6	12.0	15.9
1953–71	111.2	19.9	17.9
1953–73	141.5	26.7	18.8
1953–76	209.4	40.2	19.2

Source: Appendix A.
a. Based on the fifty-nine industries for which 1953 data were available.
b. Column 1 divided by column 2. Column 3 may differ slightly from this ratio because of rounding.

entire period was about 19 percent of the mean change. Earnings increases from 1953 to 1976 ranged from 121 percent in women's outerwear (SIC 233) to 313 percent in cement (SIC 324).

The interindustry earnings structure shows cyclical sensitivity. In chapter 4 it was noted that there are systematic differences between the union and nonunion sectors in the wage-determination process. In particular, heavily unionized industries seem less sensitive to changes in real business conditions than lightly unionized industries. In general, unionization is correlated with earnings levels, so it is not surprising that interindustry earnings variation narrows during periods of high labor demand. Such periods can produce a bidding up of earnings in low-wage (generally

Table 5-4. *Coefficients of Variation of Hourly Earnings across Industries, Selected Years, 1953–76*[a]

| | Coefficient of variation |
Year	(percent)
1953[b]	19.2
1958[b]	20.9
1958	21.1
1964	21.4
1968	20.0
1971	21.8
1973	23.0
1976	24.3

Source: See appendix A.
a. Based on ninety-three industries listed in appendix A except where noted.
b. Based on fifty-nine industries for which 1953 data were available.

nonunion) industries.[16] Table 5-4, which presents the coefficient of variation of earnings levels of the industries listed in appendix A, confirms this expectation.[17] Earnings variation widened in the 1950s, when labor demand was relatively slack, and narrowed in the late 1960s, when unemployment rates were especially low.

In short, earnings changes are highly correlated and, as noted, the earnings structure across industries changes slowly. On the other hand, considerable variation between industries can be found in earnings changes. Moreover, there are certain regularities in the change of the interindustry earnings structure. There is surely no lockstep behavior in earnings deter-

16. Michael L. Wachter, "Relative Wage Equations for U.S. Manufacturing Industries, 1947–1967," *Review of Economics and Statistics,* vol. 52 (November 1970), pp. 405–10; Michael L. Wachter, "Cyclical Variation in the Interindustry Wage Structure," *American Economic Review,* vol. 60 (January 1970), pp. 75–84; and Michael L. Wachter, "Wage Determination in a Local Labor Market: A Case Study of the Boston Labor Market," *Journal of Human Resources,* vol. 7 (Winter 1972), pp. 87–103. The expectation that wage differentials would narrow when demand pressure was high in the labor market was set forth in a theoretical paper by M. W. Reder, "The Theory of Occupational Wage Differentials," *American Economic Review,* vol. 45 (December 1955), pp. 833–52.

17. McGuire and Rapping caution about the use of cross-industry wage dispersion indexes to test the spillover hypothesis, pointing out that such indexes are sensitive to industry definition. However, the discussion in the text is not testing the hypothesis of spillover at this point; it is simply illustrating cyclical variations in earnings structure. See Timothy W. McGuire and Leonard A. Rapping, "Interindustry Wage Change Dispersion and the 'Spillover' Hypothesis," *American Economic Review,* vol. 56 (June 1966), pp. 493–501.

mination, but some evidence (see chapter 4) that, when units deviate from their position in the interindustry earnings ranking, they tend in time to fall back in line.[18]

Union-Nonunion Wage Spillovers

It is often stated that union wages set a pattern for wages in the non-union sector. And anecdotal evidence of nonunion employers that gear their wage decisions to some union reference group can easily be found.[19] On the other hand, cases can be found, especially in textiles, where the nonunion employers appear to be the pattern setters.[20] At the very least, it can be concluded that there are some spillovers in both directions between the union and the nonunion sectors.

A second obvious point is that, although there may be spillovers, earnings have not moved at the same rate in the two sectors. Chapter 2 showed that during the period 1953–76 union wages generally rose faster than nonunion wages, especially in the subperiod beginning in the late 1960s. This tendency does not suggest that the two sectors have no influence on each other; it simply indicates that the influence is not sufficiently dominant to cause uniformity in wage movements.

At an aggregate level, several studies have attempted to chart union-nonunion spillovers by inserting information about the wage relationship between the union and the nonunion sectors into wage equations for the

18. This refers to the negative *REL* coefficients in table 4-7. Similar results can be obtained from the earnings data used to construct table 5-4. Annual earnings change in each of the ninety-three industries was regressed over 1959–76 against the annual change in consumer prices (lagged one year), the inverted official unemployment rate, and the ratio of earnings in the industry to the average of earnings in all ninety-three industries (lagged one year). This last variable measures the relative earnings status of the industry and will have a negative sign if earnings remain in line. Of the ninety-three industry regressions, seventy produced negative coefficients for this variable.

19. See Eaton H. Conant, "Defenses of Nonunion Employers: A Study from Company Sources," *Labor Law Journal*, vol. 10 (February 1959), pp. 100–09, 132.

20. Southern nonunion textile employers have adopted unionlike practices of coordinated wage rounds. For example, in October 1972 Burlington, J. P. Stevens, Cone Mills, Texfi, Riegel, and Dan River all announced wage increases, followed a month later by Avondale Mills. Almost a year later, the six firms again simultaneously announced wage increases, with Avondale Mills lagging one month. See *Current Wage Developments*, vol. 25 (January 1973), pp. 4–5, and vol. 25 (October 1973), p. 8.

two sectors. As might be expected, the answers obtained are ambiguous and sensitive to the data base used and the period observed.

For example, Johnson found that a lagged union-nonunion wage differential in a union sector wage-change equation produced the expected negative coefficient.[21] That is, to the extent that wages in the union sector pulled ahead of those in the nonunion sector, forces arose to slow union wage growth. This result is similar to that obtained for the *REL* coefficient in table 4-7 above. Flanagan also found a significant negative coefficient in various union wage-change equations.[22] But both Johnson and Flanagan failed to find the opposite effect for the nonunion sector. That is, it appeared that the union sector geared its wage decisions to the nonunion sector but that the nonunion sector made such decisions independently of the union sector. This result—that there is spillover from the nonunion to the union sector but not the other way—runs counter to the impression held by many industrial relations specialists.

It turns out to be easy to upset these results using somewhat different data. Appendix table D-1, for example, presents an equation explaining nonunion wage rate changes in manufacturing (Flanagan's dependent variable) that employs Johnson's union-nonunion wage differential estimate. Unlike the Flanagan or Johnson results, a positive and significant sign for the differential is produced, suggesting a spillover from the union to the nonunion sector. Moreover, the table shows that it is possible to estimate other equations that reverse the results obtained by Johnson and Flanagan. While the lightly unionized sector (by various definitions) shows signs of a spillover effect (using Johnson's estimate of the union-nonunion differential), the heavily unionized sector does not.

The fact that contradictory results can be obtained should sound a note of caution. It is not easy to map out patterns of wage spillover using industry data. Even when significant coefficients are found, it is unclear that spillover—in the sense of wage imitation—is at work. As discussed in chapter 4, indirect pressure on wages through the product market may be an explanation. A relative increase in labor costs could lead to reduced profit margins or higher prices and reduced sales, or both. Over a period of time, these influences could strengthen employers' resistance to wage demands (union firms) or simply lead to less generous wage decisions by employers (nonunion firms).

21. George E. Johnson, "The Determination of Wages in the Union and Non-Union Sectors," *British Journal of Industrial Relations,* vol. 15 (July 1977), pp. 211–25.

22. Robert J. Flanagan, "Wage Interdependence in Unionized Labor Markets," *Brookings Papers on Economic Activity, 3:1976,* pp. 635–73.

It could be argued that the ambiguities arising from studies based on industry data result from the arbitrariness of the industry classifications. Standard industrial classification codes do not necessarily correspond to the structures of wage imitation.[23] However, there would be a conceptual problem in conducting tests for the presence of spillover from a data set gathered on the assumption that such spillovers are prevalent. In any case, wage interrelationships could vary over time, necessitating continuing adjustments in the definitions of the data sample.

Evidence of the variability in union-nonunion wage interrelationships can be adduced from data on white-collar workers in predominantly unionized firms. It is widely held that employers whose blue-collar workers are unionized award comparable pay increases to their white-collar workers to keep them from unionizing. To examine such behavior, data were gathered from *Area Wage Surveys* of the Bureau of Labor Statistics for twenty-four metropolitan areas in which the unionization rate of plant workers in manufacturing was at least 75 percent.[24] Figures could be obtained on the wage changes of male skilled maintenance workers and unskilled plant workers in manufacturing (who were heavily unionized) and manufacturing clerical workers (who were lightly unionized despite their employment in "union towns"). These data, and some results from regressions appearing in table D-2, are summarized in table 5-5.

The period covered in the table is 1967–77, years when the union-nonunion pay differential was generally rising. It is apparent from the table that, even in union towns, clerical workers in manufacturing, whose unionization rate averaged only 12 percent, did not keep up with heavily unionized skilled maintenance workers or unskilled plant workers.[25] The

23. This point is advanced in John T. Dunlop, "Policy Decisions and Research in Economics and Industrial Relations," *Industrial and Labor Relations Review,* vol. 30 (April 1977), p. 276.

24. The criteria for inclusion in the sample were the 75 percent unionization rate and complete data for the period covered. The twenty-four metropolitan areas included are Akron, Baltimore, Buffalo, Cincinnati, Cleveland, Columbus, Davenport, Dayton, Detroit, Indianapolis, Kansas City, Louisville, Memphis, Milwaukee, Minneapolis, Philadelphia, Pittsburgh, Richmond, St. Louis, San Francisco, South Bend, Toledo, Trenton, and Wichita. Data on wages were available in the form of index numbers (1967 = 100) through 1973 in Bureau of Labor Statistics, *Handbook of Labor Statistics, 1976,* bulletin 1905 (Government Printing Office, 1976), pp. 198–99, 202–03. Various *Area Wage Surveys* of the Bureau of Labor Statistics were used to estimate the index for 1977. This was done by compounding the annual rates of change reported for 1973–77. Unionization rates were drawn from *Area Wage Surveys* in bulletin 1975-28.

25. The unionization rate reported for office workers is used to represent the rate for clerical employees.

Table 5-5. *Comparison of Pay Changes of Clerical, Skilled Maintenance, and Unskilled Plant Workers in Manufacturing, Twenty-four Highly Unionized Metropolitan Areas, 1967–77*

Annual percentage change

Item	1967–71 (1)	1971–73 (2)	1973–77 (3)
Increase in pay of clerical worker	5.8	5.1	8.1
Increase in pay of skilled maintenance worker	6.5	6.7	9.2
Increase in pay of unskilled plant worker	6.4	7.1	9.4
Hypothetical difference in clerical pay increase between areas with total clerical unionization and those with no unionization			
Given skilled maintenance worker pay increase	(0.4)	(2.1)	2.3
Given unskilled plant worker pay increase	(−0.1)	3.2	2.4
Increase in rate of change of clerical pay associated with 1 percentage point increase in			
Skilled maintenance worker pay	0.5	0.4	0.4
Unskilled plant worker pay	0.6	(0.2)	(0.2)

Source: Appendix table D-2. The twenty-four areas and sources are listed in footnote 24 to this chapter. Coefficients in parentheses are based on regression coefficients that were not significant at the 10 percent level.

regression analysis suggests that a 1 percentage point increase in the rate of change in pay of either skilled maintenance workers or unskilled plant workers was associated with a considerably smaller increase in the rate of change in clerical pay.[26]

Hypothetically, had clerical workers been heavily unionized, their pay could have kept up with, or exceeded, the pay increases of skilled maintenance or unskilled plant workers after 1971. Of course, the actual rate of clerical unionization was low: the simple average of the rates for the twenty-four metropolitan areas was 12 percent, with a range of 0–49 percent.

In short, spillover did not automatically confer pay increases on clerical employees during a period of a substantial widening of the overall union-nonunion pay differential. Clerical workers in manufacturing whose pay did keep up with union increases were likely to be unionized themselves. But during the period 1960–67, when overall union-nonunion differentials were not generally widening, the pay of clerical, skilled mainte-

26. These estimates are based on the regression coefficients of the pay changes of skilled maintenance and unskilled plant workers in table D-2.

nance, and unskilled plant workers increased at about the same rate.[27] Apparently any simple notion that a constant and mechanical linkage exists when the wages of a group of mostly nonunion workers are determined in a highly unionized blue-collar environment must be abandoned. The data also suggest that the proposition that white-collar unionization is superfluous and ineffective must be questioned.[28] White-collar unionization may have had little effect on union-nonunion pay differentials in the early and mid-1960s, possibly because spillovers maintained the relative status of white-collar workers. But in this sample, at least, unionization began to benefit white-collar workers in manufacturing in the 1970s, as union pay generally rose faster than nonunion pay and they could no longer rely on spillovers from the unionized blue-collar sector.

General Evidence on Wage Imitation

Whether wage imitation exists is not really an issue. There is simply too much casual and anecdotal evidence to ignore the phenomenon. However, the existence of a phenomenon does not obviate the need to assess

27. See Bureau of Labor Statistics, *Handbook of Labor Statistics, 1975—Reference Edition* (GPO, 1975), pp. 267, 271, 273. On a base of 1967 = 100, the earnings index for clerical workers in 1960 stood at 81.1 in manufacturing and the wage index for skilled maintenance workers (male) stood at 80.9. The index for unskilled plant workers (male) was 80.2. Thus the annual rates of pay change for the three groups in 1960–67 were almost identical.

28. This was the conclusion reached by Daniel S. Hamermesh in a study of city data for 1960–67: "White-Collar Unions, Blue-Collar Unions, and Wages in Manufacturing," *Industrial and Labor Relations Review*, vol. 24 (January 1971), pp. 159–70. Since clerical unionization did not begin to affect pay change until the late 1960s, the lack of influence Hamermesh found in the earlier period is not surprising. As an experiment, data for 1971 on the annual earnings of production and nonproduction workers in manufacturing were assembled for the twenty-four metropolitan areas on which table 5-5 is based. Estimates of the 1977 values of these wages were made by increasing the nonproduction wage by the increase in clerical salaries for 1971–77 and increasing the production wage by the increase in skilled maintenance workers' pay or unskilled plant workers' pay for 1971–77. These wage increases were obtained from the data sources used for tables 5-3 and D-2. Regressions were run in the form $NPRE_{iy} = a + bPRE_{iy} + cCU_i$, where $NPRE_{iy}$ is the annual wage of nonproduction workers in area i and year y, PRE_{iy} is the annual production worker wage in area i and year y, and CU_i is the office-worker unionization rate in area i. For $y = 1971$, c is insignificant, though positive. This result is in line with the Hamermesh conclusion for the 1960s. But by 1977 the unionization regression coefficients had become both larger and significant at the 10 percent level. For further details, see table D-3.

Table 5-6. *Percentage of Workers Receiving First-Year Wage Adjustments, Classified by Magnitude of Adjustment, 1976*

Adjustment range (percent)	Major-union sector, private industries (1)	Major-union sector, manufacturing (2)	Total union sector, manufacturing (3)	Nonunion sector, manufacturing (4)
No increase	4	...	1	14
Under 4	6	5	8	12
4 and under 6	24	31	25	17
6 and under 8	11	7	13	27
8 and under 10	27	21	22	17
10 and under 12	14	16	16	9
12 and under 14	7	11	9	3
14 and over	7	8	6	1
Mean adjustment	8.4	8.9	8.4	6.0
Median adjustment	8.5	8.8	8.3	6.5

Source: *Current Wage Developments*, vol. 29 (April 1977), p. 55, and vol. 29 (September 1977), p. 54.

its importance and scope. The existence of wage imitation has often been considered important in formulating programs of wage controls or guidelines. But its importance can be evaluated only after current knowledge about it has been examined.

One point must be made at the start. Occasionally journalistic accounts of wage rounds give the impression that patterns are mechanically followed throughout the economy or at least within the union sector. Table 5-6 shows at a glance that any such suggestion is invalid. The table shows first-year wage adjustments in 1976 (a heavy bargaining year) in the major-union private sector, the major-union sector in manufacturing (where pattern following is sometimes seen as a central element in wage determination), the total union sector in manufacturing, and the nonunion sector in manufacturing. In 1976, as in other years for which data are available, a scattering of settlements is usual. The union columns in table 5-6 do not even show a clear central tendency. It is obvious that wage setters do not all reach the same decisions.[29] Whenever a macro view of the labor market is taken, the wage-imitation hypothesis must generally be expressed in terms of the influence of one settlement on another rather than the dictation of one settlement by another.

29. After years of discussions about wage rounds and key bargains, the dispersion of wage settlements may seem surprising to some readers. Indeed, the director of the Council on Wage and Price Stability characterized the dispersion of the previous year as "striking." Michael H. Moskow, "The Economic Context," *Labor Law Journal*, vol. 27 (August 1976), pp. 465–66.

For wage settlements in one unit to influence wage settlements elsewhere, there must be an information mechanism by which knowledge about wage settlements is disseminated. There are, of course, official sources of aggregate data such as the Bureau of Labor Statistics, but these sources usually provide either no information on specific settlements or only partial information. Moreover, the availability of data from official sources was decidedly more limited in the 1940s and 1950s, when the phenomenon of pattern bargaining was widely discussed.[30]

Cross-Industry Ownership Effects

An information mechanism becomes particularly important as industry lines are crossed. Firms and union officials operating in the same product markets might be expected to be aware of each other's decisions and to have strong economic incentives to coordinate those decisions; beyond that industry, these incentives would be reduced. Nevertheless, there are channels for interindustry information flows.[31]

From the employer's side, ownership patterns may provide extra-industry information. In 1972 fewer than 1 percent of all companies listed in *Enterprise Statistics* by three-digit industry classification had establishments outside their major industry. But this small minority of companies employed 48 percent of the work force of all listed firms, meaning that the large firms often have establishments in many different industrial classifications.[32] For example, firms whose principal industry was "motor vehicles and equipment" had 1,000 or more employees in other areas such as textiles, wood products, rubber and plastic products, glass, primary metals, fabricated metals, machinery other than motor vehicles, wholesale and retail trade, and services. Of the 1.4 million employees working

30. For example, the biennial survey of compensation (including fringe benefits) goes back to 1959 for manufacturing and 1966 for the rest of private nonfarm economy. The costing out of major union settlements by the BLS goes back to the mid-1950s, but the data are spotty until the mid-1960s. Hourly-earnings data for many industries go back only to 1958 or 1964. The survey of union and nonunion wage decisions in manufacturing began in 1959. A history of these indexes can be found in Bureau of Labor Statistics, *BLS Measures of Compensation,* bulletin 1941 (GPO, 1977).

31. The discussion that follows uses industry information. As already noted, the industry approach has been criticized since "wage contours" do not necessarily follow industry classification codes.

32. Bureau of the Census, *1972 Enterprise Statistics,* pt. 1: *General Report on Industrial Organization* (GPO, 1977), p. 59.

Table 5-7. *Employment Patterns in Manufacturing, 1972*

Principal industry of company	Percent of work force employed in other than principal industry[a]
Meat packing	50
Alcoholic beverages	33
Tobacco products	49
Pulp, paper, and board mills	67
Rubber products	47
Glass products	39
Blast furnaces and steel mills	39
Metal cans	51
Radio, TV, and communications equipment	57
Motor vehicles and equipment	48

Source: Bureau of the Census, *1972 Enterprise Statistics*, pt. 1: *General Report on Industrial Organization* (Government Printing Office, 1977), table 2, pp. 23–58.
a. Total work force assigned to each principal industry includes employees of single-industry companies.

for these firms, almost half worked in industries other than "motor vehicles and equipment."[33]

Cross-industry ownership is quite common, especially in manufacturing. Although it is difficult to summarize this tendency, table 5-7 presents the proportion of the work force of companies in ten major industries that was employed outside those central industries. Obviously such calculations are heavily influenced by the degree of disaggregation of the industry classification used. Workers outside an "industry" are often employed in sectors that are closely related in input-output relationships or product-market competition. Still, potential information on wage settlements is implicit in ownership patterns.

Cross-Industry Unionization Effects

A similar potential information channel exists on the union side. Table 5-8 presents a summary of industry concentration estimates for twenty large unions, based on a computer file supplied by the BLS, which allocates known union agreements by three-digit standard industrial classifications. Column 1 shows the proportion of workers covered by contracts of each union in the industry that had the greatest number of members

33. Ibid., pp. 109–11.

Table 5-8. *Indexes of Union Representation Concentration by Three-Digit Industry Classification*

Union	One-industry worker concentration ratio (percent) (1)	Four-industry worker concentration ratio (percent) (2)	Number of 3-digit industries having contracts (3)
Service Employees	26	72	26
Carpenters	58	85–87[a]	28
Electrical Workers (IBEW)	19	65	44
Operating Engineers	35	90–91[a]	26
Ladies Garment Workers	77	90	8
Laborers	53	93–94[a]	13
Hotel and Restaurant Employees	57	99	9
Meat Cutters	51	92	13
Plumbers	86	98	11
Retail Clerks	85	98	17
Machinists	37	52	85
Paperworkers	45	83	18
Clothing and Textile Workers	49	70	39
Rubber Workers	70	90	17
Steelworkers	35	61	92
Communications Workers	93	100	6
Electrical Workers (IUE)	39	78–81[a]	38
Mine Workers	98	100	2
Teamsters	58	73	106
Auto Workers	70	87	54

Source: Data from a Bureau of Labor Statistics computer tape covering private sector contracts known to the BLS in the spring of 1978. The tape contains complete listings of agreements covering 1,000 or more workers and partial listings of agreements covering fewer workers.

a. Range shown because some contracts were assigned only at the 2-digit level.

of that union.[34] Because the industry classification is somewhat arbitrary, a four-industry concentration ratio is also presented, in column 2. This is the proportion of workers covered by union agreements for each union in the four highest-ranked industries in which the union had workers under contract. Finally, column 3 is a simple count of the number of three-digit industries in which the union had any workers covered by contracts known to the Bureau of Labor Statistics.

34. The union concentration ratio in table 5-8 differs from the usual concentration ratio, which is often applied in the analysis of industrial organization. The ratio in the table refers to the concentration of the union's membership in a particular industry or group of industries. It does not measure the fraction of industry employment covered by a given union.

The table shows that some unions, such as the Mine Workers, Hotel and Restaurant Employees, and Communications Workers, are confined to a relatively small number of industries. However, other unions, such as the Steelworkers, Machinists, Electrical Workers (IBEW), Teamsters, and Auto Workers, have relatively broadly based industry membership patterns as measured by concentration, or number of industries in which they had contracts. These large unions are thus in a position to convey information on wage settlements from one industry to another.

Although the industry ownership and union concentration data suggest a potential for exchanging information on wages and wage settlements, they do not provide proof that such exchanges take place or, more important, that they lead to pattern following. Moreover, it is easy to rationalize virtually any pattern or lack of pattern by citing these or other data. For example, when the Mine Workers embarrassed the Carter administration with a large wage settlement in the spring of 1978, government officials claimed that the contract was not pattern setting.[35] The concentration of the Mine Workers in a particular sector of the economy (table 5-8) could be cited as evidence supporting this view.

On the other hand, coal mining is linked through ownership patterns to chemicals, petroleum refining, steel, nonferrous metals, and other manufacturing industries. In 1972 about 22 percent of the coal mining work force were employed by companies whose major industries were in manufacturing. Thirty-six percent of the employees of companies whose major industry was coal mining were in industries other than coal mining. There are input-output relationships between coal mining and utilities, steel, and other sectors. Coal is moved by railroad workers and teamsters. The Mine Workers were instrumental in founding the Steelworkers union and at one time had a significant membership in the chemicals industry.[36]

35. The Council on Wage and Price Stability, in commenting on the coal settlement, noted that "coal settlements have not in the past set a pattern for other agreements." But the council did note that the publicity accompanying the strike and its settlement might have some influence elsewhere. Council on Wage and Price Stability, press release, "The Inflation Impact of the 1978 National Bituminous Coal Wage Agreement," April 14, 1978, pp. 5–6.

36. John L. Lewis, first president of the CIO and president of the United Mine Workers, believed he could improve the bargaining position in mines owned by steel companies if the steel industry itself were organized. Phillip Murray, first president of the Steelworkers, was originally a UMW vice-president. The UMW supplied the initial funds to the Steel Workers Organizing Committee. District 50 of the UMW began to organize in the chemicals industry in the 1930s. It split from the UMW in 1968 and later affiliated with the Steelworkers. Gary M. Fink, ed., *Labor Unions* (Greenwood Press, 1977), pp. 76–79, 357–59.

If one wanted to rationalize a statement that a coal settlement was pattern setting, there would be plenty of supporting evidence.

Conceptual Vagueness in Wage-Imitation Studies

It is precisely this lack of a clear-cut guide to what factors contribute to, or detract from, spillover behavior that has led to severe criticism of the concept itself.[37] Investigations of pattern-following behavior usually find that deviations from the lead settlements occur as the pattern travels away from its source. This tendency has been found in case studies of steel and automobile parts.[38] The finding that deviations from the patterns were occurring required the addition of "epicycles" to the theory of patterns. For example, one author concluded that by the 1950s union rivalry was forcing a "minimum differentiation" from earlier settlements.[39] Another author, finding that supposed followers adopted a pattern before hypothesized leaders, suggested that the followers had merely

37. After a review of the literature on spillover and wage rounds, Burton and Addison conclude: "It appears difficult from the data to generate precise and generally acceptable empirical specifications of the round, and the element of judgment that this inevitably introduces means that different researchers may come up with quite different measurements of 'the' round. . . . Even if the latter problem did not arise, the apparent variability of round phenomena makes it useless as a forecasting device." John Burton and John Addison, "The Institutionalist Analysis of Wage Inflation: A Critical Appraisal," in Ronald G. Ehrenberg, ed., *Research in Labor Economics* (Greenwich, Conn.: Jai Press, 1977), vol. 1, pp. 365–66.

38. For example, Seltzer found that firms in the steel pattern outside the steel industry began to move away from the pattern in the late 1940s. George Seltzer, "Pattern Bargaining and the United Steelworkers," *Journal of Political Economy*, vol. 59 (August 1951), pp. 319–31. See also George Seltzer, "The United Steelworkers and Unionwide Bargaining," *Monthly Labor Review*, vol. 84 (February 1961), pp. 129–36. Similar findings were reported by Locks, especially for smaller firms. Mitchell O. Locks, "The Influence of Pattern-Bargaining on Manufacturing Wages in the Cleveland, Ohio, Labor Market, 1945–50," *Review of Economics and Statistics*, vol. 37 (February 1955), pp. 70–76. Levinson analyzed contracts negotiated by the Auto Workers and found "a considerable degree of flexibility" in pattern following. Harold M. Levinson, "Pattern Bargaining: A Case Study of the Automobile Workers," *Quarterly Journal of Economics*, vol. 74 (May 1960), pp. 296–317 (quotation from p. 316). Alexander also found that the Auto Workers were willing to deviate from the pattern set with the major automobile companies when bargaining in the automobile parts industry. Kenneth Alexander, "Market Practices and Collective Bargaining in Automobile Parts," *Journal of Political Economy*, vol. 69 (February 1961), pp. 15–29.

39. Benson Soffer, "On Union Rivalries and the Minimum Differentiation of Wage Patterns," *Review of Economics and Statistics*, vol. 41 (February 1959), pp. 53–60.

anticipated what the leaders would eventually do.[40] Still another hypothesis advanced to explain a seeming anomaly in wage imitation was that escalated contracts would create spillovers only when the rate of inflation was high, producing large escalator payments.[41]

Wage Imitation and Wage Controls Programs

It is important to note that, unlike many other hard-to-measure social phenomena, there may be an interest group especially concerned with demonstrating that wage imitation exists under certain circumstances. Where wage tribunals, during periods of controls or otherwise, have to make decisions, a union may wish to claim a tandem relationship.[42] For example, during the 1971–74 period of wage controls one union reportedly developed a chart from which it could search for such relationships.[43] Moreover, controls tribunals are often anxious for assistance in

40. John E. Maher, "The Wage Pattern in the United States, 1946–1957," *Industrial and Labor Relations Review,* vol. 15 (October 1961), p. 14. Criticism of this paper appears in the July 1962 issue.

41. Benson Soffer, "The Effects of Recent Long-Term Wage Agreements on General Wage Level Movements: 1950–1956," *Quarterly Journal of Economics,* vol. 73 (February 1959), pp. 36–60, especially p. 50. A related hypothesis is that "key" bargains set a pattern only in tight labor markets. Frank C. Pierson, "The Economic Influence of Big Unions," *Annals of the American Academy of Political and Social Science,* vol. 333 (January 1961), p. 105.

42. Reder noted in the early 1950s that some "patterns" are merely "instruments of propaganda" generated "for purposes of public consumption." M. W. Reder, "The Theory of Union Wage Policy," *Review of Economics and Statistics,* vol. 34 (February 1952), p. 40, n. 24.

43. This anecdote is reported in William M. Vaughn III, "Wage Stabilization in the Food Industry," in John T. Dunlop and Kenneth J. Fedor, eds., *The Lessons of Wage and Price Controls—The Food Sector* (Harvard University, Graduate School of Business Administration, 1977), pp. 154–55. When arbitrators are called upon to set wages, they often appeal to wage comparisons. See Richard Ulric Miller, "Arbitration of New Contract Wage Disputes: Some Recent Trends," *Industrial and Labor Relations Review,* vol. 20 (January 1967), p. 255; and Gary A. Hall, "American Wage Arbitration, 1950–74" (Ph.D. dissertation, University of Tennessee, 1976), pp. 34–37. The Miller and Hall studies are basically updates of an earlier investigation by Irving Bernstein, which came to similar conclusions. See his *Arbitration of Wages* (University of California Press, 1954), pp. 28–30.

Although arbitrators often refer to wage comparisons as a criterion for wage decisions, they may have no clear guidelines for determining which comparison is relevant. See Sylvia Wiseman, "Wage Criteria for Collective Bargaining," *Industrial and Labor Relations Review,* vol. 9 (January 1956), p. 256. This ambiguity provides the arbitrator with flexibility. Moreover, it is not clear how the comparison should be made. For example, an arbitrator might choose either that pay be equalized or that rates of pay change be equalized. Robert E. Sibson, "Wage

finding patterns, since this reduces caseloads (all cases in the pattern can be handled at one time), produces an equitable solution, or explains away an inflationary settlement. A famous magician once described his art of fooling the audience as "more akin to a seduction than to anything else . . . a pleasant experience for both parties."[44] During periods of controls or guidelines, a union is often tempted to play the magician's role and management is often willing to play the magician's helper.[45]

In any case, there are factors that weaken deliberate wage imitation across broad sectors of the economy. Collective bargaining did not become widespread until the late 1930s and the 1940s, and both union and management bargainers were new to the technique of wage setting. In what has been characterized as a "rush to consolidate [their] bargaining structures" some unions may have found it expedient to follow wage patterns.[46] If decisionmakers are not sure how to react to a new situation, the safest rule may be to react the same way as everyone else.

Reinforcing this tendency were the wage controls of World War II. The wartime authorities placed great emphasis on wage relationships in considering requests for wage increases.[47] To the extent that wage relationships had existed previously, the authorities could simplify their administrative procedures by handling tandem cases all at once. Precedents are fundamental to any judicial or quasi-judicial process, so applicants for wage increases had an incentive to find comparison groups that had previously received favorable treatment. Moreover, the authorities used

---

Comparisons in Bargaining," *Labor Law Journal,* vol. 4 (June 1953), pp. 423–32. Wage comparisons may sometimes be used for after-the-fact justifications of pay decisions.

44. James Randi, "The Psychology of Conjuring," *Technology Review,* vol. 80 (January 1978), p. 63.

45. The experience of the Pay Board during the Nixon controls was that employers usually "sincerely" advocated approval of the wage increases they had negotiated, apparently for fear of jeopardizing a long-term relationship with the union. The business members of the Pay Board usually took a tough line on general principles of wage control but in specific wage cases often found themselves voting with the labor members. Arnold R. Weber and Daniel J. B. Mitchell, *The Pay Board's Progress: Wage Controls in Phase II* (Brookings Institution, 1978), pp. 263–66.

46. Arnold R. Weber, "Stability and Change in the Structure of Collective Bargaining," in Lloyd Ulman, ed., *Challenges to Collective Bargaining* (Prentice-Hall, 1967), p. 22. Weber characterizes the immediate post–World War II period as the "heyday of 'pattern' bargaining," although he expresses some skepticism concerning the effectiveness of such patterns.

47. See Daniel Quinn Mills, *Government, Labor, and Inflation: Wage Stabilization in the United States* (University of Chicago Press, 1975), pp. 23–31.

particular wage cases to establish formulas for the entire economy. The most famous of these was the "Little Steel" formula of 1942.[48]

It was natural that this linkage of wage settlements would continue immediately after the war. In a major dispute during the transition to wage decontrol, a steel settlement provided an 18½-cent increase, which set a pattern for other industries. The 18½-cent round is worth exploring because it occurred at a time when notions about settlements and wage patterns were being formulated in the industrial relations literature. This episode undoubtedly influenced subsequent thinking.

After VJ Day, plans were implemented to phase out detailed wage controls. As major labor disputes arose, fact-finding boards were appointed to recommend settlements. At the same time, the National War Labor Board was replaced by a transitional National Wage Stabilization Board (NWSB). In January 1946 a fact-finding board recommended a wage settlement of 19½ cents for General Motors. The Steelworkers, who had reached an impasse with U.S. Steel, then demanded the same 19½ cents, a demand that steel management refused. President Truman recommended 18½ cents, which was again accepted by the union and rejected by management. A three-week strike ensued, which ended when the President signed an executive order permitting the NWSB to approve settlements that were in accord with government recommendations or industry or area patterns. The steel industry accepted the 18½-cent figure, which was later applied to disputes in automobiles, electrical equipment, coal mining, and railroads. However much the spread of 18½ cents may have impressed observers at the time, this incident was not typical collective bargaining.[49]

Even in this peculiar postwar atmosphere, observers noted that deviations from patterns occurred in subsequent wage rounds.[50] Before these tendencies toward diversity could fully work themselves out, Korean War wage controls were imposed.[51] The new controls reinforced linkage

48. Based on movements in prices, the Little Steel formula permitted an increase in wages 15 percent above the level of straight-time earnings prevailing in January 1941. Ibid., p. 26.

49. "Postwar Work Stoppages Caused by Labor-Management Disputes," *Monthly Labor Review,* vol. 63 (December 1946), pp. 876–92.

50. Seltzer, "Pattern Bargaining," p. 327.

51. A description of Korean War wage controls can be found in Mills, *Government, Labor, and Inflation,* pp. 31–36. For an analysis of the rules on interplant wage inequities during the Korean War, see Harold G. Ross and Melvin Rothbaum, "Interplant Wage Inequities," *Industrial and Labor Relations Review,* vol. 7 (January 1954), pp. 200–10. Such rules built wage comparisons into the program.

between settlements.[52] After the Korean War, however, formal wage controls were not imposed again until 1971. And the initial phases of this program, with the exception of a special arrangement for construction, did not place as heavy an emphasis on wage relativities as the earlier programs had.[53]

In summary, two institutional factors in the 1940s and early 1950s stimulated wage imitation. One was the very newness of collective bargaining in many sectors of the economy. The other was the imposition of wage controls placing heavy emphasis on wage relationships. Unless there is a sudden surge in unionization such as that of the 1930s and 1940s, the first factor will not be repeated. And even though programs of wage controls and guidelines may come and go in the future, they are not likely to be as detailed and as focused on wage relativities as in the 1940s and 1950s.[54]

Fringe Benefits and Wage Imitation

Since the early literature on wage imitation, the complexity of labor contracts has greatly increased. Although economists may conceive of

52. For example, Garbarino asserts that the tandem linkage of General Electric and Westinghouse to General Motors was reinforced during the Korean War controls, despite efforts by the two electrical companies to sever the relation. After controls ended, the two did not resume their effort to break away until 1960. Joseph W. Garbarino, *Wage Policy and Long-Term Contracts* (Brookings Institution, 1962), pp. 98–102. In discussing the Korean War wage controls experience while it was in progress, Clark Kerr found that "essentially what the [Wage Stabilization] Board has done is to take the top national bargains and turn them into governmental policy" (p. 382). Dale Yoder commented on the Kerr paper, noting that "the development and imposition of patterns appear inevitable in wage controls." Clark Kerr, "Governmental Wage Restraints: Their Limits and Uses in a Mobilized Economy," *American Economic Review,* vol. 42 (May 1952, *Papers and Proceedings, 1951*), pp. 369–84. The Yoder comment appears on p. 401.

53. The Pay Board had no interplant inequity exception. Its tandem rule was generally confined to relationships within industries. Weber and Mitchell, *The Pay Board's Progress,* pp. 70–73, 425–28. Although the new leadership of the Cost of Living Council beginning with Phase III (early 1973) had a commitment to the use of wage relativities, the official Pay Board rules were never substantially altered.

54. Programs based on detailed tandem relationships and wage relativities are likely to require substantial bureaucracies. This feature acts as a check on their implementation. For example, the Carter administration's wage guideline program announced in October 1978 made little provision for exceptions to the standard based on such considerations. Initial rules of the Carter program can be found in Council on Wage and Price Stability, *Fact Book: Wage and Price Standards* (COWPS, October 31, 1978).

the labor contract as primarily a schedule of wage rates, the actual schedule of wages usually takes up only a small amount of space in a typical union agreement. The rest is devoted to fringe benefits, work rules, safety procedures, union security arrangements, and so forth. This has reduced the degree to which union agreements can be easily copied, especially across industry lines. While wage rate increases are often summarized in the press by a single number (such as 18½ cents), the whole package is much more difficult to evaluate.

Fringe benefits, in particular, provide a way for firms to deviate from patterns, a possibility that was recognized in the early literature.[55] A health and welfare plan has many different features. A worker may know that he is covered by a hospitalization plan, but it will be difficult for him to judge whether that plan is "better" or "worse" than a plan offered by some other employer. Medical policies can differ in the kinds of services covered, the duration of benefits, the rates at which reimbursements are made, and so on. A superior policy for one individual might be inferior for another, depending on factors such as age, marital status, and health.

It might be expected that deviations from patterns could be made most easily in fringe benefits. Table 5-9 provides data supporting this supposition based on a 1974 survey of fringe and wage compensation in unionized private nonfarm establishments. Column 1 shows the coefficient of variation (standard deviation divided by the mean) for straight-time earnings of nonoffice workers in fifteen industry groupings for which a large enough number of establishments were available to make such a computation. Column 2 makes the same computation for private fringe benefits excluding social security and other legally required payments. In every case, the coefficient of variation for fringe benefits is substantially wider than that for straight-time wages.[56] That is, the element of

55. Seltzer, "Pattern Bargaining," pp. 327–28; Locks, "The Influence of Pattern Bargaining," p. 76. More recent writers have also commented on the scope for deviations from patterns by means of fringe benefits and nonwage components of contracts. See Robert M. MacDonald, "Collective Bargaining in the Postwar Period," *Industrial and Labor Relations Review*, vol. 20 (July 1967), p. 563, n. 4; and Bevars Mabry, "The Economics of Fringe Benefits," *Industrial Relations*, vol. 12 (February 1973), p. 98. Mabry states: "The more uniform wage pattern can lessen intra-institutional rivalry, while at the same time the monopoly power of the union can be used to benefit its more favorably placed members through differential fringe benefits."

56. An F-test for the figures in column 2 revealed statistically significant differences relative to the wage figures in column 1 at the 5 percent level in every industry except wholesale groceries, which contains only eleven observations. Hence a very wide difference in the coefficients of variation would be needed to support a finding of a significant difference.

Table 5-9. *Fringe Benefit versus Wage Variability for Unionized Nonoffice Employees, Selected Industries, 1974*

		Coefficient of variation			
			Private fringe benefits[a]		Number of establish-
		Straight-time earnings	Including pensions	Excluding pensions	ments in sample
SIC	Industry	(1)	(2)	(3)	(4)
201	Meat packing	0.25	0.64	0.64	22
271	Newspapers	0.17	0.32	0.39	19
26	Paper manufacturing	0.20	0.42	0.48	36
28	Chemicals	0.21	0.63	0.70	94
331	Steel	0.12	0.31	0.32	32
36	Electrical	0.22	0.56	0.51	52
371	Motor vehicles	0.20	0.56	0.52	27
372	Aircraft	0.14	0.47	0.38	14
401	Railroads	0.08	0.71	0.27	18
42	Trucking	0.15	0.28	0.32	42
481	Telephones	0.18	0.32	0.29	13
49	Utilities	0.13	0.35	0.40	41
504	Wholesale groceries	0.29	0.56	0.70	11
54	Food stores	0.21	0.51	0.51	30
15 16 17	Construction	0.17	0.53	0.63	97

Source: Calculated from data from the biennial survey of employer expenditures for employee compensation on a computer tape provided by the Bureau of Labor Statistics. The survey is described in Bureau of Labor Statistics, *BLS Measures of Compensation*, bulletin 1941 (GPO, 1977), chap. 4.

a. Excludes premiums and overtime for shift, weekend, and holiday work, since these vary with hours worked in different establishments.

compensation for which comparisons are easily made shows less variation across establishments than the element for which comparisons are difficult. Since some of the variation in fringe benefits could be due to erratic funding of pension plans, the test was repeated for private benefits excluding pension,[57] but the same result (column 3) was obtained: fringe-benefit variation is wider than straight-time variation. Private benefits accounted for 18 percent of private compensation of unionized

57. Employers may commit themselves to additional pension benefits without immediately funding the obligation; in a particular year the amount of money paid into a pension fund could understate or overstate actual obligations. Changes in actuarial and related assumptions can also affect the funding in a particular year. I am indebted to Victor J. Sheifer of the Bureau of Labor Statistics for pointing out this peculiarity of pension data.

nonoffice workers in 1974, permitting significant room for deviations from wage patterns.[58]

Other elements of the contract besides the fringe benefits in table 5-9 can be varied, even if a wage pattern is followed. For example, escalator clauses can differ substantially in the amount of money payable per percentage increase in the consumer price index. Clever changes in the wording can make the formulas of escalators sound similar but in fact result in different outcomes.[59] And it is hard to imagine how work rules could be compared across industries, particularly those that are closely related to industry technology. For that matter, even wage rates are difficult to compare outside the realm of sharply defined crafts.[60] Of course, some sort of average hourly-earnings figure may be available, but skill mix can cause this to vary widely, as can other factors.

Observed Imitation of Major Contract Settlements

Once industry lines are crossed, in short, patterns become difficult to follow. However, there do seem to be certain spheres of influence surrounding certain major contract settlements. Usually, when a major contract is signed, the press briefly reports the general wage change. *Current Wage Developments,* a monthly journal of the Bureau of Labor Statistics, provides a summary of union contracts so that a search can be made for

58. Bureau of Labor Statistics, *Employee Compensation in the Private, Nonfarm Economy, 1974,* bulletin 1963 (GPO, 1977), p. 33. The figure is derived by dividing pay for leave, retirements, and other fringe benefits (excluding social security, unemployment insurance, and workmen's compensation) by total compensation (with the same exclusions). The figure for manufacturing is somewhat higher than the all-industries estimate.

59. Escalators can be limited with "caps" (which place an absolute limit on the payment) and "corridors" (which require a specific amount of inflation to activate the escalator). Escalators frequently provide a certain cents-per-hour increase per index point increase in the consumer price index, but the value of this increment can be varied by changing the base year in which the CPI is measured. Or the standard formula can be used, but with "percentage point" quietly substituted for index point. As long as the CPI is substantially above its base-year level, the percentage point formula will give smaller cents-per-hour increases at a given rate of inflation. The most creative escalator in recent years appeared in the 1976 General Electric contracts. It provided for a 1-cent-per-hour increase for each 0.3 percentage (not index) point increase in the CPI up to 7 percent and above 9 percent with no credit for the gap between 7 and 9 percent. See "Wage Highlights," *Current Wage Developments,* vol. 28 (July 1976), p. 1.

60. See H. M. Douty, "The Impact of Trade Unionism on Internal Wage Structures," in J. L. Mey, ed., *Internal Wage Structure* (Amsterdam: North-Holland, 1963), pp. 233–41.

other agreements containing a similar general wage change. Table 5-10 shows the result of a search of contracts negotiated after the "big three" automobile companies and the United Auto Workers came to an agreement in 1973. The Auto Workers settled for a reported "3 percent plus 12 cents" in the first year, a very modest-sounding contract meant to please the Phase IV wage authorities. But the contract actually provided about a 10 percent annual rate of wage increase because of an escalator clause.[61]

In the twelve months following these agreements, many other contracts were signed in the motor vehicle and machinery industries, where the UAW is an important influence. The table shows that the big three auto companies signed contracts providing for identical summary wage increases with the Auto Workers, and General Motors and Chrysler with the Electrical Workers (IUE). As it happened, however, in 1973 General Motors was able to wring some concessions from the Electrical Workers regarding employees outside the auto parts component of GM's operations. Contracts outside the immediate automobile sector show variation from the 3-percent-plus-12-cents pattern. And variations in escalator clause (*COLA*) formulas produced still more divergences. Generally, the table suggests that the sphere of influence around the automobile settlements extends into truck manufacturing, farm implements, auto parts, and other machinery. However, the fact that an employer is in the sphere by no means requires mechanical subservience to the pattern. Deviations occur as the pattern spreads out from the center. And were it possible to summarize adjustments in fringe benefits for the contracts listed in table 5-10, the deviations would probably be still more apparent.[62]

Another major contract that is often viewed as pattern setting is the Teamsters' National Master Freight Agreement and related settlements.[63]

61. See Daniel J. B. Mitchell, "Union Wage Determination: Policy Implications and Outlook," *Brookings Papers on Economic Activity, 3:1978*, p. 573. This estimate does not take account of fringe benefits.

62. This conclusion is similar to those reached by Alexander, "Market Practices," pp. 28–29, and Levinson, "Pattern Bargaining," pp. 316–17.

63. Early in 1978 the Teamsters' contract became a major focus of the Carter administration's "deceleration" program on the grounds that this contract (which was due for renegotiation in 1979) would set a pattern for all other unions. Barry Bosworth, then director of the Council on Wage and Price Stability, stated that if "we could get the Teamsters to agree to 20 percent for three years, the United Auto Workers would sign a contract for the same thing. So would steel. Each of these unions wants what the other one has got." See Hobart Rowen, "Bosworth Says U. S. Fumbles Rail Talks," *Washington Post,* June 16, 1978.

Table 5-10. *Contracts Negotiated after 1973 Automobile Settlement*

Employer and union[a]	First-year general wage change[b]
Big three automobile companies and UAW	
Chrysler—UAW	3% + 12¢ + COLA
Ford—UAW	3% + 12¢ + COLA
General Motors—UAW	3% + 12¢ + COLA
Other contracts, machinery and motor vehicles	
International Harvester—UAW	3% + 12¢ + COLA
Caterpillar—UAW	3% + 4¢ + COLA
Deere—UAW	3% + 12¢ + COLA
General Motors—IUE	
Auto parts workers, Delco	3% + 12¢ + COLA
Other Delco workers	Wage cuts for new hires
Frigidaire	10¢ (previous wage cuts for new hires eliminated)
Eaton—UAW	25¢ + COLA
Chrysler—IUE	3% + 12¢ + COLA
Dana Corp.—UAW	3% + 16¢ + COLA
Mack Trucks—UAW	27¢ + COLA
Eaton—MESA	25¢ + COLA
Eaton—AIW	17¢ + COLA
Allis-Chalmers—UAW	3% + 8¢ + COLA
Massey-Ferguson—UAW	3% + 12¢ + COLA
Budd Co.—UAW	3% + 4¢ + COLA
Champion Spark Plug—UAW	3% + 16¢ + COLA
Dana Corp., Spicer Axle Div.—AIW	15–25¢ + COLA
Borg-Warner, York Div.—UAW	25¢ + COLA
Growth International, Inc.—UAW	18¢ + COLA
Caterpillar—IAM	24–30¢ + COLA
Jeep—UAW	3% + 7¢ + COLA
Kelsey-Hayes—UAW	3% + 12¢ + COLA
Rockwell International (Automotive)—UAW	3% + 4¢ + COLA
Burroughs—UAW	2.8% + COLA
FMC Corp.—UAW	20¢ + COLA
White Motor Corp., Truck Div.—UAW	3% + 12¢ + COLA
Diamond Reo Trucks—UAW	2% (+1% later in year) + COLA
National Twist Drill and Tool Co.—UAW	15¢ + COLA
Eltra Corp., Prestolite Div.—UAW	20¢ + COLA
ESB, Inc., Automotive Div.—UAW	24¢ + COLA
Maytag—UAW	3% + COLA
Kelsey-Hayes—AIW	3% + 26¢ + COLA
Motor Wheel Corp.—AIW	38¢
Clark Equipment Co., Automotive Div.—UAW	3% + 4¢ + COLA
Clark Equipment Co., Transmission Div.—AIW	26¢ + COLA
Tecumseh Products Co., Marion Div.—UAW	12–30¢ + COLA

Table 5-10 (*continued*)

Employer and union[a]	First-year general wage change[b]
White Farm Equipment—UAW	3% + 8¢ + COLA
Teledyne Wisconsin Motor—UAW	35¢ + COLA
Deere—IAM	3% + COLA
Bendix—UAW	3% + 12¢ + COLA
Teledyne Continental Motors—UAW	11¢ + COLA
Avco-Lycoming Div.—UAW	6% + COLA
Paris Mfg. Co.—UAW	40¢
J. I. Case Co.—UAW	3% + 8¢ + COLA
Sundstrand—UAW	33¢ + COLA
AFC Industries, Carter Carburetor Div.—UAW	25¢ (+25¢ in inequity adjustments) + COLA
Trico—Trico Workers Union	4% + COLA

Source: *Current Wage Developments*, October 1973–September 1974. Most of the information was drawn from the section "Selected Wage and Benefit Changes." In a few cases, this information was supplemented by the section "Wage Highlights."

a. UAW: United Automobile, Aerospace, and Agricultural Implement Workers of America;
    IUE: International Union of Electrical, Radio, and Machine Workers;
    MESA: Mechanics Educational Society of America;
    AIW: Allied Industrial Workers of America;
    IAM: International Association of Machinists and Aerospace Workers.
b. *COLA*: provision for cost-of-living adjustments through an escalator clause.

This agreement, which represents an amalgamation and restructuring of what once were regional agreements, was estimated to cover 300,000 local cartage and 100,000 over-the-road truck drivers and related workers in late 1978.[64] In 1976, after a brief strike, a three-year contract was signed guaranteeing wage increases of 65 cents an hour in the first year and 50 cents in the second and third years. An escalator clause with a complicated shifting formula was also included. Table 5-11 shows the outcome of that agreement and other Teamster and related agreements in trucking, food processing, construction, and warehousing (including wholesale and retail food warehousing). These are sectors in which the Teamsters have many members. The basic 65-50-50-cent pattern shows up in trucking and some of the warehousing contracts, but not in Teamster contracts in food processing. And the construction agreements apparently follow those in local building trades settlements. As with the Auto Workers, there is a Teamsters sphere of influence, although the

64. The estimate is reported in Lena W. Bolton, "Heavy Bargaining Returns in 1979," *Monthly Labor Review*, vol. 101 (December 1978), p. 21. On the development of national bargaining in trucking, see Arthur A. Sloane, "Collective Bargaining in Trucking: Prelude to a National Contract," *Industrial and Labor Relations Review*, vol. 19 (October 1965), pp. 21–40.

Table 5-11. *Selected Contracts Negotiated after 1976 National Master Freight Agreement*

Employer and union[a]	General wage change over life of contract[b]
Trucking	
Trucking Employers, Inc.—IBT	65¢, 50¢, 50¢ with *COLA*
Western States Truck Line Maintenance Employers—IAM	65¢, 50¢, 50¢ with *COLA*
Continental Trailways—ATU	$.60–$1.20 over 3 years with *COLA*
United Parcel Service—IBT	65¢, 50¢, 50¢ with *COLA*
Southwestern States Master Rail-Truck Agreement—IBT	65¢, 50¢, 50¢ with *COLA*
Bowman Transportation Co. (Atlanta)—USWA	65¢, 55¢, 50¢ (other terms unknown)
National Automobile Transporters—IBT	("Similar to National Master Freight")
Eastern Area Tank Haul Agreement—IBT	65¢, 50¢, 50¢ with *COLA*
Food processing	
Anheuser-Busch—IBT	75¢, 75¢, 75¢
Schlitz, Miller, Anheuser-Busch, California Brewers—IBT	75¢, 75¢, 75¢ with *COLA*
Dried Fruit Industries (Fresno and Monterey)—IBT	30¢, 25¢, 25¢ with *COLA*
Dried Fruit Industries (Santa Clara and San Benito)—ILWU	40¢, 30¢, 30¢ with *COLA*
California Processors—IBT	30–52¢, 53¢, 52¢
Agripac, Inc.—IBT	12%, 6%–5¢, 6% with *COLA*
Ice Cream Council (Chicago)—IBT	50¢, 40¢, 35¢ (hourly workers); no increase and two reopeners (drivers)
Associated Milk Dealers (Chicago)—IBT	37.5¢
St. Louis Dairies—IBT	80¢, 30¢, 40¢ (plant workers); 60¢, 35¢, 35¢ (office workers); 32.5¢, 15¢, 17.5¢ (retail route drivers)
Campbell Soup—IBT	7.5% (under reopener)
Del Monte—IBT	26% regulars; 12% seasonals, 6%, 6% with *COLA*
Associated Producers and Packers (western Wash.)—IBT	20–60¢, 5%, 5% with *COLA*
Frozen Food Employers (northern Calif.)—IBT	35–50¢, 35–50¢, 35–50¢
Chicago Bakery Employers—IBT	25¢, 20¢, 20¢
Greater N.Y. Milk Dealers—IBT	$16.50 a week, $10 a week
Construction	
Associated General Contractors (upstate N.Y.)—IBT	50¢, 45¢, 70¢
New England Road Builders—IBT	35¢, 45¢, 42.5¢
Contractors Assn. of Eastern Pa.—IBT	40¢, 55¢
Mid America Regional Bargaining Assn. (Chicago)—IBT	75¢, 75¢

Table 5-11 (*continued*)

Employer and union[a]	General wage change over life of contract[b]
Contractors Assn. of Westchester Cty. (N.Y.)—IBT	No increase
Associated General Contractors (Arizona)—IBT	30¢, 30¢, 55¢ (same increments as LIU and IUOE)

Warehousing, wholesale, retail

Seattle Warehouse Distributors—IBT	65¢, 45¢, 40¢ with *COLA*
Food Wholesalers (Del.)—IBT	65¢, 50¢, 50¢, with *COLA*
Industrial Employers and Distributors (central and northern Calif.)—IBT	70¢, 45¢, 45¢ with *COLA*
Lumber and Mill Employers Assn. (San Francisco)—IBT	65¢, 50¢, 50¢ with *COLA*
Wholesale Grocery Assn. (Minneapolis)—IBT	65¢, 50¢, 50¢ with *COLA*
Wholesale Tobacco Distributors (N.Y.)—IBT	37.5¢ (under reopener). Appears to follow deferred increases in retail food in New York City area)
Kroger Co., grocery dept. (Cincinnati)—RCIA	65¢, 55¢, 55¢ with *COLA*
Detroit Lumbermen's Assn.—IBT	45¢, 45¢, 45¢ with *COLA*
Missouri-Illinois Food Distributors—IBT	99.5¢, 58¢, 50¢ with *COLA*
Major and independent oil companies (drivers) (northern Ill. and northern Ind.)—IBT	75¢, 75¢, 75¢
Food Employers Council, S. Calif.	
Warehouse and drivers—IBT	65¢, 50¢, 50¢ with *COLA*
Office employees—IBT	25¢, 25¢, 25¢ with *COLA*
Meat cutters—MCBW	40¢, 45¢, 50¢ with *COLA* (note: *COLA* in these contracts appears more limited than under National Master Freight)
New York Heating Oil Assn.—IBT	50¢, 25¢ with *COLA*
Metro Detroit Food Employers—IBT	65¢, 50¢, 50¢ with *COLA*
Wholesale Beer Distributors, S. Calif.—IBT	70¢, 45¢, 40¢

Source: *Current Wage Developments*, April 1976–March 1977. Excludes contracts negotiated before National Master Freight Agreement.

    a.   IBT: International Brotherhood of Teamsters, Chauffeurs, Warehousemen and Helpers of America;

    IAM: International Association of Machinists and Aerospace Workers;

    ATU: Amalgamated Transit Union;

  USWA: United Steelworkers of America;

  ILWU: International Longshoremen's and Warehousemen's Union;

    LIU: Laborers' International Union of North America;

  IUOE: International Union of Operating Engineers;

  RCIA: Retail Clerks International Association;

  MCBW: Amalgamated Meat Cutters and Butcher Workmen of North America.

    b. *COLA*: provision for cost-of-living adjustments through an escalator clause.

divergence from the major trucking pattern seems greater within the Teamsters union than was the divergence from the major settlements within the Auto Workers.

Recent Empirical Studies of Wage Imitation

Various efforts have been made to capture the channels of wage imitation econometrically. Flanagan experimented with individual contract data (similar to those used in chapter 4) but was unable to obtain satisfactory results.[65] However, the contracts he used covered a wide variety of industries. In the multi-industry context, as noted earlier, it is often difficult to specify exactly what wage imitation would mean or how it would be implemented. More promising is some work on the construction industry. Since construction workers are generally organized by craft, intercraft wage rivalry seems a distinct possibility.[66] Moreover, since construction workers frequently change employers, their fringe benefits are usually financed by fixed contributions per hour into various multiemployer benefit funds.[67] Such institutional arrangements make it easier to compare benefits, which is complicated in the industrial sector.

Despite the expectation that structures of wage imitation should be easily identifiable in construction, the statistical evidence is mixed. Shulenburger establishes a procedure for determining "key" bargaining units in construction and then attempts to determine their influence on nonkey units. In some periods, wage contours appear to exert an influence; in others, no influence can be detected. The ability to predict wage changes using the spillover approach also appears to vary across

65. "Wage Interdependence," pp. 667–72.

66. For a review of wage determination in construction, see Daniel Quinn Mills, *Industrial Relations and Manpower in Construction* (MIT Press, 1972), chap. 3.

67. The Davis-Bacon Act of 1931 requires that federal construction contractors pay "prevailing" (often union) wage rates, and the Department of Labor thus continually surveys and publishes construction wage rates by craft. Detailed data on construction wages and fringe benefits by craft and city appear quarterly in *Current Wage Developments*. Finally, as an outgrowth of the wage relativities orientation of the construction wage control authorities during 1971–74, a computerized data file on construction wages was developed and is apparently in use by construction contractors. "Construction Data Bank Ready for 1978 Bargaining Season," *Daily Labor Report* (January 20, 1978), p. A–5. In short, the ability to make wage comparisons and the mechanisms for doing so are quite evident in construction.

crafts.[68] These results lead Shulenburger to doubt the utility of the wage relativities approach employed in the construction wage controls of 1971–74.[69] On the other hand, Ross found a high degree of wage interdependence in construction and also found that the relativities approach to wage controls added considerably to wage restraint while controls were in effect.[70]

The empirical debate about construction mirrors the more aggregative literature elsewhere. Using 1948–60 data, Eckstein and Wilson found evidence of manufacturing wage rounds and key bargains.[71] But the wage-round hypothesis broke down in a later analysis that included the mid-1960s.[72] Using data from 1956 to 1970 and a different methodology, Mehra found no evidence of significant wage spillovers and patterns in manufacturing.[73] After looking at the more casual evidence of the automobile pattern in table 5-10, the reader may wonder whether the Mehra tests were not too strict.[74] However, the basic point—that wage imitation is statistically an elusive concept—is hard to dispute.

68. This method of determining the key units is discussed in David B. Shulenburger, "Prior Identification of 'Key' Wage Determining Units," *Industrial Relations,* vol. 16 (February 1977), pp. 71–82. His results using these key units appear in his "Wage Leadership and Patterns of Wage Settlement in Construction," Industrial Relations Research Association, *Proceedings of the Thirtieth Annual Winter Meeting* (Madison, Wis.: IRRA, 1978), pp. 185–92; and "A Contour Theoretic Approach to the Determination of Negotiated Wage Change in the Building Construction Industry," *Economic Inquiry,* vol. 16 (July 1978), pp. 395–410.

69. "Wage Leadership," pp. 191–92.

70. Clark G. Ross, "The Construction Wage Stabilization Program," *Industrial Relations,* vol. 17 (October 1978), pp. 308–14.

71. Otto Eckstein and Thomas A. Wilson, "The Determination of Money Wages in American Industry," *Quarterly Journal of Economics,* vol. 76 (August 1962), pp. 379–414. Critical comments appear in the November 1967 issue.

72. O. Eckstein, "Money Wage Determination Revisited," *Review of Economic Studies,* vol. 35 (April 1968), pp. 133–43, especially p. 139.

73. Y. P. Mehra, "Spillovers in Wage Determination in U.S. Manufacturing Industries," *Review of Economics and Statistics,* vol. 58 (August 1976), pp. 300–12.

74. Mehra's technique is essentially to strip industry wage data of external influences such as labor-market conditions and serial correlation. The remaining residuals should be uncorrelated across industries unless some sort of spillover mechanism is operative. However, it is possible that hourly-earnings data cannot support such an elaborate cleaning and stripping since they may contain sufficient errors of measurement and concept to cause the loss of any spillover effects. Surely, the fact that large firms and bargaining units often operate in more than one industry classification (even at the two-digit SIC level) should lead to some spillover, as Mehra defines it. His finding none makes his methodology questionable. For ex-

Implications of Patterns and Wage Imitation

As has been discussed in this chapter, there has been much debate about wage imitation in the literature on labor economics. It is thus reasonable to ask whether the debate is essentially exhausted. Are there further points on wage imitation that researchers could profitably pursue? Apart from future research, does the current state of knowledge on wage imitation have implications for anti-inflation programs?

Economic Theory and Future Research

In view of the ambiguous nature of the statistical evidence, should wage imitation and pattern bargaining be dropped from the tool kit of labor economists? The answer depends on one's judgment, but to me it is no. The casual, anecdotal, and case-study evidence supporting wage imitation simply cannot be dismissed. It appears that wage imitation does take place and that it is important in certain spheres (especially within firms, plants, and narrowly defined units), but that its influence diffuses as it reaches the outer edges of the spheres. Its importance seems to vary in different times and circumstances, a characteristic difficult to deal with in econometrics, where stable relationships are generally assumed.[75]

Apart from empirical questions, recent developments in the theoretical literature lend some support to wage imitation as a labor-market influence. There has been much interest recently in efforts to formulate

---

ample, since General Motors operates in both "transport equipment" and "electrical machinery," there should be some detectable spillover between these two industries.

My experiments using residuals from wage-change equations, which cleaned the annual change in earnings of the influence of the inverted unemployment rate and price change lagged one year, revealed considerable intercorrelation of residuals across industries. The intercorrelated industries, however, often had little obvious direct relation to one another besides a significant correlation coefficient. This is a dilemma for the investigator. If too much data cleaning is done, there is nothing left to explain and the residuals are simply noise. If not enough data cleaning is done, the propensity for cross-industry wage changes to be correlated will assert itself. In that case, the investigator will not be able to distinguish between spillover effects and the effects of common, cross-industry explanatory influences.

75. In principle, anything can be estimated, including shifting coefficients, provided a model explaining these shifts can be produced. In fact, such estimation is easier to prescribe than to carry out. Authors of elaborate models that are adjusted to capture every "blip" in the data lay themselves open to charges of "mining the data."

theories of long-term relationships between employers and employees. Various explanations of such long-term relationships can be advanced, ranging from unions (which push for job security) to the costs of employee turnover to both firms and workers.[76] If the concept of a long-term relationship is accepted, then there must be standards by which both parties judge the fairness of the other's performance under particular circumstances.

It has been suggested that, when demand is falling, the fair solution demanded of employers by employees is protection of the real wage.[77] Employees cannot assess the effect of wage cuts in averting layoffs and are (rightly) suspicious of employers' offers to limit layoffs in exchange for wage concessions. Such suspicions would explain the tendency of firms to deal with drops in demand through layoffs rather than wage cuts. However, the real wage criterion is not entirely satisfactory. In the early 1930s, despite the fall in prices, workers resisted nominal wage cuts. Indeed, that experience (and similar episodes in previous depressions) led to the widespread acceptance of downward wage inflexibility in macroeconomic models. In the mid-1970s, when the price level suddenly shot up, the real wages of many workers declined. Many employers apparently do not feel bound to maintain workers' purchasing power.

Fairness could just as well be judged in a relative instead of an abso-

76. An early paper in the cost-of-turnover literature is Walter Y. Oi, "Labor as a Quasi-Fixed Factor," *Journal of Political Economy,* vol. 70 (December 1962), pp. 538–55. Some researchers have examined costs and search strategies directly; for example, Joseph C. Ullman, "Interfirm Differences in the Cost of Search for Clerical Workers," *Journal of Business,* vol. 41 (April 1968), pp. 153–65; comments appear in the January 1970 issue. The implications of long-term contractual relationships are explored in Michael L. Wachter and Oliver E. Williamson, "Obligational Markets and the Mechanics of Inflation," discussion paper 7 (University of Pennsylvania, Center for the Study of Organizational Innovation, November 1977). I am indebted to Arthur M. Okun for providing me with three chapters of an unpublished manuscript, "Short-Run Fluctuations in Perspective," which deals with these issues. Recent work on the impact of unionization on hospitals suggests that turnover is reduced by unions; Brian Becker, "Hospital Unionism and Employment Stability," *Industrial Relations,* vol. 17 (February 1978), pp. 96–101. The Becker finding supports the more general results reported in R. B. Freeman, "Job Satisfaction as an Economic Variable," *American Economic Review,* vol. 68 (May 1978, *Papers and Proceedings, 1977*), pp. 135–41, especially p. 140.

77. One interpretation is that workers are averse to taking risks and that their employers "insure" them against real wage reductions by paying a lower initial wage. H. M. Polemarchakis and L. Weiss, "Fixed Wages, Layoffs, Unemployment Compensation, and Welfare," *American Economic Review,* vol. 68 (December 1978), p. 909. Other references appear in this paper.

lute sense. Workers could demand of their employers that they not be treated worse than anyone else in adverse circumstances, and they might be satisfied with being treated the same as everyone else in auspicious periods. Knowledge of how others are being treated is likely to be greater within a plant than within an industry and within an industry than throughout the economy. To the extent that employers and unions cross industry lines, spheres of influence wider than industries could be created in certain sectors. In short, the notion of equal treatment is at least as promising a candidate for judging fairness as the real wage, and it could contribute to an understanding of seemingly anomalous behavior in the labor market.

Bargaining theory may also benefit from further study of wage imitation. Although there seems to be a tendency within industries for greater uniformity in wages than in fringe benefits, there have been episodes in which benefit imitation has occurred as well. For example, when supplemental unemployment benefits (SUB) plans were first adopted, several industries picked up the idea.[78] This was probably because the initial SUB plans were analogous to a technological innovation that spreads from firm to firm as information about it is disseminated. However, a complementary explanation is also possible.

When economists think of collective bargaining in the abstract, they often conceive of the process as a negotiation about a single magnitude, such as total labor costs per hour.[79] But actual bargaining is frequently subdivided into separate issues. In a major bargaining situation, subcommittees will hammer out deals on particular aspects of the contract, such

78. Supplemental unemployment benefits provide laid-off workers with income to supplement their normal unemployment compensation. The demand for SUB grew out of early pressure for a "guaranteed annual wage" and from the adverse effect on higher-paid union workers of ceilings on state unemployment compensation benefits. The automobile contracts are usually viewed as having set the pattern for SUB. Norma Pope and Paul A. Brinker, "Recent Developments with Guaranteed Annual Wage: The Ford Settlement," *Labor Law Journal*, vol. 19 (September 1968), pp. 555–62. However, the idea had been around in various forms for some time, and other unions made similar demands more or less coincident with those of the UAW. For example, the National Maritime Union announced its intention to make such demands before the automobile negotiations were formally under way. "Developments in Industrial Relations," *Monthly Labor Review*, vol. 78 (April 1955), p. 460. As is often the case, determining the true pattern setter is not easy.

79. Bargaining theorists are usually content to talk about a wage as the magnitude under negotiation. For example, see Pao Lun Cheng, "Wage Negotiation and Bargaining Power," *Industrial and Labor Relations Review*, vol. 21 (January 1968), pp. 163–82.

as pensions and health insurance. The contract is assembled in pieces. To the economist, the statement (often reported in the press) that the parties have settled everything except pensions or some other issue seems peculiar. How can other issues be closed if one remains open? Or how can one issue remain open if everything else is closed? Is not the remaining issue simply a residual that can be determined by subtracting the cost of all other components of the settlement from the agreed-upon level of total costs?

The complexity of the modern labor contract often does force this type of decentralized bargaining behavior. A primary objective of both parties must be to minimize bargaining costs—strikes and impasses. Every item cannot be bargained about at once. And a procedure of first bargaining about costs and then dividing the pie would lead to complicated bargaining about what the costs of particular benefits actually would be. To reduce the risk of complicating the bargaining and stumbling into an unnecessary dispute, decentralized bargaining is needed. And to end the decentralized process, there may be tacit agreements to accept as "relevant" pieces of settlements reached elsewhere. Since wages are most easily measurable, the wage component of the contract is most likely to be affected by external wage developments. But occasionally innovations in fringe benefits or other aspects of the contract may also reflect external influences.

In short, pattern bargaining and imitation may assist the parties in assembling a contract by moving certain issues out of the way so that others can be tackled. Total labor costs need not be determined through wage imitation, but portions of the package may be. Doing what others are doing is a way of reducing the costs of transactions between labor and management. Thus the tendency for wages to be more prone to imitation than fringe benefits is not necessarily labor-management deception of workers who have difficulty comparing benefits. It can play a socially useful role in reducing the incidence of strikes.

Wage Guidelines and Wage Controls

There are clearly fruitful research projects related to wage imitation that have yet to be undertaken. Imitative behavior may shed light on elements of economic theory besides wage determination. But any new insights must be kept in perspective. Empirical studies of wage imitation produce ambiguous results, and models of such behavior give different results, depending on assumptions. If wage imitators look at each other,

202 UNIONS, WAGES, AND INFLATION

the effect could be destabilizing and inflationary. But if there are simply leaders and followers and a one-way flow of imitation, no destabilizing effect should be expected. The chief problem for policymakers faced with this uncertainty is how to mesh public policy on wage determination with general anti-inflation efforts.

This issue is acute both when the government tries to influence and moderate wage decisions and when it institutes formal wage controls. For example, in early 1978 the Carter administration embarked on a modest voluntary "deceleration" program for wages and prices. No uniform numerical guideline for wage increases was proposed; it was simply urged that they be more moderate than they had been in the recent past.[80] In practice, the approach turned into government rhetoric aimed at a few key contracts that were believed to set wage patterns, especially the Teamsters agreement scheduled for renegotiation in 1979. Public policy implicitly relied on the pattern-bargaining formulation of the wage-imitation hypothesis and on the assumption that wage patterns could be manipulated to meet government objectives.

The pitfalls of such an approach are evident. The evidence in table 5-11 suggests that there is a Teamsters sphere of influence, although outside trucking and warehousing the influence is diffused at best. Thus, while a multiplier effect can be attributed to the Teamsters negotiations, a domino theory of economywide wage determination, with the Teamsters as the first domino, is not justified. Restraints on the Teamsters might have ripple effects. But it is also conceivable that other negotiators—seeing that the Teamsters were being subjected to abnormal pressure—would decide that the Teamsters wage outcome was no longer relevant to other wage settlements. And the singling out of a particular settlement for government attention could produce a backlash—that is, a larger settlement then would otherwise have occurred—with possible adverse ripple effects.[81] In short, there are enough uncertainties about wage imitation to make such government efforts risky. The Carter administration apparently came to this conclusion in October 1978 and substituted a program of more general guidelines for the earlier deceleration approach.

80. The program as originally announced called for wage and price increases to decelerate relative to their rates of increase over the previous two years. "Carter's Voluntary Wage-Price Program Is Generally Disliked by Business, Labor," *Wall Street Journal*, January 23, 1978.
81. For example, the leader of a union singled out for government attention would feel compelled to demonstrate to the membership that the union negotiating team had not yielded to outside pressure.

In principle, comprehensive guidelines and formal controls move away from the wage imitation approach in that they apply to everyone (or to broad sectors) rather than to a few key contracts. No particular group is officially singled out, although some may receive more attention than others. Of course, a major issue in any such program is whether union cooperation will be forthcoming. To that extent, any big union contract that happens to come up for renegotiation automatically becomes a key since the outcome is a test of the guidelines or controls mechanism. In ignoring or following the rules, the parties to such a contract can set a pattern of noncompliance or compliance for other units.[82]

A purely voluntary guidelines program would be difficult to operate if it were based mainly on detailed wage relativities and wage imitation. This is because such programs usually have only a small staff to monitor compliance. Formal controls, however, can run the gamut from a legally enforced numerical guideline to a detailed case-by-case approach in which relative wages play an important role. This choice is nowhere better illustrated than in the structure of controls adopted during the 1971–74 economic stabilization program.

The program contained two diverse elements. In construction, the Construction Industry Stabilization Committee (CISC) operated on a case-by-case basis with heavy emphasis on wage relativities and no numerical guideline. The operators of that program believed that a cause of wage inflation in construction was a distortion in the wage structure that had developed because of demand pressure in the 1960s.[83] If traditional differentials could be restored, it was reasoned, the inflationary pressure would stop.

In contrast, after a brief freeze of virtually all wages and prices, a system of wage review was established in 1971 for the rest of the labor force and administered by a tripartite Pay Board. The board adopted a more "regu-

82. The strike and ultimate settlement of the airline machinists in 1966 is usually cited as the case that broke the 3.2 percent wage guidepost of the Kennedy-Johnson administrations. John Sheahan, *The Wage-Price Guideposts* (Brookings Institution, 1967), pp. 57–60.

83. Unfortunately, little has been published on the administrative aspects of the CISC. The official final report of the entire 1971–74 program hardly mentions it. See Thomas R. Goin, "Phase II Wage Stabilization Policies and Concepts," and Richard Mullins, "Phases III–IV Wage Stabilization Policies," in Department of the Treasury, Office of Economic Stabilization, *Historical Working Papers on the Economic Stabilization Program: August 15, 1971 to April 30, 1974* (GPO, 1974), pt. 1, pp. 325–406, 409–26. Apparently, the CISC authorities wished to distinguish their program from other parts of the 1971–74 effort and decided against inclusion in the official history.

latory" approach than the CISC. In essence, the board created a series of rules and exceptions to those rules and established an appeals procedure for "gross inequities." The contrast between the two approaches was not absolute, however, since one exception to the 5.5 percent wage guideline enunciated by the Pay Board was for tandem relationships.[84]

The Pay Board's program has been attacked by those favoring the wage-relativities approach. But at least two difficult and troubling questions about the applicability of wage relativities as the principle behind a system of wage controls remain from the 1971–74 experience. Until these questions can be satisfactorily answered, policymakers must be reluctant to implement a comprehensive wage relativities program.

The first question is how large a role wage relativities play in wage inflation compared with other influences. Construction is the prime example of a sector in which distortions in relativities may have helped create wage inflation. If the relativities approach is taken to its extreme, forces other than wage relativities should have had little part in construction wage inflation except through the relativities mechanism. If this is true, when construction wage controls were lifted in early 1974, there should have been no upsurge in wage inflation. That is, the wage authorities had spent almost three years stabilizing wage differentials so that, in principle, external factors, such as the raging inflation of 1973–75, should not have set off renewed wage pressure in construction. Just as in the rest of the economy, however, major wage settlements in construction accelerated markedly after controls were lifted. First-year construction settlements in the major-union sector averaged 5.0 percent in 1973 and 11.0 percent in 1974. For all industries, excluding construction, the figures were 6.0 percent and 9.5 percent.[85] Clearly, removing distortions in relative wages will not relieve an "absolute" distortion caused by price inflation.

The second question is the applicability of the wage-relativities approach to sectors other than construction. At the beginning of Phase III (January 1973) an attempt was made to move the entire controls program —not just construction—away from the regulatory approach of the Pay Board. In particular, the Pay Board's 5.5 percent guideline was to be scrapped because "no single standard or wage settlement can be equally applicable at one time to all parties in an economy so large, decentralized,

84. Weber and Mitchell, *The Pay Board's Progress,* pp. 70–73, 425–28.
85. *Current Wage Developments,* vol. 27 (April 1975), p. 48; vol. 26 (June 1974), pp. 46, 61.

and dynamic."[86] The new authorities were never able to scrap it, however, no matter how much they disliked it, because there was nothing specific with which to replace it.

One of the characteristics of a large decentralized economy is that it is difficult to regulate without a bureaucracy. No large bureaucracy was available in 1971–74, nor is one likely to be available in the future. If direct intervention to moderate wage inflation is to be attempted, a few simple rules, which large numbers of wage-setting units can follow, are needed. A vague injunction not to make wage decisions that might upset wage differentials would be as meaningless as a prescription to make only wage adjustments that would restore stable differentials. There is no handy formula that tells the parties which differentials are important. Without general rules, each case must be judged individually.

The issue of the applicability of the wage-relativities approach in construction to other sectors of the economy is best illustrated by the experience of wage controllers in the food sector. At the beginning of Phase III, a new tripartite committee modeled after the construction committee was established in the food sector (retailing and manufacturing). The food committee had a variety of objectives besides wage restraint. However, the wage restraint component of the food program was initially operated case by case, and the committee quickly found itself with a large backlog of wage requests. It was forced to adopt Pay Board rules on an interim basis and eventually permanently. Among the rules was the much maligned 5.5 percent numerical wage standard. Despite assertions that Pay Board costing rules and standards were strange to wage setters in the food industry, these wage setters proved reluctant to abandon the Pay Board's reporting forms, which embodied these concepts. Indeed, the management members of the committee feared that relativities-oriented forms might create patterns where none existed. Ironically, because the controllers were loath to acknowledge the importance of the 5.5 percent standard, they were unable to change it when it was outmoded by price inflation.[87]

86. Statement of the Labor Management Advisory Committee to the Cost of Living Council, February 26, 1973, cited in Vaughn, "Wage Stabilization," p. 157.

87. The material in the text is based on a description in Vaughn, "Wage Stabilization," especially pp. 158–77. Vaughn, however, is a supporter of the relativities approach to wage control and sees the experience quite differently. See also Albert Rees, "Tripartite Wage Stabilizing in the Food Industry," *Industrial Relations*, vol. 14 (May 1975), pp. 250–58. Note that the comments in the text refer only to the wage-restraint aspects of the wage program in the food industry, not to aspects such as reform of collective bargaining.

If general wage controls or guidelines are imposed in the future, they should not cling to a single view of wage determination. When wage setters are asked about influences on wage determination, they inevitably mention wage comparisons. But this is not a sufficient foundation upon which to build an economywide system of controls, especially if there is resistance to establishing a large bureaucracy to administer it. Broad programs require broad rules. Since relativities and patterns seem to be important in some situations, exceptions to the broad rules can be formulated with these concepts in mind. If the parties are given some leeway in the regulations, they ought to have scope at least for maintaining internal wage differentials.[88] Moreover, a relativities approach can be followed at the industry level in particular sectors where it seems appropriate.

A numerical guideline has the virtue of simplicity. It gives the parties an idea of what is expected, even if the actual elaboration of how to "cost" wage increases and where exceptions may be permitted is complicated. Such figures as the Pay Board's 5.5 percent are remembered when the detailed rules are not.

A guideline can be viewed as a suggestion of normal wage behavior intended to supplant other prevailing notions. It is sometimes said that a guideline becomes a floor for wage negotiations, although statistical evidence on this point is seldom explored. But even without guidelines, some units get less than "normal" wage increases and some get more. The trick under a guideline program—or a program of controls that uses a guideline—is to find a mechanism for labeling those who receive more as "exceptions" so that the rules will not appear to have been violated.[89] That is,

88. A numerical guideline can permit maintenance or adjustment of internal wage differentials by the parties unless the standard is very tight. Some groups can be given more than the standard provided others are given less. Even if the standard is expressed as a percentage, nothing prevents the parties from maintaining cents-per-hour differentials internally. Beyond this, exceptions can be permitted for intraplant inequities, as was done under Pay Board rules. See Weber and Mitchell, *The Pay Board's Progress*, pp. 78–80. Maintenance of external relationships requires some sort of tandem rule. The Pay Board chose not to have an exception for interplant inequities, but earlier programs have included them and future programs could revive them.

89. Vaughn states that the 5.5 percent guideline became a floor for bargaining during Phase II ("Wage Stabilization," p. 153). But Weber and Mitchell were unable to find evidence to support such an assertion, although undoubtedly in a large economy there must have been some units that would have negotiated just under 5.5 percent without controls and were pulled up to that level (Weber and Mitchell, *The Pay Board's Progress*, pp. 375–77). When asked about labor's willingness to accept the Carter administration's 7 percent guideline, AFL-CIO President George Meany noted that "there are some unions that would be tickled to death to get 7 percent." (Meany's statement is reported in a press release of the AFL-CIO dated November

a numerical guideline does not necessarily imply a rigid rule or inflexible standards. Flexibility is desirable.

Conclusions

Although the literature on wage imitation is largely descriptive, important theoretical insights concerning wage determination and other phenomena may be gained from further study. Empirical analysis of wage-settlement data suggests that spheres of influence surround some major-union contracts such as the automobile, trucking, and metals settlements. On the other hand, it appears that the farther a unit is from the center of such a sphere, the greater the scope for deviation from the pattern. Fringe benefits can be a mechanism for such deviations. As for econometric efforts to capture union-nonunion wage spillovers, the results so far have been mixed and contradictory. Imitation seems to be important in some periods and situations but not in others. Why these variations occur may lead to interesting speculations, but no clear answers emerge.

An important issue for public policy is whether wage imitation has a clear-cut leader-follower structure or whether wage setters watch each other in a complex system of mutual interaction. A leader-follower structure is not inherently inflationary or destabilizing, but a mutual interaction system could be.

If controls are based on a leader-follower hypothesis, government attention naturally turns to a few key settlements. But there is little evidence that the entire wage structure can be manipulated by concentrating pressure on a few union agreements. The alternative concept of mutual interaction of wages and wage relativities leads to a case-by-case approach to wage intervention in a comprehensive program. Such a program applied throughout the economy would involve large bureaucracies or lengthy administrative delays, which would be unlikely to gain and retain public support. The use of a numerical wage guideline avoids the need to choose between competing models of wage imitation. But since wage imitation is a real phenomenon, even if it is difficult to define or measure, such guidelines should be interpreted flexibly. Ultimately, wage intervention is an art, not a science, and the watchword of the art must be "pragmatism."

1, 1978, related to a news conference held the day before.) The mere announcement of a wage guideline does not automatically guarantee a minimum raise of that amount.

VI

Concluding Observations and
Future Directions

IN THE PRECEDING chapters, a variety of topics related to wage determination and collective bargaining were discussed. For the convenience of the reader, the highlights of those chapters are summarized below. This is followed by a general discussion of whether U.S. wage-setting arrangements are inflationary. Since guidelines, controls, and the like are periodically considered as anti-inflation options, the third section discusses direct government intervention in private wage determination. Finally, some new developments in the analytics of wage setting are reviewed and a promising area for future research is suggested.

Highlights of the Study

Six major empirical characteristics of the union sector were reviewed in preceding chapters. They were trends in union membership relative to the total work force, comparison of trends in union earnings and non-union earnings, differences between union earnings and nonunion earnings in their responsiveness to business-cycle pressures, differences between the responsiveness of earnings in the two sectors to price inflation, the union wage premium relative to the nonunion sector, and the phenomenon of wage imitation. Obviously, other characteristics might have been discussed, but these six are most directly relevant for economic policy.

The Extent of Unionization

Unionization covers a distinct minority of the work force. Even with the well-publicized expansion into the public sector, the union share of employment has declined since the mid-1950s. The big growth period for unionization came in the 1930s and 1940s and was associated with a change in workers' attitudes and in public policy, galvanized by the Great Depression. Shifts in the composition of the labor force toward a service economy and toward the greater participation of women have been reflected in shifts in union membership patterns. But unions have not kept up with these trends. Unless there is another abrupt revolution in social attitudes, the relative decline in the unionization of the work force can be expected to continue.

Union representatives have stated that increased management resistance and the use of sophisticated legal and human relations techniques are major obstacles to increased unionization. Since the Wagner Act was passed in 1935, nonunion employers have unquestionably become more adept at using available legal channels to fend off union organization drives. But such explanations cannot be the whole story. There was strong employer resistance during the period of rapid union growth. And in recent years unions themselves have come up with some innovative tactics involving the exertion of financial leverage.[1] However, with a given set of social background conditions, unionization efforts seem to realize diminishing returns.

Union-Nonunion Earnings Trends since the Korean War

One of the most striking characteristics of wage setting since the Korean War has been the tendency for the union-nonunion earnings differential to widen, though this has not occurred in every subperiod. Nor has every unionized industry raised its earnings level relative to every nonunion industry. But the trend has been sufficiently general to require some comment.

Economists have sometimes regarded unions as analogous to monopolistic firms. It is assumed that, although unions operate in the labor market, their influence can be analyzed with the same models that are usually

1. The Clothing Workers have called upon members of the board of directors of a recalcitrant employer to resign their posts, threatening financial pressure on other firms with which these directors are associated. Unions have pension, strike, and other funds that can be used to exert such leverage. It has also been suggested that unions should insist that pension funds not be invested in firms resisting unionization. The latter tactic raises legal questions about fiduciary responsibilities, however, and since there are many sources of funds for investment other than pensions, it might not be very effective. "Embattled Unions Strike Back at Management," *Business Week* (December 4, 1978), pp. 54–69; and Jeremy Rifkin and Randy Barber, *The North Will Rise Again: Pensions, Politics, and Power in the 1980s* (Beacon Press, 1978).

applied to product-market enterprises. The creation of a product monopoly initially raises the price of the product relative to the costs of production. But thereafter a textbook product monopoly should exert no influence on the rate at which the price increases relative to other prices. This argument, when applied to union wages, suggests that an earnings differential between union and nonunion workers should have been created during the period of rapid union growth and simply maintained thereafter. The fact that this behavior is inconsistent with the empirical evidence suggests that the union-as-monopoly model is misleading.

Textbook monopoly firms have a clear goal: the maximization of profits. Unions have no such simple goal. Sophisticated models of union "utility functions" that include as arguments employment (or membership) and wage rates can be developed. But the meaning of the utility-function concept for an organization composed of diverse interest groups is questionable. Moreover, while profit-maximization models lead to a single course of behavior, utility-maximization models can be used to justify a broad range of outcomes. For example, a union that pushes up wages despite employment losses can always be said to have a bias toward wages rather than employment.[2]

Once monopoly models and utility functions have been scrapped, nothing in economic theory says that union-nonunion earnings differentials could not rise for many years to come, just as they have risen for many years in the past. Nor does anything say that the differential will not stop growing or even that it will not shrink. A continued increase might reduce the proportion of the work force covered by unions, just as some of the past reduction might be attributed to the past increase in the union-nonunion wage differential. But there is nothing inherent in unions as institutions that can accurately forecast the level of the union-nonunion earnings differential in 1990. Indeed, since collective bargaining involves two parties, analysis of the outcome of that process cannot be based only on the union side; management resistance must play some part.

On the management side, profit maximization can be used to explain behavior. Profit maximization suggests that employers might be willing to let the union wage premium drift upward slowly even as they resist short-run wage gains. Opportunities for cost absorption are better in the long run than in the short run. Firms can substitute capital for labor or

2. Daniel J. B. Mitchell, "Union Wage Policies: The Ross-Dunlop Debate Reopened," *Industrial Relations,* vol. 11 (February 1972), pp. 46–61.

even nonunion for union labor as time passes. In industries where employers' ability to pay differs, weak firms may shrink or even disappear, leaving the product market open to the remaining firms, which may then find it easier to pass along wage costs to the consumer.

All of these adaptations entail some loss of employment relative to the employment level that would otherwise have prevailed. Absolute employment losses need not be involved, but if they are, nothing innate in unions' behavior suggests that such employment losses would not be acceptable to them. Union leaders may see no connection between a sequence of short-run wage decisions and a long-run employment trend.

The possibility of an ever-expanding gap in earnings between the union and nonunion sectors is unnerving to anyone familiar with compound interest. Indeed, the suggestion that the gap cannot continue to widen indefinitely may be more arithmetical than theoretical. Empirical evidence indicates that industries and bargaining units that have experienced relatively rapid wage gains will *tend* to lag in future wage determination (the negative *REL* coefficient of chapter 4). A prudent forecaster would probably predict an eventual halt in the widening of union-nonunion earnings differentials, but there is little to suggest precisely when this might happen.

Union-Nonunion Wage Behavior and the Business Cycle

Both the union and the nonunion sectors modify their wage-setting behavior in response to real business fluctuations. Neither sector, however, acts as if it were part of a classical labor market with homogeneous labor being rented through an auction system. In particular, nominal wages do not start falling the moment excess supplies of labor appear.

In the union sector such indexes as the outcomes of representation elections and strike activity show a sensitivity to real economic conditions, but wage adjustments seem less sensitive to business-cycle fluctuations than in the nonunion sector. What wage sensitivity the union sector has exhibited is concentrated in short-term contracts, whose number has declined in relation to contracts of long duration. This difference in sensitivity between the union and nonunion sectors leads to cyclical adjustments of the union-nonunion earnings differential apart from any long-term trends. In general, a recession widens the pay gap between union and nonunion workers.

Why should there be a difference in wage-change behavior between the union and the nonunion sectors? First, it must be noted that an industry's propensity for unionization is positively correlated with other industry characteristics such as the size of the establishment, the capital intensity of the production process, and the proportion of male employees. The characteristics of heavily unionized industries suggest longer employee-employer relationships than generally exist in other industries.

In the context of such long relationships, short-run real business fluctuations may not seem an appropriate standard for wage determination. When unions are involved, the concept of equity of wage determination in long-term employer-employee relationships is reinforced. Equity is hardly a well-defined or easy-to-apply principle. But certainly the idea that wage increases should be more restrained in periods of economic slack is not in accord with usual notions of equity.[3]

A second important point is that union pay rates tend to be above market levels. Normally, a queue of workers will be ready to accept work at the current union wage. During periods of high unemployment, the queue will lengthen, but its length is not of special interest to either the union or the employer. Of course, when labor markets are extremely tight (low unemployment rates), even unionized firms may experience labor shortages and be forced to respond with wage increases. But under normal circumstances, labor availability will be adequate regardless of the ups and downs of the business cycle. Union wages are therefore quite insulated from labor-market supply and demand pressure.

Fluctuations in real business conditions may be correlated with fluctuations in employers' ability to pay. For most firms recessions mean reduced sales and profits. When union wages are sensitive to economic slack, it is likely to stem from employers' reactions and resistance. Union bargaining power may be affected indirectly by the business cycle through reduced work opportunities for strikers or members of their families. Anecdotal evidence of union willingness to make wage concessions in order to save well-defined work opportunities can be found. But such concessions most often occur when a plant closing is imminent and the union is well aware of the problem. Concessions are also sometimes made in industries where past employer resistance has been weak and unions cannot count on the employer to restrain wage outcomes. Without employer resistance—an integral part of collective bargaining—a union must either learn to re-

3. In periods of economic slack, short workweeks and reduced opportunities for overtime become common. It could therefore be argued that, to maintain income, this particular definition of equity demands a compensatory increase in the hourly wage!

strain itself (and become sensitive to industry needs) or face its own eventual demise.

Union-Nonunion Wage Behavior and Price Inflation

Price changes affect the rate of wage change in both the union and the nonunion sectors. Generally, however, wage determination shows some signs of "money illusion" in broad econometric studies. That is, a 1 percent increase in prices seems to bring forth less than a 1 percent increase in wages, all other influences being constant. But in union situations, where the parties have shown an interest in prices by installing a cost-of-living escalator, scheduled wage increases and the escalator clause together yield the expected one-for-one relationship.[4]

There is some evidence that the responsiveness of wages to price inflation is greater in the union than in the nonunion sector. But many union workers are not covered by escalated contracts so that the gap between the sectors is not wide, if it is significant at all. The explanation of the differences that can be observed may again lie with long-term employer-employee relationships and concomitant concepts of equity. Industrial relations observers have always found that workers resist explicit cuts in their nominal wages. De facto cuts in real wages resulting from rising prices may be more acceptable than such explicit nominal cuts, but it would be surprising if workers were unconcerned about de facto cuts. Thus workers can be expected to take advantage of the union mechanism, when it is available, to resist falling purchasing power.

The Union Wage Premium

Measurement of unions' effect on pay levels has fascinated labor economists for many years. Most observers would agree that unions provide their members with services in the form of industrial jurisprudence. However, it hardly seems plausible that industrial jurisprudence is the only service rendered. Workers expect unions to provide them with higher wages and fringe benefits than they would otherwise receive. They are willing to bear the costs of strikes to back up their unions' demands. The

4. As noted in chapters 2 and 4, escalator clauses usually provide less than full protection against inflation (the 1 percent price increase resulting in less than a 1 percent wage increase because of the escalator formula). However, the text here refers to the *combination* of escalator and fixed wage increases.

gains might be illusory and wages might end up at the market level, but it seems unlikely that there would be no union wage effect.

The most widely cited estimate of the union-nonunion wage differential is the 10–15 percent reported for the 1950s in H. Gregg Lewis's celebrated study.[5] Economists were comfortable with this estimate because 10–15 percent does not seem large. It allows the observer both to acknowledge that unions have some effect on wages and to believe that classical influences set wages. However, the widening of the union-nonunion differential since the period observed by Lewis requires some boosting of this estimate. By the mid-1970s, 20–30 percent seemed a more likely range, especially for production and nonsupervisory workers.

Estimates of the type just described are usually made on the assumption that the union is an exogenous wage-raising influence. Of course, few economic institutions are truly exogenous, that is, totally uninfluenced by the economy they influence. While there is always the possibility that high-wage workers simply purchase more union services, creating the illusion of a union wage premium, this possibility is more beguiling than probable.

The interindustry pattern of unionization was established by the late 1940s. It grew from worker unrest in the depression, the resultant public policies that promoted collective bargaining, and World War II wage controls. For most workers, the choice is not whether to purchase union services but where to work. A blue-collar worker who finds himself in the automobile industry will almost certainly work under a union contract. A worker who takes a job in banking almost certainly will not.

There has been ample opportunity for union-nonunion wage premiums to change since the 1940s, but little opportunity for a change in the interindustry pattern of unionization. Wages and unionization are not really simultaneously determined today. And models that assume simultaneous and continuous determination must be viewed with suspicion. They are sensitive to the precise specification of the simultaneous structure and can yield confusing and contradictory results. The simple exogenous models are more believable.

Wage Imitation

The observation that wages are often evaluated in terms of other wage rates has long been incorporated in industrial relations texts. This can be

5. H. G. Lewis, *Unionism and Relative Wages in the United States: An Empirical Inquiry* (University of Chicago Press, 1963), p. 193.

viewed as simply a peculiar feature of the labor market or as a rational response to decisionmaking under uncertain conditions. Where there are long-term employer-employee relationships, for example, neither party is likely to be in a position to define exactly what the relationship implies for the indefinite future or in all possible contingencies. A long-term commitment to fair treatment by employers—especially if a union is to police the commitment—requires some agreement on what is fair. Certainly, following what others are doing could be one definition of fairness. In the judicial setting, after all, the concepts of precedents and equal treatment are entrenched.

However, acceptance of the principle of wage imitation by labor-market analysts does not require acceptance of any particular model of how that imitation is accomplished. There are two main versions of wage-imitation models. In one version, units look at each other's wages and attempt to achieve target wage differentials. A world of mutual interaction in which everyone is watching everyone is potentially unstable; there may be no consensus on what the long-term wage differentials should be. This version suggests that an external spark such as a sudden increase in labor demand could set off a wage explosion like that in the construction industry in the late 1960s and early 1970s. Certainly, explaining the behavior of construction wages during that period would require reference to that type of wage imitation.

A second version involves one-way causal flows. In this version there are "key" wage determination units that set patterns for other units. The model can be based either on adaptive attempts to maintain wage differentials by follower units or solely on the wage increment. Either view suggests that the course of wage determination can be easily affected throughout the economy by manipulating a few wage-setting units.

Unfortunately, beyond the observation that wage changes across industries are highly correlated, it is difficult to distinguish one version of wage imitation from another. In fact, it is difficult to distinguish wage imitation from the tendency of wages throughout the economy to be influenced by common causes such as the rate of price inflation. For this reason, the wage-imitation concept is of greater use to practitioners of industrial relations than to those making economic policy. Policymakers should be cautious about building their strategies on the elusive wage-imitation concept.

The limited empirical evidence available suggests that there are spheres of wage imitation, which emanate from certain major-union contracts, and that deviations from the pattern are likely as the perimeter of the sphere is approached. Clearly, a multiplier effect should be attributed to certain union agreements: for instance, the contracts with the big three automobile companies affect workers outside those companies. But what is not known is the ultimate extent of the multiplier. Nor is it certain that key contracts significantly influence each other. Casual evidence suggests that they do under some circumstances but not under others. Imitation may take the form of making components of the compensation package similar to some other contract rather than following the other contract's absolute value.

Essential to wage imitation is a mechanism for spreading information about wages. Within a plant or other place of work, such information is likely to be readily available, especially where wages are set by union contract so that occupational wage rates are known to all members of the unit. Once industry lines are crossed, information is more difficult to obtain. Even here, however, there are potential channels of information. Some of the large unions cross industry lines, and large firms often have operations in several industries.

While cross-industry channels of information are available, the complexity of the information has increased. Fringe benefits are particularly hard to compare. There are many ways in which seemingly similar wage *rates* can hide differences in actual compensation. Units may appear to follow patterns while actually deviating from them. Even in the earliest studies of pattern bargaining, such deviations were reported.

Finally, it must be recalled that structures of wage imitation have been reinforced—and possibly created in some instances—during periods of wage control. This reinforcement was especially apparent during the controls of World War II and the Korean War. Any comprehensive program of controls will soon have a substantial caseload of requests for wage increases. It is administratively convenient for the authorities to group requests together according to some type of tandem-relationship criterion so that many cases can be handled with a single decision. Units seeking wage hikes have an incentive to produce evidence of links with units that have already received above-standard increases.

Inflation and Wage Determination

Theories of inflation fall along a spectrum ranging from pure excess-demand models to structural explanations. The pure excess-demand view attributes price inflation to monetary and fiscal policies that raise the level of aggregate demand above the capacity of the economy to produce. Under such circumstances, prices are bid up as markets attempt to clear. Many variations of this view are possible. For example, some monetarists would deny that fiscal policy creates excess demand, except to the extent that budget deficits lead to monetary expansion. It is not necessary to assume that all product markets are perfectly competitive to believe in the excess-demand view. Even monopolies will raise prices continually if government policy keeps expanding demand.

In contrast, the structural view of inflation pictures general price increases as symptoms of a struggle between various interest groups over the distribution of income. If the sum of the claims on income made by all groups exceeds the actual income being generated at current prices, prices will rise. Such theories are more common among European than American economists and sometimes have a Marxist tinge.[6] They probably account for the fact that Americans refer to "wage and price control" and Europeans prefer the phrase "incomes policy." Incomes policy in Europe is frequently seen as a way of attempting to reconcile competing claims for income by persuading the major interest groups to accept a common agreement. Sometimes the structural view is supplemented by the idea that workers do not save enough so that wage increases lead to excess consumption and insufficient saving. When intended saving falls short of intended investment in the Keynesian model, the economy is stimulated. If the economy is operating near full capacity, such stimulation is inflationary.

The excess-demand view, with its emphasis on governmental monetary and fiscal policy, includes neither collective bargaining nor wage determination as a cause of inflation. Economic stimulation by government policy initially expands the demand for goods and services. A by-product of this first-round effect is the expansion of the derived demand for labor as employers seek to produce those goods and services. A combination of rising prices and growing excess demand for labor leads to wage increases. But the wage increases are seen as a result of inflation, not as a cause.

The structural view, in contrast, is compatible with a wage-push mechanism of inflation. Organized labor is seen as one of the aggressive interest groups, perhaps the most aggressive. European observers on the right and on the left have been able to agree on a wage-push mechanism,

6. See Daniel J. B. Mitchell, "Incomes Policy and the Labor Market in France," *Industrial and Labor Relations Review*, vol. 25 (April 1972), p. 315.

though with different moral interpretations. Those on the left interpret inflation as one of the perversities of capitalism; that is, when workers struggle to increase their wages to a "just" level, inflation is engendered, robbing them of their well-deserved gains. Those on the right may view wage demands as the work of left-wing union militants who do not understand the importance of an adequate profit level to finance investment and future growth.

The structural and excess-demand views can be reconciled by making monetary and fiscal policies endogenous rather than exogenous—if for political reasons these policies accommodate or rationalize wage demands, inflation will be unchecked.[7] In effect, the individual decisions of micro-level wage setters, when summed up, become the basis of monetary and fiscal policy. Those who make monetary and fiscal policy know that if they attempt to restrict demand to restrain inflation increased unemployment and economic slack will result. According to this accommodating view, since recessions are not popular, the authorities resist causing them.

Applied to the United States, however, the reconciliation of structural and excess-demand views of inflation through a model of accommodation is not wholly satisfying. Monetary and fiscal policies have not always avoided creating recessions. Despite resistance to slamming on the aggregate-demand brakes, it is sometimes done. For example, in the recession of 1974–75 the unemployment rate was allowed to rise as high as 9 percent while industrial production dropped by 17 percent from its peak-to-trough value.[8]

Moreover, a look at the early 1960s, when prices were rising by well under 2 percent a year, suggests that collective bargaining is not incompatible with price stability. Thus theories suggesting that collective bargaining or wage determination or pressure from interest groups spontaneously generates inflation must be approached with caution. The politicization of income distribution found in some European countries is less of a factor in the United States. Inflation is usually the cause of such politicization rather than the result.

7. John R. Hicks, "Economic Foundations of Wage Policy," *Economic Journal,* vol. 65 (September 1955), p. 391, described the shift toward accommodative monetary policy as a move from the gold standard to the "labour standard."

8. The unemployment rate (seasonally adjusted) peaked at 9 percent in May 1975. Industrial production fell 17 percent between September 1974 and January 1975 despite the resumption of work after a coal strike ended in December. Bureau of Economic Analysis, *Business Statistics, 1977* (Government Printing Office, 1978), pp. 19, 69.

To explain the initiating cause of inflation in the United States, an excess-demand theory is crucial. The buildup of inflation in the late 1960s was certainly a demand phenomenon. In fact, collective bargainers at first failed to appreciate the trend in price inflation and permitted their wage decisions to lag behind the more responsive nonunion sector, making it difficult to construct a wages-were-the-villain model for that period. But the excess-demand view alone is not entirely satisfactory. Experience in the mid-1970s showed that exogenous pricing elements—crop shortages, oil cartels, and dollar devaluation—could substantially affect overall price changes. Those who relied on a demand approach alone greatly underestimated the acceleration of inflation that began in 1973, when exogenous pricing elements began to play a major role.[9]

If the initiating causes of American inflation are mainly monetary and fiscal policies and occasional exogenous price shocks, wages might appear to play little part in the process. This is because the analysis so far, like much of the literature on inflation, has been concerned only with finding initiating causes, and wage determination is not one of them. But it is an important element in explaining the perpetuation of inflation. The wage-price spiral is not a figment of some editorial writer's imagination; it is very real and flourishing in the modern American economy.

It is difficult to stop inflation once it has started. On the basis of past experience, wage setters have every reason to suspect that inflation will continue. In writing long-term contracts, they will therefore extrapolate from the past for the future. Even in the nonunion sector—where annual wage determination is common—current price changes will play a role in determining current wage changes. If inflation has been accelerating so fast that past estimates of inflation turn out to have been too low, wage decisions will include catch-up elements as well as trend extrapolations. In short, ongoing inflation tends to go on, and accelerating inflation tends to accelerate. Monetary and fiscal restraints can be applied to slow the process, but wage determination as a whole is not very sensitive to economic slack and in the major-union sector is even less sensitive. Monetary and fiscal restraints will help inflation only over an extended period; at first they will affect only some wages and prices. As these first-round effects filter through into general reductions of the rate of price inflation, they will have a wider effect on wage determination. As the wider effect filters through into price determination, further wage restraint will follow.

9. Commodity inflation was estimated to account for 45 percent of the rise in the consumer price index in 1973. Joel Popkin, "Commodity Prices and the U.S. Price Level," *Brookings Papers on Economic Activity, 1:1974*, p. 256.

But the time needed to attain some anti-inflation goal may stretch into years.

The monetary and fiscal authorities may be willing to resist political pressure to avoid recession for a time, but the longer the time required to attain a given goal, the greater these counterpressures will be. If the restraints work only gradually and if their effect can be easily masked by exogenous price shocks, the time available for monetary and fiscal restraint to achieve the goal may be shorter than is necessary.

Direct Intervention in Wage Setting

Beginning with World War II, there have been three episodes of formal wage and price controls and two episodes of "voluntary" wage-price guidelines. Between these episodes were periodic vague calls for restraint or ad hoc interventions in particular wage or price decisions. All of the formal episodes have certain common elements such as administrative problems and public relations. All were instituted because it was believed that monetary and fiscal policy alone would not achieve economic objectives in an efficient (least-cost) manner. But there were significant differences between the direct intervention programs as well.

The General Issue

The wage-price controls of World War II were part of a general effort to allocate resources to military needs. In principle, a system composed only of monetary and fiscal restraint and taxes on nonessential products can be imagined, but in a wartime emergency it is difficult to find the correct combination of general and specific taxes and monetary policy to carry out the required allocation of resources. So a system of quantitative allocation, rationing, and direct wage-price controls was used. The policy worked in that the war was won and inflation was checked during the war. But it did not result in stable prices in the immediate postwar period.[10]

The controls in effect during the Korean conflict were more modest because the economic resources devoted to the military effort were smaller in proportion to overall economic activity. Inflation restraint

10. Consumer prices rose 8.5 percent in 1945–46 and 14.4 percent in 1946–47. Bureau of Labor Statistics, *Handbook of Labor Statistics, 1975—Reference Edition,* bulletin 1965 (GPO, 1975), p. 316.

rather than resource allocation was the major emphasis. Although the Korean War program is often viewed as ineffective,[11] once controls were fully in effect, consumer prices were quite stable, and when the controls were lifted, prices did not leap upward. The period immediately after the controls ended was one of stable, even falling, prices, which contradicts the conventional wisdom that bubbles of repressed inflation explode when controls are lifted.[12] From an anti-inflation viewpoint, therefore, the economic policy that accompanied the Korean conflict was "successful."

Wage-price guideposts during the early 1960s operated in a period of economic expansion after a period of economic slack. The surge in aggregate demand that accompanied the Vietnam military buildup led to the program's demise in early 1966. However, an interesting "what if" question remains. Had excess-demand pressure been checked, so that the economy continued to operate at about the 1964 level, would the guideposts have contributed to restraining inflation and prolonging the expansion? The fact that union wage adjustments did not fully anticipate the rate of inflation in the mid-1960s suggests that inflationary expectations had not been allowed to develop.

Much the same question could be asked about the 1971–74 controls. Like the earlier guideposts, they were established in anticipation of a recovery from a period of economic slack. In part it was hoped that the controls would persuade wage and price setters to reflect the slack more fully in their behavior. The inevitable catch-up wage increases left over from the late 1960s could be labeled special cases so that they would not contribute further to inflationary expectations. And the controls of Phase II (November 1971–January 1973) did seem to have a calming effect.[13] However, in retrospect demand policy seems to have been ex-

11. Mills states that the Wage Stabilization Board "had little if any discernible effect in controlling wages" and that "price increases were generally allowed . . . to offset the wage increases." Daniel Quinn Mills, *Government, Labor, and Inflation: Wage Stabilization in the United States* (University of Chicago Press, 1975), p. 36.

12. Consumer prices rose 0.5 percent from 1953 to 1954 and fell 0.4 percent from 1954 to 1955. Bureau of Economic Analysis, *Business Statistics, 1977*, p. 229.

13. For example, the use of escalator clauses did not increase during Phase II despite regulations encouraging them. Nor was there a wage bulge when Phase III began despite the virtual decontrol of most smaller wage-setting units. See Arnold R. Weber and Daniel J. B. Mitchell, *The Pay Board's Progress: Wage Controls in Phase II* (Brookings Institution, 1978), pp. 368–72; and Arnold R. Weber and Daniel J. B. Mitchell, "Further Reflections on Wage Controls: Comment," *Industrial and Labor Relations Review*, vol. 31 (January 1978), p. 157.

cessively expansionary in 1972. More important, exogenous food, oil, and devaluation price shocks destroyed the program as the authorities vainly sought to hold back an engulfing tide of inflation. Again the "what if" question arises. Suppose that demand policy had been less expansionary in 1972 and that there had not been crop shortages and the 1973 war in the Mideast. If under these circumstances the administration had gradually removed the Phase II controls,[14] would expectations about inflation have remained sanguine?

In general, economists oppose wage-price controls and guidelines because they "create distortions" and because they "don't work." Seldom are these verdicts based on detailed analyses or even on the right questions. Controls and guidelines do create distortions, although these are usually concentrated on the price side of the program rather than the wage side. It is clear that these distortions mount up in time, however, so that the controls, or intervention, option can only be considered on a temporary basis.

The important question about controls or guidelines is whether they can dampen inflationary expectations quickly enough to avoid heavy costs of distortion. In any event, the distortions argument cuts both ways. Monetary and fiscal restraint also creates distortions. The distortions of controls and guidelines tend to be in the form of shortages, those produced by monetary and fiscal restraint to be excess supplies and underutilized resources (including labor). Most monetarists will attribute the depression of the 1930s to the improper use of monetary policy, but they do not draw from that monumental distortion the conclusion that monetary policy should not be used,[15] or that monetary policy inevitably entails mistakes that cause depressions. Rather they conclude that monetary policy must be used correctly. Surely the controls and guidelines options should be afforded the same benefit of the doubt. If applied,

14. The actual shift to Phase III was abrupt, apparently because administration officials feared that the Pay Board and the Price Commission of Phase II were becoming entrenched. In view of the general public suspicion of both agencies, this fear is difficult to understand. However, the abrupt shift led to confusion about the degree to which controls were still in effect, aroused apprehension that the authorities were no longer trying to stop inflation, and probably hastened dollar devaluation. Thus the shift from Phase II was itself inflationary. On the administration's motives, see George P. Shultz and Kenneth W. Dam, "Reflections on Wage and Price Controls," *Industrial and Labor Relations Review,* vol. 30 (January 1977), pp. 143–44.

15. Milton Friedman and Anna Jacobson Schwartz, *A Monetary History of the United States, 1867–1960* (Princeton University Press for the National Bureau of Economic Research, 1963), chap. 7.

direct intervention should be used correctly—that is, briefly and with the specific aim of checking the wage-price spiral during periods of moderate or slackening demand.

A permanent system of wage-price controls would ultimately turn the economic system into a bureaucratic, centralized regime in which commodity rationing, with all the inconveniences and costs entailed, would become the normal state of affairs. Most people would find this highly undesirable. Even voluntary guidelines operated over an extended period could produce extreme economic rigidities. If controls or guidelines are used for transitional purposes, they must be administered flexibly. They should not be expected to hold back the consequences of excessive aggregate demand stimulation or to prevent exogenous price shocks from affecting consumer purchasing power.

Past programs of controls or guidelines make it clear that the implicit emphasis in direct intervention programs is on the wage side. The point of effective control is a wage standard expressed in absolute terms: 3.2 percent, 5.5 percent, 7.0 percent. Prices are generally subject to cost–pass-through rules of varying stringency. But since labor is a large element in total aggregate costs and since most prices are simply costs to producers at later stages of production, restraint of prices is primarily conditioned on restraint of wages. This is not because wages are the villain and prices the victim, but because wages are easier to define administratively and the labor market is less subject to distortion. A rule that prices should increase by no more than 3.2 percent would have quickly resulted in product shortages, even in the early 1960s. The same type of rule applied to wages did not have that effect on the labor market.[16]

Numerical Guidelines

When interventions in the labor market are undertaken, various approaches can be used. As noted above, a general numerical standard for wage increases has been the practice in recent programs. Although the number chosen may be rationalized in various ways, such standards perform several common functions.[17] Increases below the standard are per-

16. See Daniel J. B. Mitchell and Ross E. Azevedo, *Wage-Price Controls and Labor Market Distortions* (UCLA Institute of Industrial Relations, 1976), for further discussion of product versus labor market distortions.

17. For a discussion of the rationales (productivity, cost-of-living increases, and so forth), see D. Quinn Mills, "The Problem of Setting General Pay Standards: An Historical Review," Industrial Relations Research Association, *Proceedings of the Twenty-sixth Annual Winter Meeting* (Madison, Wis.: IRRA, 1974), pp. 9–16.

mitted with little or no review. Unless the standard is set far below the going rate of wage increase, many increases will be automatically allowed, reducing the difficulty of administration. A numerical standard—although it may be encrusted with exceptions and costing rules—is a simple concept. Because it is easily understood, it facilitates compliance. Finally, a numerical standard can be viewed as a suggested norm. It suggests to the parties that they should look beyond last year's price increase (or average wage increase) for a guide to their behavior. It gives them a new number to think about. If the wage standard is not too far from what the parties might otherwise have chosen and if they are convinced that the program will slow inflation, the guideline can calm inflationary fears.

A wage guideline has the virtue of applying to every unit. It does not single out—as some informal jawboning efforts have done—a few wage determination units as pattern setters for everyone else. A deliberate focus on a few units alleged to be key contracts is presumably based on a theory of pattern bargaining. But (as pointed out in chapter 5) not enough is known about wage imitation to justify this type of approach. There is no guarantee that a domino theory of the labor market (affect one unit, affect them all) would work in actual application. In contrast, a broadly applied numerical guideline does not depend on any particular theory of wage imitation.

Another form of intervention could be case-by-case reviews of requests for wage increases without the application of a specific numerical standard. The authorities might have a numerical target in mind for the average settlement but would not seek to apply it in any particular instance. This approach, which was tried during the 1971–74 controls program in selected sectors, rests on the theory that distortions in wage relationships must be removed before wage inflation can be slowed, and it assumes that the authorities intuitively know what stable wage relativities should be. Beyond this, the case-by-case approach presents severe administrative problems. A theory of distorted wage relationships suggests that all wage setters, even the very small ones, should be included. This would make the potential caseload in such a program enormous if it were applied at the economywide level. World War II controls resembled this type of intervention but involved a complex network of industry and regional wage review boards and a large accompanying bureaucracy. Except in national emergencies on the scale of World War II, public support for such economywide efforts would be doubtful. If economywide programs of controls or guidelines are considered, the choice is likely to be a numerical standard or no program at all.

Future Research in Wage Determination

The growth of unionization in the 1930s and 1940s provoked an outburst of institutional literature on wage determination. Case studies and empirical investigations revealed a variety of phenomena that were hard to reconcile with the standard textbook exposition of marginal productivity theory. This engendered tension between theorists and institutionalists over the appropriate analytical approach to the subject. Many young labor economists in the 1960s developed a distaste for the study of wage determination and turned to such topics as human capital, labor-market participation, and demographics.

However, wage determination could not be ignored as long as there was concern about inflation. Since inflation is perceived as a macroeconomic problem, those who remained interested in wage determination tended to engage in aggregate empirical research. The Phillips curve, with its myriad modifications, was born. Although some theoretical justifications were developed for the existence of the Phillips curve, the unstable nature of the estimates raised new questions and the feeling that aggregate wage equations had been pushed as far as they could be and that new insights were needed.

Fortunately, future developments in economic theory may provide insights into past peculiarities in the labor market. The image of a homogeneous labor force with costless mobility and perfect information must be abandoned. If mobility were costless to buyers and sellers in the labor market, employees would not be afraid of losing their jobs and employers would not worry about turnover. Even if workers and employers had perfect information about current conditions, they could hardly be expected to have such information about the future. If labor were homogeneous—even within occupations—employers would not set standards for hiring new employees (high school diplomas, experience, scores on tests) or engage in other forms of screening. The fact that there are costs of mobility to both worker and employer opens the door to new theories of long-term implicit employer-employee relationships.[18]

18. For some examples of this new literature, see David Mayers and Richard Thaler, "Sticky Wages and Implicit Contracts: A Transactional Approach" (UCLA Graduate School of Management, 1978); Michael L. Wachter and Oliver E. Williamson, "Obligational Markets and the Mechanics of Inflation," discussion paper 7 (University of Pennsylvania, Center for the Study of Organizational Innovation, 1977); and Donald F. Gordon, "A Neo-Classical Theory of Keynesian Unemployment," *Economic Inquiry,* vol. 12 (December 1974), pp. 431–59.

Various explanations of turnover costs can be adduced. If employees are not homogeneous, costly screening may be needed to replace those who quit. Also, human capital theory suggests that employees with "specific" talents (skills useful only to a particular employer) require training, the cost of which is likely to be borne by the employer.[19] Employers should attempt to limit such training or screening costs by paying their employees wage premiums to discourage quitting. From the employees' viewpoint, imperfect knowledge of the labor market means that a job search, which could involve a prolonged period without full income, must be undertaken if a job is lost. And there is the risk that any new job might turn out to be less satisfactory than the worker had expected.

In many cases, because jobs involve long-term relationships, the initial wage and benefit level offered by an employer is not the only consideration—a worker might also be interested in future treatment. What will happen if business falls off and fewer workers are needed? What will happen if prices increase, reducing the real wage? What kinds of internal opportunities for training and advancement will be offered, since internal mobility is less costly than external mobility?

Obviously, no one can predict the future exactly, and explicit contracts between workers and employers covering every conceivable contingency are impossible or too costly. But "looser" implicit agreements that include the observance of the norms of fairness, such as rules for resolving problems posed by unforeseen contingencies, are possible. As a result, social norms of employer obligations have been developed. Most people consider an employer who lays off an older worker whose productivity has declined to be cold-hearted; the "good" employer is expected to provide such a worker with employment until retirement.

Generally, the observed rules for employers suggest that reduced variance of income is part of the implicit contract and that the longer the employee remains with the employer, the more binding the contract becomes. This may mean that there is a difference between employers and employees in the amount of risk they will take. Some observers have suggested that the implicit labor contract contains "insurance" for the employee provided by the employer against undue income fluctuation.[20]

19. Unlike general human capital, specific human capital is valuable only to a single employer, who must provide the necessary and costly training to acquire it and cannot "charge" the worker an implicit tuition to make up the costs. See Gary S. Becker, *Human Capital: A Theoretical and Empirical Analysis, with Special Reference to Education*, 2d ed. (Columbia University Press, 1975), pp. 19–37.

20. Costas Azariadis, "Implicit Contracts and Underemployment Equilibria," *Journal of Political Economy*, vol. 83 (December 1975), pp. 1183–1202.

As long as contracts are implicit, cheating is possible. Without involuntary servitude, employers must rely primarily on wage premiums and nonvested fringe benefits to discourage turnover when the labor market is buoyant. The social norms include little about the obligations of workers to their employers. And in soft labor markets, nonunion workers must rely on social norms to induce their employers to honor the implicit contracts. Exploitation (cheating) by employers is obviously tempting when job opportunities elsewhere are limited: wages might not be kept up with inflation and working conditions might deteriorate. Of course, an expected improvement in labor-market conditions might restrain an employer's practice of such cheating. Disillusioned workers might leave when other opportunities increased, and the employer would have acquired a bad reputation, inhibiting future recruitment.

However, restraints on cheating are not perfect. If contracts are implicit, there can be honest disagreements about the proper response to contingencies. The social norms may be contradictory. For example, the principle of "equal pay for equal work" conflicts with the notion that an employer should help tide workers over periods of illness or bereavement. A worker whose productivity has been temporarily reduced for such a reason but who is receiving full pay is not performing equally with other workers. In any case, the social norms do not provide clear guidance on how long an employer is expected to look the other way when workers develop serious psychological problems, suffer from alcoholism, or simply turn out to be less productive than expected.

The implicit-contract view of the employer-employee relationship contributes much to an understanding of collective bargaining. Unions grew in popularity in the 1930s when an unforeseen contingency—the depression—made workers particularly vulnerable to what they perceived as exploitation. The threat of job loss in the 1930s was especially menacing. Although apparently real hourly earnings were almost maintained (a sign that social norms influenced employers' behavior even during the depression), family incomes fell as a result of unemployment and reduced hours. The need for an agent to police implicit contracts when labor markets were very slack and to offset income losses evidently was strongly felt.

Unions tend to make implicit social norms explicit. Labor contracts typically spell out the behavior required of employers in the event of layoffs or inflation. Seniority clauses protecting the most senior workers reflect the social norm that the employer owes the most to employees who have remained with the firm the longest. Escalator clauses explicitly deal with protection against price increases. And to handle the many contingencies for which formulas are not easily established, arbitrators are assigned to make equitable decisions.

Arbitrators interpret the employer-employee contract when it is made explicit in the written union-management agreement. In principle, labor arbitrators who hear cases arising during the life of the contract base their decisions mainly on the specific terms to which the parties have agreed. But arbitrators also look for tacit understandings established by past practice. Besides explicit and implicit agreements, they inevitably face questions of equity that involve the social norms of fairness. For example, an agreement may provide for discharge of employees for just cause, but it is left to the arbitrator to determine in a particular circumstance if there was just cause.

Analysis based on long-term implicit contracts may also shed some light on wage-imitation behavior. In a world of uncertainty in which worker productivity cannot be precisely measured, there is no simple way to determine what pay a job should carry or how large a pay increase should be offered. Since in the formal legal system, concepts of precedent and equal treatment are important, it may be inferred that they should also be important in implicit employer-employee relationships. Then the fair solution to wage setting might be to maintain some historic wage relationship (precedent) or follow someone else's decision (equal treatment). Even if a wage decision was made independently of other decisions, there might well be a need to rationalize the outcome by reference to some other group. This would show that the implicit contract was being honored and that wage decisions were not being made arbitrarily.

The macro aspects of the labor market, which are hard to reconcile with simple micro theory, may also be illuminated by the implicit contract approach. Even in the nonunion sector, wage change is not especially responsive to the unemployment rate. In a perfect labor market that clears every day, such behavior would be incomprehensible, but in a long-term relationship, a tendency to ignore short-term fluctuations seems much more reasonable. If the implicit contract is more binding for experienced and older workers and if workers place a value on smoothing their income fluctuations, the preference for layoffs (starting with the most junior employees) rather than wage cuts is also understandable. Under a layoff-by-seniority system, the more senior the worker is, the less the chance that his or her income will be adversely affected by a business decline. Thus implicit contracts have relevance to the analysis of aggregate unemployment fluctuations.

Clearly the implicit-contract approach could permit a reconciliation of institutionalist observation and economic analysis. The researcher of the future must therefore be prepared to take a middle path between pure theory and pure observation. There is no point in spinning models of the labor market that explain nonexistent phenomena. So the labor-market researcher must have a solid grasp of institutional practices. But there is also no justification for the assumption of some industrial relations scholars that economics has little to offer in explaining labor-market arrangements. Once economic models incorporate uncertainty, information and turnover costs, and screening problems, many new insights will be developed.

Industries and Data Availability

DATA on average hourly earnings for ninety-three industries were used to create tables 2-4 and 2-5 and for certain computations in other chapters. Complete earnings data for all industries in the sample were available for 1958–76, but for 1953–57 they were available for only fifty-nine industries. These data include overtime and similar premiums but do not include expenditures on fringe benefits such as pensions and health and welfare programs. They cover only production and nonsupervisory workers.[1] The sources of these data are the Bureau of Labor Statistics and its volumes on *Employment and Earnings*.[2]

Table A-1 lists the ninety-three industries and provides information on data availability for certain variables used in chapters 3, 4, and 5. Estimates of unionization rates using the contract file (see chapter 2) were available for all ninety-three industries.[3] Unlike other sources of unionization rates, the contract file does not guarantee that the estimated unionization cannot be more than 100 percent. In two industries, such excessive rates were estimated. These figures result from inaccurate estimates by the Bureau of Labor Statistics or from the allocation of workers to one industry, some of whom may belong in another industry.[4] For purposes of

1. Hourly earnings estimates are determined by dividing payroll by hours paid for. Thus vacations and other hours paid for but not worked are included in the denominator. As a result, the gradual trend toward increased time off with pay is not reflected in the estimates.

2. Data were taken from Bureau of Labor Statistics, *Employment and Earnings, United States, 1909–75*, bulletin 1312-10 (Government Printing Office, 1976), pp. 1–675; and *Employment and Earnings*, vol. 24 (March 1977), pp. 94–107. The estimate for hourly earnings in 1976 for SIC 482 (telegraph) was obtained by telephone from the Bureau of Labor Statistics.

3. The computer printout of union coverage provided by the Bureau of Labor Statistics did not provide an estimate for SIC 4011 (railroads). An estimate was obtained from Lena W. Bolton, "Bargaining Calendar to Be Heavy in 1977," *Monthly Labor Review*, vol. 99 (December 1976), p. 16. The printout estimate for SIC 352 (farm machinery) was increased to reflect three unallocated contracts at International Harvester.

4. The two instances in which such excessive estimates occurred were SIC 321 (flat glass) and SIC 231 (men's and boys' suits).

dichotomizing the work force, as in tables 2-4 and 2-5, such estimates pose no real problem, although in regression analysis some difficulties arise (see appendix B).[5]

As discussed in chapter 2, unionization rates were also obtained from an article by Freeman and Medoff.[6] In general, where industry codes used by Freeman and Medoff were more detailed than those used in the ninety-three-industry breakdown, employment weights from *Employment and Earnings* were used to combine the detailed industry groups. For the compensation survey, 1970 was used to obtain employment weights. For the current population survey results, employment weights were taken for 1974.[7]

5. In chapter 3 in particular, the unionization rate enters into a series of estimates produced by regression analysis. One method of dealing with the excessive estimates would have been to truncate them artificially at 100 percent. However, no corrections could be made for rates that were less than 100 percent but that were based on either overestimates or underestimates of the number of workers covered by union contracts. Hence, it was decided to use the unadjusted figures. The other two sources of unionization estimates do not permit rates above 100 percent, but this does not make them free from error.

6. Richard B. Freeman and James L. Medoff, "New Estimates of Private Sector Unionism in the United States," *Industrial and Labor Relations Review,* vol. 32 (January 1979), pp. 143–74.

7. Employment weights from *Employment and Earnings* for compensation survey estimates were used for the following industries: SIC 27 (except 271), 30 (except 301), 301, 31 (except 314), 34, 42, and 494–7. Employment weights from *Employment and Earnings* for current population survey estimates were used for the following industries: SIC 30 (except 301), 301, 357, and 42. Employment weights were taken directly from the current population survey estimates appearing in the Freeman and Medoff paper for SIC 494–7, 50 (except 504), 504, 52, 53, 54, 551–2, 56, 57. In the compensation survey estimates, the unionization rate for SIC 237–8 was estimated from data from SIC 238 only.

Table A-1. *List of Industries and Availability of Data*

		Variable[a]					
Standard industrial classification number	Industry	Average hourly earnings in 1953 (AHE53)	Annual earnings of black females (BFSOC)	Union and nonunion wages (UNCP and NONCP)	Unionization rate from compensation survey (UNEEC)	Unionization rate from current population survey (UNCPS)	Capital-labor ratio (KLDEP)
SIC 10	Metal mining	X	n.a.	X	n.a.	X	X
SIC 12	Bituminous coal	X	n.a.	X	X	X	X
SIC 131–2	Crude petroleum and natural gas extraction	X	X	X	n.a.	X	X
SIC 15	General building construction	X	X	X	X	X	X
SIC 16	Heavy construction	X	X	X	n.a.	X	X
SIC 17	Specialty trade contractors	X	X	X	X	X	X
SIC 19	Ordnance	X	X	n.a.	X	X	n.a.
SIC 201	Meat packing	X	X	X	X	X	X
SIC 202	Dairies	n.a.	X	X	X	X	X
SIC 203	Canning	X	X	X	X	X	X
SIC 204	Grain products	X	X	n.a.	X	X	X
SIC 205	Bakeries	X	X	X	X	X	X
SIC 206	Sugar refining	X	X	n.a.	X	n.a.	X
SIC 207	Confectionery products	X	X	X	X	X	X
SIC 208	Beverages	X	X	X	X	X	X
SIC 209	Miscellaneous food products	n.a.	X	X	X	X	X
SIC 21	Tobacco products	X	X	X	X	X	X
SIC 22	Textile products	X	X	X	X	X	X
SIC 231	Men's suits	X	X	n.a.	X	n.a.	X
SIC 232	Men's furnishings	X	X	X	X	n.a.	X
SIC 233	Women's outerwear	X	X	X	X	n.a.	X

SIC	Industry						
SIC 234	Women's underwear	X	X	X	X	n.a.	X
SIC 235	Hats	n.a.	X	n.a.	X	n.a.	X
SIC 236	Children's outerwear	X	X	X	X	n.a.	X
SIC 237–8	Fur products	n.a.	X	X	X	n.a.	X
SIC 239	Miscellaneous fabrics	n a	X	X	X	X	X
SIC 24	Lumber	X	X	X	X	X	X
SIC 25	Furniture	X	X	X	X	X	X
SIC 26	Paper products	X	X	X	X	X	X
SIC 27	Printing and publishing except newspapers (271)	X	X	X	X	X	X
SIC 271	Newspapers	X	X	X	X	X	X
SIC 28	Chemicals	X	X	X	X	X	X
SIC 29	Petroleum	X	X	X	X	X	X
SIC 30	Rubber products except tires (301)	X	X	X	X	X	X
SIC 301	Tires	X	X	X	X	X	X
SIC 31	Leather products except footwear (314)	X	X	X	X	X	X
SIC 314	Footwear	X	X	X	X	X	X
SIC 321	Flat glass	n.a.	X	n.a.	X	n.a.	X
SIC 322	Glassware	n.a.	X	X	X	n.a.	X
SIC 324	Cement	X	X	n.a.	X	n.a.	X
SIC 325	Clay	n.a.	X	X	X	X	X
SIC 326	Pottery	X	X	X	X	X	X
SIC 327	Concrete, gypsum, plaster	n.a.	X	X	X	n.a.	X
SIC 328–9	Other stone and nonmetallic	n.a.	X	n.a.	n.a.	X	X
SIC 331	Steel	X	X	n.a.	X	X	X
SIC 332	Iron and steel foundries	n.a.	X	X	X	n.a.	X
SIC 333–4	Nonferrous metal	n.a.	X	X	X	n.a.	X
SIC 335	Nonferrous drawing and rolling	X	X	X	X	n.a.	X
SIC 336	Nonferrous foundries	n.a.	X	X	X	n.a.	X
SIC 339	Miscellaneous metals	n.a.	X	X	X	n.a.	X
SIC 34	Fabricated metal except cans (341)	X	X	X	X	n.a.	X

(continued)

Table A-1 (*continued*)

Standard industrial classification number	Industry	Variable[a]					
		Average hourly earnings in 1953 (AHE53)	Annual earnings of black females (BFSOC)	Union and nonunion wages (UNCP and NONCP)	Unionization rate from compensation survey (UNEEC)	Unionization rate from current population survey (UNCPS)	Capital–labor ratio (KLDEP)
SIC 341	Metal cans	X	X	X	X	n.a.	X
SIC 351	Engines	n.a.	n.a.	X	X	X	X
SIC 352	Farm machinery	n.a.	X	X	X	X	X
SIC 353	Construction machinery	n.a.	X	X	X	X	X
SIC 354	Metal-working machinery	X	X	X	X	X	X
SIC 355	Special industry machinery	X	X	X	X	n.a.	X
SIC 356	General industry machinery	n.a.	X	X	X	n.a.	X
SIC 357	Office machines and computers	n.a.	X	X	X	X	X
SIC 358	Service industry machinery	n.a.	X	X	X	n.a.	X
SIC 359	Miscellaneous machinery	n.a.	X	X	X	X	X
SIC 36	Electrical equipment	X	X	X	X	X	X
SIC 371	Motor vehicles	X	X	X	X	X	X
SIC 372	Aircraft	X	X	X	X	X	X
SIC 373	Shipbuilding	X	X	X	X	X	X
SIC 374	Railroad equipment	X	n.a.	X	X	X	X
SIC 375–9	Other transportation equipment	n.a.	X	X	n.a.	X	X
SIC 38	Instruments	X	X	X	X	X	X
SIC 39	Miscellaneous manufactures	X	X	X	X	X	X
SIC 4011	Class I railroads	X	X	n.a.	X	X	X
SIC 411	Local transit	n.a.	X	n.a.	X	n.a.	X
SIC 413	Intercity transit	n.a.	X	n.a.	X	n.a.	X

SIC	Industry						
SIC 42	Trucking and warehousing	n.a.	X	X	X	X	X
SIC 481	Telephones	X	X	X	X	X	X
SIC 482	Telegraph	X	X	X	n.a.	X	X
SIC 483	Radio and television broadcasting	n.a.	X	X	n.a.	X	X
SIC 491	Electrical utilities	X	X	X	X	X	X
SIC 492	Gas utilities	X	X	X	X	X	X
SIC 493	Combination utilities	X	X	X	X	X	X
SIC 494–7	Water, steam, sanitary	n.a.	n.a.	X	X	X	X
SIC 50	Wholesale trade except groceries (504)	n.a.	X	X	X	X	X
SIC 504	Wholesale groceries	n.a.	X	X	X	X	X
SIC 52	Building materials stores	n.a.	X	X	X	X	X
SIC 53	General merchandise, retail	X	X	X	X	X	X
SIC 54	Food stores	n.a.	X	X	X	X	X
SIC 551–2	Motor vehicle dealers	n.a.	X	X	X	X	X
SIC 56	Apparel stores	X	X	X	X	X	X
SIC 57	Furniture stores	n.a.	X	X	X	X	X
SIC 591	Drug stores	n.a.	X	X	X	X	X
SIC 598	Fuel and ice dealers	n.a.	n.a.	X	X	X	X
SIC 60	Banking	n.a.	X	X	X	X	X
SIC 701	Hotels	n.a.	X	X	X	X	X
SIC 721	Laundries	n.a.	X	X	X	X	X

Source: See footnote 2 to this appendix.

X Data available.

n.a. Not available.

a. The variables are defined more fully in appendix B.

Regression Analysis and Data Sources
for Chapter 3

Definitions and Sources of Variables

A large number of variables were used in preparing the tables in chapters 2 and 3 and the regressions in this appendix. The abbreviations for these variables and their definitions and sources are listed below. Some of the variables were not available for all the industries listed in table A-1, which indicates the industries for which data were missing.

AHEij   Average hourly earnings in year 19ij. Data from 1953 to 1974 are from Bureau of Labor Statistics, *Employment and Earnings, United States, 1909–75,* bulletin 1312-10 (Government Printing Office, 1976), pp. 1–675. Data for 1976 are from *Employment and Earnings,* vol. 24 (March 1977), table C-2.

BFSOC   Average annual earnings of black females who worked all four quarters of 1972. In some cases, because the data source was more aggregated than the industry code used for the regressions and tabulations, aggregate figures were substituted. Figures refer only to earnings from the major industry of employment and do not include employers' contributions to pensions, health and welfare funds, and so forth. The data were drawn from social security payroll tax records. Bureau of Labor Statistics, *Annual Earnings and Employment Patterns of Private Nonagricultural Employees, 1971 and 1972,* bulletin 1928 (GPO, 1976), table B-24.

BLK76   The proportion of nonwhite workers in total payroll employment for 1976. In some cases, because the data source was more aggregated than the industry code used for the regressions and tabulations, aggregate figures were substituted. *Employment and Earnings,* vol. 24 (March 1977), p. 9.

236

BMSOC   Same as *BFSOC*, but for black males.

ED   Median educational attainment, in years, of males and females, by industry in 1970, weighted by $1 - PFEM$ and *PFEM*, respectively. In some cases, because the data source was more aggregated than the industry code used for the regressions and tabulations, aggregate figures were substituted. Bureau of the Census, *Census of Population, 1970,* Final Report PC(2)-7B, *Industrial Characteristics* (GPO, 1973), table 3.

ESSIZ   Employees per establishment in 1974. Bureau of the Census, *County Business Patterns, 1974, U.S. Summary,* CPB-74-1 (GPO, 1977), table 1B. Data for class 1 railroads (SIC 4011) were taken from the same source as *AHE53–AHE74,* p. 778.

KLDEP   Depreciation deduction by active corporations in 1973 as proportion of 1973 employment. In some cases, because the data source was more aggregated than the industry code used for the regressions and tabulations, aggregate figures were substituted. Depreciation from Internal Revenue Service, *Statistics of Income, 1973, Corporation Income Tax Returns* (GPO, 1977), table 1. Employment figures from same source as *AHE53–AHE74.*

KLDEPA   Depreciable assets per employee in 1973. From same sources as *KLDEP.*

NONCP   Total hourly compensation of nonunion, nonoffice employees in 1974 from the 1974 biennial survey of compensation. A summary of this survey can be found in Bureau of Labor Statistics, *Employee Compensation in the Private Nonfarm Economy, 1974,* bulletin 1963 (GPO, 1978). However, detailed industry figures are not published and were drawn from a computer tape supplied by the BLS. Total compensation includes wages, overtime and shift premiums, employers' contributions to health, welfare, pension, and similar funds, and payments legally required of employers such as social security payroll taxes.

NONFR   Private hourly fringe compensation of nonunion, nonoffice employees in 1974. From same source as *NONCP.* Private fringe benefits exclude payments legally required of employ-

	ers such as social security payroll taxes. Also excluded—to remove the influence of different business-cycle influences across industries—are overtime and shift premiums.
NONST	Straight-time hourly wage of nonunion, nonoffice employees. From same source as *NONCP*.
PFEM	The proportion of female employees in total payroll employment in 1976. *Employment and Earnings,* vol. 24 (March 1977), pp. 9, 70–76.
PFRIN	Private fringe benefits as a proportion of private compensation in 1971. Private fringe benefits and compensation exclude payments legally required of employers such as social security payroll taxes. Bureau of the Census, *Annual Survey of Manufactures, 1970–71* (GPO, 1973), pp. 143–50.
QT76	Average of monthly quit rates in 1976. Quit rates are the number of voluntary separations as a percentage of total payroll employment. *Employment and Earnings,* vol. 24 (March 1977), pp. 122–25.
TOTCP	Total hourly compensation of nonoffice employees in 1974. From same source as *NONCP*.
TOTFR	Private hourly fringe compensation of nonoffice employees in 1974. From same source as *NONCP*.
TOTST	Straight-time hourly wage of nonoffice employees in 1974. From same source as *NONCP*.
UNCP	Total hourly compensation of union, nonoffice employees in 1974. From same source as *NONCP*.
UNCPS	The proportion of employees in an industry reported to be union members in the current population surveys for May 1973, 1974, and 1975, reported in Richard B. Freeman and James L. Medoff, "New Estimates of Private Sector Unionism in the United States," *Industrial and Labor Relations Review,* vol. 32 (January 1979), pp. 143–74. Data were not available for all industries. A list of the industries for which data could be obtained can be found in table A-1; see also footnote 7, appendix A.
UNEEC	The proportion of employees in an industry covered by collective bargaining agreements based on a biennial survey of compensation expenditures for 1968, 1970, and 1972. From same source as *UNCPS*.
UNE76	Ratio of employees reported covered by union agreements to

total payroll employment in 1976. The number of covered employees was taken from a summer 1977 computer printout of "key" and "nonkey" listings made available by the Bureau of Labor Statistics. Key listings are for agreements covering 1,000 or more workers and are believed to be virtually complete for the private sector. Nonkey listings are those covering smaller agreements and are only partially complete. Since estimates of the number of workers covered by an agreement are made at the time a report of the agreement is received, it seemed appropriate to divide by 1976 rather than 1977 employment because of the lag inherent in the workers-covered estimates. Employment is from the same source as *AHE76*. Three unclassified International Harvester agreements were assigned to farm machinery (SIC 352). The BLS printout omitted railroad workers. An estimate of the number of workers covered in the railroad industry was taken from Lena W. Bolton, "Bargaining Calendar to Be Heavy in 1977," *Monthly Labor Review,* vol. 99 (December 1976), p. 16.

UNFR Private hourly fringe compensation of union, nonoffice employees in 1974. From same source as *NONCP*.

UNST Straight-time hourly wage of union, nonoffice employees in 1974. From same source as *NONCP*.

WFSOC Average annual earnings of white (nonblack) females who worked all four quarters of 1972. From same source as *BFSOC*.

WMSOC Same as *WFSOC*, but for white (nonblack) males. From same source as *BFSOC*.

Regression Analysis

The results of regression analysis across a detailed industry sample of employee earnings and quit rates were reported in chapter 3. In all cases, the dependent variable was regressed against six explanatory variables: one of three indexes of the unionization rate discussed in chapter 2 (the contract file [*UNE76*], the compensation survey [*UNEEC*], or the current population survey [*UNCPS*]); the proportion of nonwhite workers in the work force (*BLK76*); the average establishment size in the industry

(*ESSIZ*); the proportion of female workers in the work force (*PFEM*); the ratio of depreciation to employment (*KLDEP*); and weighted median years of educational attainment in the industry (*ED*). Definitions and sources of these variables were given above.

The industry sample contained ninety-three industries, which are listed in table A-1. However, missing observations prevent the use of all industries in the sample. In particular, *KLDEP* could not be estimated for ordnance (SIC 19), eliminating that industry from all regressions. Hence the largest sample size for the regressions is ninety-two observations. Two of the three unionization rate series, *UNEEC* and *UNCPS*, were also not available for all industries. In some cases, observations were missing for employee compensation. Hourly earnings data were not available for all industries before 1958. The regressions for 1953 are thus for a smaller sample than those for later years. Also, the number of regressions that involved explicit measures of union and nonunion compensation was limited by missing observations. Quit rate data were not available for many industries; most of the missing observations were for industries other than manufacturing.

As noted in chapter 3, the three unionization rate measures produce different regression results. An interesting question is whether the differences are due to discrepancies in the industry samples over which the regressions were run (because of missing observations) or whether they are due to divergent estimates of unionization. Several tables are presented in this appendix to deal with that question.

Regressions Underlying Table 3-10

Tables B-1, B-2, B-3, B-6, B-7, and B-8 present the regression equations from which the figures in table 3-10 were derived. Columns 1–7 in the six tables present results for all the industries for which data on the particular unionization rate series in the table were available; they are for years beginning in 1958. Columns 8 and 9 present the results for industries for which earnings data before 1958 were available. Shown are regressions for 1953 and 1976. Comparison of the results from these regressions permits analysis of trends over the entire 1953–76 period.

Note that in all fifty-four cases except one, the unionization rate (*UNE76*, *UNEEC*, or *UNCPS*) produces the expected positive coefficient. Only six of the positive coefficients are statistically insignificant. The proportion of female workers (*PFEM*) always produces the expected negative and significant sign. Establishment size (*ESSIZ*) fails to produce a significant coefficient. Weighted median education (ED) always produces the expected positive sign but is not often significant. Similarly, the proportion of nonwhite workers ($BLK76$) produces the expected negative sign in all cases, but its coefficient sometimes falls below significance at the 10 percent level. The ratio of depreciation per employee ($KLDEP$)—a capital-intensity proxy—tends to be significant in the expected positive direction. However, the association is stronger in the later years in tables B-2 and B-3.

Of greatest concern in this study is the unionization rate coefficient, the b coefficient of chapter 3. Tables B-4, B-5, B-9, and B-10 explore the discrepancy between the coefficient obtained when $UNE76$ (from the contract file) is used as the index of the unionization rate and the coefficients obtained with the other two indexes, $UNEEC$ (from the compensation survey) and $UNCPS$ (from the current population survey). There are two possible sources of the discrepancy. Since $UNEEC$ and $UNCPS$ are not available for all industries, it is possible that the differences in the estimated b coefficients are due to the different samples used for the regressions. And since the values of the three indexes are not identical for the industries for which complete data are available, the discrepancies in the b coefficients could be due to measurement differences.

Tables B-4 and B-9 (columns 2 and 5, 4 and 6) show that, if the sample used for the $UNE76$ estimates is made identical to that used for the $UNEEC$ estimates, changes in the resulting b coefficients are comparatively minor; the discrepancies are due mainly to measurement differences. In contrast, tables B-5 and B-10, when the same columns are compared, suggest that the discrepancies in b coefficients obtained from $UNE76$ and $UNCPS$ are due to combinations of sample effects and measurement effects in most cases. For the regressions run on the smaller samples for which 1953 data on earnings were available, the regressions using $UNCPS$ produce insignificant b coefficients. Tables B-5 and B-10 show that the insignificance results from the use of $UNCPS$ rather than from the sample of industries. That is, when $UNE76$ is substituted for $UNCPS$ using the same sample, the b coefficients are significant.

Regressions Underlying Table 3-11 and the Quit-Rate Discussion in Chapter 3

Tables B-11, B-12, and B-13 present the regressions used to construct table 3-11, as well as regression results for quit rates ($QT76$) discussed in chapter 3. Columns 1–4 of the tables contain equations "explaining" the annual incomes of four-quarter workers for four major demographic groups: white (nonblack) males, white (nonblack) females, black males, and black females. In addition to the three measures of the unionization rate, the tables employ the same five explanatory variables previously used to explain industry average hourly earnings.

Two of the explanatory variables must be reinterpreted when used to explain demographic earnings. The proportions of black and female workers (*BLK76* and *PFEM*) carry various types of information. They may reflect certain industry characteristics not represented in the other variables. They may also reflect "crowding" effects on earnings caused by the concentration of blacks and females (for whatever reasons) in particular industries. In industry earnings equations, they may simply correct for the tendency of blacks and women to earn less than whites and men. But when specific demographic earnings are used as the dependent variables, this last type of correction is no longer a source of variance. Hence the *BLK76* and *PFEM* variables can reflect the other kinds of information but not the simple earnings difference correction.

In all twelve earnings regressions, unionization has the expected positive sign. In only one case is the coefficient statistically insignificant. Establishment size has a positive and significant influence for females but not for males. This influence was obscured by the hourly-earnings regressions in the previous tables, in which the earnings of males and females were aggregated. Capital intensity as measured by *KLDEP* has a positive effect on all workers. This is consistent with the regressions on hourly earnings for the 1970s. The education variable is always significant at the 5 percent level in tables B-11, B-12, and B-13, although it tended to be less significant in the hourly-earnings regressions. This is probably because the education variable is more consistent with a data set covering all workers than with one covering only those included in the production and nonsupervisory classification to which hourly-earnings statistics refer.

A higher proportion of female workers tends to lower the annual earnings of women and blacks. The effect of *PFEM* on the earnings of white males is ambiguous. In the equations involving *UNCPS*, a negative influence appears. This finding appears to be related more to the industry sample than to the *UNCPS* variable.[1] The proportion of black workers in employment seems to lower the earnings of white males in the two larger samples involving *UNE76* and *UNEEC*.

1. If the same sample is used with the *UNE76* variable, a negative and significant coefficient for *PFEM* also appears.

Unionization and education have a negative influence on quit rates ($QT76$), and the proportion of female workers has a positive effect in the equations that include $UNE76$ and $UNEEC$. Only the education variable has a significant impact in the equation that includes $UNCPS$, which is for a much smaller number of industries. However, the insignificant unionization coefficient appears to be partly the result of differences in the unionization estimate.

Table B-14 compares the unionization coefficients obtained using $UNEEC$ and $UNCPS$ with those obtained with $UNE76$. In general, the discrepancies in the coefficients when $UNEEC$ and $UNE76$ are used are due mainly to the differences in measurement of the two variables rather than to sample variation. When $UNE76$ and $UNCPS$ are compared (columns 3 and 5), the results are more ambiguous. If $UNE76$ is substituted for $UNCPS$, unionization becomes a significant variable in the two instances when equations with $UNCPS$ produce insignificant unionization coefficients. However, the discrepancies seem due to a combination of sample variation and measurement differences.

Regressions Underlying Table 3-9

Tables B-15, B-16, and B-17 present the regression results from which the figures of table 3-9 were calculated. The regressions explain hourly compensation in three forms: straight-time pay, private fringe benefits, and total compensation. Note that total compensation exceeds the sum of private fringes and straight-time pay by an amount equal to legally required fringe benefits and certain shift premiums. The tables break down the three forms of compensation into union, nonunion, and total payments in the industries covered. Only industries for which both union and nonunion data were available are included.

An important question arises when union effects on earnings are examined using a data set that does not distinguish between union and nonunion pay. It is desirable to know if there is a bias in the coefficient of unionization (the b coefficient). As pointed out in chapter 3, this coefficient can be viewed as an estimate of the mean union-nonunion pay differential. However, it will be biased if differences in unionization rates affect union and nonunion pay.

If the unionization variable is positively correlated with union pay but not correlated with nonunion pay, the b coefficient will be biased upward relative to the mean union-nonunion differential. This can be seen in table B-15. The variable *UNE76* has a strong and significant relation with union straight-time pay (*UNST*) but no significant relationship with nonunion straight-time pay (*NONST*). The mean union-nonunion differential is $4.79 − $3.73 = $1.06. But the *b* coefficient in column 3 implies a difference of $1.22, an upward-biased estimate. The same phenomenon occurs when private fringe benefits or total compensation is used as the dependent variable.

Generally, labor economists have expected unionization to have a positive influence on union pay. Unions that have organized the most workers in an industry could be expected to be more powerful than those with only a small proportion of employment covered by contracts. There is no clear expectation about the union influence on nonunion pay, however, since opposing influences can be hypothesized. Table B-15 seems to be in line with the expected results. However, tables B-16 and B-17, which use *UNEEC* and *UNCPS* as the unionization rate instead of *UNE76,* do not give the expected results. Unionization is not significantly and positively correlated with union pay in those tables.

Table B-18 suggests that these divergent outcomes result from measurement differences between the unionization rates rather than variations in the samples. This means that the biases inherent in the indirect means of estimating the union effect on pay depend heavily on the particular variables used. In particular, the associations usually observed between unionization and industry pay are not necessarily upward-biased estimates of the mean union-nonunion pay differential within those industries.

It is important to note that the regressions in tables B-15, B-16, and B-17 use explanatory variables that refer to industrywide characteristics. The estimates of the *b* coefficients could thus be biased by any systematic relationships between union or nonunion status and the labor-force or other pay-related characteristics of establishments within the industries. Even if the estimated *b* coefficients are not upward-biased estimates of mean union-nonunion differentials within industries, they may be upward-biased estimates of the actual effect of unionization on those differentials.

Table B-1. Regression Equations Relating Average Hourly Earnings to UNE76 and Other Selected Variables

	Dependent variable								
Explanatory variable	AHE76 (1)	AHE74 (2)	AHE73 (3)	AHE71 (4)	AHE68 (5)	AHE64 (6)	AHE58 (7)	AHE76 (8)	AHE53 (9)
Constant	5.47*	4.32*	4.24*	3.75*	2.70*	1.98*	2.03*	5.37*	1.89*
UNE76	1.49*	1.18*	1.07*	0.81*	0.69*	0.65*	0.52*	1.33*	0.33*
BLK76	-2.41	-2.17	-2.32*	-2.13*	-1.83*	-1.62*	-1.58*	-3.52*	-1.82*
ESSIZ	(-0.00)	(-0.00)	(-0.00)	(-0.00)	(-0.00)	(-0.00)	(-0.00)	(-0.00)	(-0.00)
PFEM	-3.75*	-3.03*	-2.74*	-2.29*	-1.65	-1.47*	-1.17*	-3.84*	-0.87*
KLDEP	0.0001*	0.0001*	0.0001*	0.00004*	0.00003*	0.00003*	0.00002*	0.0001*	(0.00)
ED	(0.04)	(0.07)	(0.04)	(0.04)	(0.06)	(0.08)	(0.03)	(0.08)	(0.02)
$\bar{R}^2$	0.78	0.76	0.75	0.72	0.72	0.74	0.70	0.78	0.69
Standard error	0.61	0.51	0.48	0.42	0.32	0.28	0.24	0.65	0.19
Number of observations	92	92	92	92	92	92	92	58	58
Mean of dependent variable (dollars)	5.31	4.50	4.16	3.64	3.03	2.54	2.10	5.49	1.76

Coefficients in parentheses not significant at 10 percent level.
* Significant at 5 percent level or better.

Table B-2. *Regression Equations Relating Average Hourly Earnings to UNEEC and Other Selected Variables*

Explanatory variable	Dependent variable								
	AHE76 (1)	AHE74 (2)	AHE73 (3)	AHE71 (4)	AHE68 (5)	AHE64 (6)	AHE58 (7)	AHE76 (8)	AHE53 (9)
Constant	3.08*	2.50	2.73*	2.44*	1.62*	(0.91)	1.06	3.73*	1.60*
UNEEC	2.02*	1.53*	1.30*	1.03*	0.87*	0.93*	0.85*	1.94*	0.45*
BLK76	−2.67	−2.43	−2.59*	−2.37*	−2.04*	−1.91*	−1.89*	−3.23	−1.85*
ESSIZ	(−0.00)	(−0.00)	(0.00)	(−0.00)	(−0.00)	(−0.00)	(−0.00)	(−0.00)	(−0.00)
PFEM	−3.24*	−2.65*	−2.42*	−2.02*	−1.43*	−1.24*	−0.94*	−3.31*	−0.77*
KLDEP	0.0001*	0.00004	0.00005*	0.00003	(0.00)	(0.00)	(0.00)	0.0001*	(0.00)
ED	0.20	0.19	(0.14)	(0.13)	0.13*	0.15*	0.09*	(0.16)	(0.03)
$\bar{R}^2$	0.76	0.73	0.72	0.70	0.69	0.72	0.71	0.75	0.64
Standard error	0.64	0.54	0.52	0.44	0.34	0.29	0.24	0.70	0.21
Number of observations	87	87	87	87	87	87	87	55	55
Mean of dependent variable (dollars)	5.27	4.47	4.14	3.62	3.01	2.52	2.08	5.42	1.75

Coefficients in parentheses not significant at 10 percent level.
* Significant at 5 percent level or better.

Table B-3. *Regression Equations Relating Average Hourly Earnings to UNCPS and Other Selected Variables*

Explanatory variable	Dependent variable								
	AHE76 (1)	AHE74 (2)	AHE73 (3)	AHE71 (4)	AHE68 (5)	AHE64 (6)	AHE58 (7)	AHE76 (8)	AHE53 (9)
Constant	(2.79)	(2.18)	2.43	2.30	(1.45)	(0.71)	(0.98)	(3.23)	1.44*
UNCPS	2.17*	1.51*	1.22*	0.87*	0.77*	0.86*	0.72*	(1.15)	(0.09)
BLK76	(−1.81)	(−1.38)	(−1.60)	(−1.56)	(−1.36)	(−1.23)	−1.31*	(−2.94)	−1.62*
ESSIZ	(−0.00)	(−0.00)	(0.00)	(−0.00)	(−0.00)	(−0.00)	(−0.00)	(−0.00)	(−0.00)
PFEM	−3.87*	−3.36*	−3.07*	−2.70*	−2.01*	−1.74*	−1.40*	−4.91*	−1.37*
KLDEP	0.0001*	0.00005	0.00005	(0.00)	(0.00)	(0.00)	(0.00)	0.0001	(0.00)
ED	0.24	0.23*	0.19	0.16	0.16*	0.18*	0.11*	0.29	0.07
$\bar{R}^2$	0.70	0.67	0.65	0.63	0.64	0.68	0.67	0.71	0.71
Standard error	0.71	0.60	0.57	0.50	0.38	0.32	0.27	0.73	0.19
Number of observations	68	68	68	68	68	68	68	44	44
Mean of dependent variable (dollars)	5.35	4.54	4.20	3.68	3.04	2.55	2.10	5.63	1.79

Coefficients in parentheses not significant at 10 percent level.
* Significant at 5 percent level or better.

Table B-4. *Effect of Industry Sample and Unionization Data Source on b Coefficients, UNE76 and UNEEC*

Year	Coefficient of UNE76				Coefficient of UNEEC	
	92 industries[a] (1)	87 industries[b] (2)	58 industries[a] (3)	55 industries[b] (4)	87 industries[a] (5)	55 industries[c] (6)
1976	1.49*	1.47*	1.33*	1.36*	2.02*	1.94*
1974	1.18*	1.16*	...	...	1.53*	...
1973	1.07*	1.06*	...	...	1.30*	...
1971	0.81*	0.79*	...	...	1.03*	...
1968	0.69*	0.68*	...	...	0.87*	...
1964	0.65*	0.65*	...	...	0.93*	...
1958	0.52*	0.52*	...	...	0.85*	...
1953	...	...	0.33*	0.34*	...	0.45*

* Significant at 5 percent level or better.
a. From table B-1.
b. From regressions not shown.
c. From table B-2.

Table B-5. *Effect of Industry Sample and Unionization Data Source on b Coefficients, UNE76 and UNCPS*

Year	Coefficient of UNE76				Coefficient of UNCPS	
	92 industries[a] (1)	68 industries[b] (2)	58 industries[a] (3)	44 industries[b] (4)	68 industries[c] (5)	44 industries[c] (6)
1976	1.49*	1.85*	1.33*	1.76	2.17*	(1.15)
1974	1.18*	1.46*	...	...	1.51*	...
1973	1.07*	1.32*	...	...	1.22*	...
1971	0.81*	0.95*	...	...	0.87*	...
1968	0.69*	0.80*	...	...	0.77*	...
1964	0.65*	0.74*	...	...	0.86*	...
1958	0.52*	0.54*	...	...	0.72*	...
1953	...	...	0.33*	0.29*	...	(0.09)

Coefficients in parentheses not significant at 10 percent level.
* Significant at 5 percent level or better.
a. From table B-1.
b. From regressions not shown.
c. From table B-3.

Table B-6. *Regression Equations Relating Average Hourly Earnings to UNE76 and Other Selected Variables, in Industries for Which Union and Nonunion Pay Data Are Available*

Explanatory variable	Dependent variable								
	AHE76 (1)	AHE74 (2)	AHE73 (3)	AHE71 (4)	AHE68 (5)	AHE64 (6)	AHE58 (7)	AHE76 (8)	AHE53 (9)
Constant	4.75*	3.78*	3.66*	3.35*	2.57*	1.99*	2.26*	3.57*	1.63*
UNE76	1.90*	1.47*	1.33*	1.00*	0.79*	0.69*	0.49*	2.28*	0.43*
BLK76	-2.74	-2.22	-2.28*	-2.19*	-1.99*	-1.89*	-1.91*	-3.18	-1.72*
ESSIZ	(-0.00)	(-0.00)	(-0.00)	(-0.00)	(0.00)	(0.00)	(0.00)	0.002	(-0.00)
PFEM	-3.44*	-2.87*	-2.62*	-2.20*	-1.60*	-1.42*	-1.13*	-3.51*	-0.87*
KLDEP	0.0001*	0.0001*	0.0001*	0.00004*	0.00003*	0.00003*	0.00002*	0.0001*	(0.00)
ED	(0.09)	(0.11)	(0.09)	(0.07)	(0.07)	(0.07)	(0.01)	0.22	(0.04)
$\bar{R}^2$	0.79	0.77	0.75	0.72	0.73	0.76	0.72	0.82	0.73
Standard error	0.59	0.51	0.48	0.44	0.33	0.28	0.24	0.60	0.18
Number of observations	77	77	77	77	77	77	77	49	49
Mean of dependent variable (dollars)	5.18	4.41	4.08	3.58	2.98	2.49	2.06	5.35	1.75

Coefficients in parentheses not significant at 10 percent level.
* Significant at 5 percent level or better.

Table B-7. *Regression Equations Relating Average Hourly Earnings to UNEEC and Other Selected Variables, in Industries for Which Union and Nonunion Pay Data Are Available*

					Dependent variable				
Explanatory variable	AHE76 (1)	AHE74 (2)	AHE73 (3)	AHE71 (4)	AHE68 (5)	AHE64 (6)	AHE58 (7)	AHE76 (8)	AHE53 (9)
Constant	3.80*	3.11*	3.23*	2.99*	2.24*	1.62*	1.82*	3.89	1.86*
UNEEC	2.01*	1.49*	1.24*	0.89*	0.74*	0.76*	0.69*	1.71*	(0.22)
BLK76	-3.46*	-2.87*	-2.91*	-2.67*	-2.39*	-2.29*	-2.27*	-3.61	-1.88*
ESSIZ	(0.00)	(0.00)	(0.00)	(0.00)	0.0008	0.0007	0.0006	(0.00)	(0.00)
PFEM	-3.06*	-2.60*	-2.42*	-2.05*	-1.47*	-1.28*	-0.98*	-3.32*	-0.89*
KLDEP	0.0001*	0.00004	0.00004	0.00004	(0.00)	(0.00)	(0.00)	0.0001	(0.00)
ED	(0.13)	(0.13)	(0.10)	(0.08)	(0.08)	(0.05)	(0.03)	(0.15)	(0.02)
$\bar{R}^2$	0.77	0.74	0.72	0.69	0.71	0.74	0.74	0.73	0.67
Standard error	0.61	0.53	0.51	0.45	0.35	0.28	0.23	0.72	0.21
Number of observations	73	73	73	73	73	73	73	46	46
Mean of dependent variable (dollars)	5.13	4.36	4.04	3.55	2.96	2.47	2.04	5.25	1.72

Coefficients in parentheses not significant at 10 percent level.
* Significant at 5 percent level or better.

Table B-8. Regression Equations Relating Average Hourly Earnings to UNCPS and Other Selected Variables, in Industries for Which Union and Nonunion Pay Data Are Available

Explanatory variable	Dependent variable								
	AHE76 (1)	AHE74 (2)	AHE73 (3)	AHE71 (4)	AHE68 (5)	AHE64 (6)	AHE58 (7)	AHE76 (8)	AHE53 (9)
Constant	4.16*	3.37*	3.44*	3.15*	2.32*	1.63*	1.87*	3.59	1.56*
UNCPS	1.92*	1.30*	1.05	(0.70)	(0.58)	0.64*	0.52*	(0.96)	(−0.01)
BLK76	(−2.58)	(−2.03)	(−2.19)	(−2.07)	−1.98*	−1.88*	−1.93*	(−3.17)	−1.82*
ESSIZ	(0.00)	(0.00)	(0.00)	(0.00)	(0.00)	0.001	0.001	(−0.00)	(0.00)
PFEM	−3.86*	−3.38*	−3.09*	−2.71*	−2.00*	−1.72*	−1.36*	−5.00*	−1.41*
KLDEP	0.0001*	0.00005	0.0001	(0.00)	(0.00)	0.00002	0.00002	(0.00)	(0.00)
ED	(0.13)	(0.14)	(0.11)	(0.09)	(0.09)	(0.10)	(0.04)	(0.27)	(0.07)
$\bar{R}^2$	0.69	0.66	0.64	0.63	0.66	0.70	0.70	0.71	0.74
Standard error	0.72	0.61	0.59	0.51	0.38	0.31	0.25	0.74	0.18
Number of observations	60	60	60	60	60	60	60	39	39
Mean of dependent variable (dollars)	5.22	4.44	4.11	3.62	2.99	2.50	2.05	5.51	1.78

Coefficients in parentheses not significant at 10 percent level.
* Significant at 5 percent level or better.

Table B-9. *Effect of Industry Sample and Unionization Data Source on b Coefficients for UNE76 and UNEEC from Tables B-6 and B-7*

Year	Coefficient of UNE76				Coefficient of UNEEC	
	77 industries[a] (1)	73 industries[b] (2)	49 industries[a] (3)	46 industries[b] (4)	73 industries[c] (5)	46 industries[c] (6)
1976	1.90*	1.86*	2.28*	2.34*	2.01*	1.71*
1974	1.47*	1.44*	...	...	1.49*	...
1973	1.33*	1.31*	...	...	1.24*	...
1971	1.00*	0.97*	...	...	0.89*	...
1968	0.79*	0.76*	...	...	0.74*	...
1964	0.69*	0.68*	...	...	0.76*	...
1958	0.49*	0.49*	...	...	0.69*	...
1953	...	...	0.43*	0.46*	...	(0.22)

Coefficients in parentheses not significant at 10 percent level.
* Significant at 5 percent level or better.
a. From table B-6.
b. From regressions not shown.
c. From table B-7.

Table B-10. *Effect of Industry Sample and Unionization Data Source on b Coefficients for UNE76 and UNCPS from Tables B-6 and B-8*

Year	Coefficient of UNE76				Coefficient of UNCPS	
	77 industries[a] (1)	60 industries[b] (2)	49 industries[a] (3)	39 industries[b] (4)	60 industries[c] (5)	39 industries[c] (6)
1976	1.90*	2.00*	2.28*	2.14*	1.92*	(0.96)
1974	1.47*	1.54*	...	...	1.30*	...
1973	1.33*	1.41*	...	...	1.05	...
1971	1.00*	1.03*	...	...	(0.70)	...
1968	0.79*	0.75*	...	...	(0.58)	...
1964	0.69*	0.65*	...	...	0.64*	...
1958	0.49*	0.41*	...	...	0.52*	...
1953	...	...	0.43*	0.30*	...	(−0.01)

Coefficients in parentheses not significant at 10 percent level.
* Significant at 5 percent level or better.
a. From table B-6.
b. From regressions not shown.
c. From table B-8.

Table B-11. *Regression Equations Relating Annual Earnings and Quit Rates to UNE76 and Other Selected Variables*

Explanatory variable	Dependent variable				
	WMSOC (1)	WFSOC (2)	BMSOC (3)	BFSOC (4)	QT76 (5)
Constant	(3,539.1)	(1,097.5)	(2,147.6)	(218.36)	9.24*
UNE76	1,813.9*	960.03*	1,692.3*	1,114.0*	−1.04*
BLK76	−4,713.6	(872.99)	(−1,713.0)	(2,263.1)	(−0.65)
ESSIZ	(−0.10)	0.53*	(0.11)	0.52*	(−0.00)
PFEM	(136.97)	−2,545.9*	−2,059.5*	−1,879.2*	1.73*
KLDEP	0.14*	0.12*	0.11*	0.12*	(−0.00)
ED	603.91*	421.59*	475.08*	424.03*	−0.64*
$\bar{R}^2$	0.40	0.68	0.53	0.53	0.61
Standard error	1,095.56	720.02	962.71	931.15	0.67
Number of observations	92	92	92	85	51
Mean of dependent variable[a]	11,009	6,048	7,741	5,599	1.53

Coefficients in parentheses not significant at 10 percent level.
* Significant at 5 percent level or better.
a. Earnings in dollars; quit rate in percent.

Table B-12. *Regression Equations Relating Annual Earnings and Quit Rates to UNEEC and Other Selected Variables*

Explanatory variable	Dependent variable				
	WMSOC (1)	WFSOC (2)	BMSOC (3)	BFSOC (4)	QT76 (5)
Constant	(1,031.2)	(−1,254.8)	(−1,412.0)	(−1,636.4)	8.92*
UNEEC	2,443.4*	1,749.8*	3,235.0*	1,859.3*	−1.28*
BLK76	−5,582.0*	(936.12)	−(2,917.5)	(1,445.8)	(0.49)
ESSIZ	(−0.09)	0.51*	(0.01)	0.47*	(0.00)
PFEM	(775.57)	−1,947.6*	−1,212.4*	−1,486.0*	1.63*
KLDEP	0.13*	0.10*	0.07	0.10*	(−0.00)
ED	757.45*	557.04*	685.40*	538.06*	−0.59*
$\bar{R}^2$	0.38	0.72	0.59	0.54	0.65
Standard error	1,122.62	664.67	921.12	939.36	0.61
Number of observations	87	87	87	81	49
Mean of dependent variable[a]	10,988	7,720	5,982	5,625	1.49

Coefficients in parentheses not significant at 10 percent level.
* Significant at 5 percent level or better.
a. Earnings in dollars; quit rate in percent.

Table B-13. *Regression Equations Relating Annual Earnings and Quit Rates to UNCPS and Other Selected Variables*

Explanatory variable	Dependent variable				
	WMSOC (1)	WFSOC (2)	BMSOC (3)	BFSOC (4)	QT76 (5)
Constant	(−169.68)	(−1,591.7)	(−785.39)	(−2,570.6)	9.24*
UNCPS	(1,437.2)	1,875.6*	3,493.7*	2,260.0*	(−1.42)
BLK76	(−3,655.0)	(1,566.4)	(−2,800.4)	(522.27)	(−0.78)
ESSIZ	(−0.06)	0.46*	(0.02)	0.50*	(−0.00)
PFEM	−1,648.6	−2,999.8*	−1,691.3*	(−1,035.5)	(1.15)
KLDEP	0.13*	0.10*	0.10*	0.12*	(−0.00)
ED	942.10*	618.42*	656.79*	605.52	−0.58*
$\bar{R}^2$	0.44	0.70	0.58	0.54	0.51
Standard error	1,194.45	738.80	936.94	930.08	0.79
Number of observations	68	68	68	64	35
Mean of dependent variable[a]	10,992	6,092	7,757	5,572	1.63

Coefficients in parentheses not significant at 10 percent level.
* Significant at 5 percent level or better.
a. Earnings in dollars; quit rate in percent.

Table B-14. *Effect of Changes in Industry Sample and Unionization Data on Unionization Coefficient, UNE76, UNEEC, and UNCPS*

Dependent variable	Coefficient of UNE76			Coefficient of UNEEC, industries of table B-12[c] (4)	Coefficient of UNCPS, industries of table B-13[d] (5)
	Industries of table B-11[a] (1)	Industries of table B-12[b] (2)	Industries of table B-13[b] (3)		
WMSOC	1,813.9*	1,896.4*	1,643.1*	2,443.4*	(1,437.2)
WFSOC	960.03*	1,016.0*	1,140.0*	1,749.8*	1,875.6*
BMSOC	1,692.3*	1,761.8*	2,252.7*	3,235.0*	3,493.7*
BFSOC	1,114.0*	1,097.1*	1,737.9*	1,859.3*	2,260.0*
QT76	−1.04*	−0.96*	−1.08	−1.28*	(−1.42)

Coefficients in parentheses not significant at 10 percent level.
* Significant at 5 percent level or better.
a. From table B-11.
b. From regressions not shown.
c. From table B-12.
d. From table B-13.

Table B-15. *Regression Equations Relating Hourly Wages, Fringe Benefits, and Compensation to UNE76 and Other Selected Variables*

Explanatory variable	Dependent variable								
	UNST (1)	NONST (2)	TOTST (3)	UNFR (4)	NONFR (5)	TOTFR (6)	UNCP (7)	NONCP (8)	TOTCP (9)
Constant	4.91*	6.78*	5.53*	(0.45)	(0.44)	(0.50)	5.63*	7.42*	6.28*
UNE76	0.97*	(0.13)	1.22*	0.37*	(0.04)	0.38*	1.42*	(0.20)	1.69*
BLK76	(−2.47)	−3.92*	−2.57*	(−0.22)	(−0.51)	(−0.41)	(−2.57)	−4.41*	−2.98
ESSIZ	(−0.00)	(0.00)	(−0.00)	(0.00)	(0.00)	0.0004*	(−0.00)	(0.00)	(0.00)
PFEM	−2.79*	−1.73*	−2.63*	−0.59*	(−0.19)	−0.45*	−3.70*	−2.14*	−3.36*
KLDEP	(0.00)	0.0001	(0.00)	(0.00)	0.00003*	0.00001*	(0.00)	0.0001*	(0.00)
ED	(0.07)	(−0.19)	(−0.05)	(0.01)	(−0.01)	(−0.00)	(0.08)	(−0.21)	(−0.06)
$\bar{R}^2$	0.47	0.44	0.67	0.46	0.23	0.64	0.53	0.43	0.71
Standard error	0.83	0.61	0.54	0.20	0.19	0.14	0.98	0.78	0.65
Number of observations	77	77	77	77	77	77	77	77	77
Mean of dependent variable (dollars)	4.79	3.73	4.26	0.54	0.30	0.43	5.53	4.17	4.86

Coefficients in parentheses not significant at 10 percent level.
* Significant at 5 percent level or better.

Table B-16. *Regression Equations Relating Hourly Wages, Fringe Benefits, and Compensation to UNEEC and Other Selected Variables*

Explanatory variable		Dependent variable							
	UNST (1)	NONST (2)	TOTST (3)	UNFR (4)	NONFR (5)	TOTFR (6)	UNCP (7)	NONCP (8)	TOTCP (9)
Constant	5.46*	6.19*	4.88*	(0.53)	(0.09)	(0.31)	6.06*	6.30*	5.23*
UNEEC	(0.07)	(0.23)	1.00*	(0.19)	0.28*	0.37*	(0.45)	(0.61)	1.58*
BLK76	(−2.54)	−3.71*	−2.93*	(−0.20)	(−0.57)	(−0.46)	(−2.77)	−4.27*	−3.49*
ESSIZ	(−0.00)	(0.00)	(0.00)	(0.00)	(0.00)	0.001*	(−0.00)	(0.00)	(0.00)
PFEM	−2.88*	−1.63*	−2.45*	−0.59*	(−0.10)	−0.38*	−3.73*	−1.92*	−3.05*
KLDEP	(0.00)	0.0001*	(0.00)	(0.00)	0.00002*	(0.00)	(0.00)	0.0001*	(0.00)
ED	(0.03)	(−0.16)	(−0.01)	(0.01)	(0.01)	(0.00)	(0.05)	(−0.14)	(−0.00)
$\bar{R}^2$	0.44	0.42	0.64	0.39	0.27	0.60	0.49	0.42	0.68
Standard error	0.84	0.61	0.55	0.21	0.19	0.14	1.00	0.78	0.67
Number of observations	73	73	73	73	73	73	73	73	73
Mean of dependent variable (dollars)	4.75	3.70	4.22	0.53	0.29	0.42	5.48	4.13	4.81

Coefficients in parentheses not significant at 10 percent level.
* Significant at 5 percent level or better.

Table B-17. *Regression Equations Relating Hourly Wages, Fringe Benefits, and Compensation to UNCPS and Other Selected Variables*

Explanatory variable	Dependent variable								
	UNST (1)	NONST (2)	TOTST (3)	UNFR (4)	NONFR (5)	TOTFR (6)	UNCP (7)	NONCP (8)	TOTCP (9)
Constant	5.11*	6.78*	5.28*	(0.49)	(0.49)	(0.41)	5.73*	7.44*	5.85*
UNCPS	(-0.19)	(-0.09)	(0.93)	(0.33)	(-0.00)	0.46*	(0.32)	(-0.02)	1.56*
BLK76	(-2.17)	-4.12*	(-2.60)	(-0.15)	-0.69*	(-0.48)	(-2.26)	-4.86*	(-3.14)
ESSIZ	(-0.00)	(0.00)	(0.00)	(0.00)	0.0001*	0.001*	(-0.00)	(0.01)	(0.00)
PFEM	-3.99*	-1.70*	-3.11*	-0.72*	(0.09)	-0.45*	-4.97*	-1.99*	-3.78*
KLDEP	(0.00)	0.0001*	(0.00)	(0.00)	0.00003*	(0.00)	(0.00)	0.0001*	(0.00)
ED	(0.10)	(-0.19)	(-0.02)	(0.01)	(0.02)	(0.00)	(0.12)	(-0.21)	(-0.02)
$\bar{R}^2$	0.43	0.41	0.58	0.37	0.39	0.56	0.46	0.43	0.61
Standard error	0.90	0.60	0.63	0.23	0.14	0.16	1.09	0.73	0.77
Number of observations	60	60	60	60	60	60	60	60	60
Mean of dependent variable (dollars)	4.91	3.75	4.31	0.56	0.28	0.43	5.66	4.16	4.89

Coefficients in parentheses not significant at 10 percent level.
* Significant at 5 percent level or better.

Table B-18. *Effect of Changes in Industry Sample and Unionization Data on Unionization Coefficient, UNE76, UNEEC, and UNCPS*

| Dependent variable | Coefficient of UNE76 | | | Coefficient of UNEEC, 73 industries[c] | Coefficient of UNCPS, 60 industries[d] |
	77 industries[a]	73 industries[b]	60 industries[b]		
UNST	0.97*	0.83	1.05	(0.07)	(−0.19)
NONST	(0.13)	(0.04)	(0.11)	(0.23)	(−0.09)
TOTST	1.22*	1.10*	1.35*	1.00*	(0.93)
UNFR	0.37*	0.34*	0.42*	(0.19)	(0.33)
NONFR	(0.04)	(0.04)	(−0.04)	0.28*	(−0.00)
TOTFR	0.38*	0.35*	0.42*	0.37*	0.46*
UNCP	1.42*	1.24*	1.55*	(0.45)	(0.32)
NONCP	(0.20)	(0.08)	(0.08)	(0.61)	(−0.02)
TOTCP	1.69*	1.54	1.88*	1.58*	1.56*

Coefficients in parentheses not significant at 10 percent level.
* Significant at 5 percent level or better.
a. From table B-15.
b. From regressions not shown.
c. From table B-16.
d. From table B-17.

Supplemental Regression Results and Data Sources for Chapter 4

The Cyclical Responsiveness of Various Industrial-Relations Indicators

Chapter 4 refers to statistical evidence of the cyclical responsiveness of certain measures relating to industrial relations. These include charges of unfair labor practices filed against labor and management with the National Labor Relations Board (NLRB), the number and outcomes of NLRB representation elections, and the annual change in the number of workers involved in work stoppages. A series of regressions relating to these measures can be found in tables C-1, C-2, and C-3, respectively.

In table C-1, the number of unfair labor practices charged and filed each fiscal year is regressed against three variables: *RFISGNP*, *ΔRFISGNP*, and *TIME*. The variable *RFISGNP* is the ratio of real GNP (1972 dollars) to its logarithmic trend on a fiscal-year basis. The trend was estimated for 1950–76. Therefore, *RFISGNP* is an indicator of the level of real economic activity. The variable *ΔRFISGNP* is the annual (fiscal year) change in *RFISGNP*. The variable *TIME* is a time trend set equal to 1 in 1954, which captures any secular trends in the dependent variables. The regressions indicate that high values of *RFISGNP* tend to depress the number of charges filed. High values of *ΔRFISGNP* (economic expansion) seem to be associated with an increase in the number of charges filed against employers and unions, although only in the former case is the relation statistically significant.

Table C-2 uses the same explanatory variables as table C-1 to explain the number of NLRB representation elections held per fiscal year and the proportion of such elections won by unions. It presents the results for all elections, elections held in manufacturing (a center of unionization), and elections involving only one union. In one-union elections the choice is between union and nonunion status. In contrast, in elections involving more than one union there are often jurisdictional disputes where the workers are really choosing *which* union they wish to represent them rather than *if* a union should represent them. The variable *RFISGNP* is positively associated with both the number of union elections and the union win rate. This relation is significant for the union win rate in all elections, manufacturing elections, and one-union elections. However, it is only significant for the number of elections held in the case of manufacturing elections.

Table C-3 presents equations explaining the annual change in the number of workers (in thousands) involved in all work stoppages ($\Delta ALLWK$), stoppages primarily involving a wage, hours, or benefits issue ($\Delta WAGWK$), and stoppages resulting from a contract renegotiation ($\Delta RENWK$).[1] Explanatory variables are the ratio of real GNP (1972 dollars) to its logarithmic trend, *RGNP* (trend fitted over 1947–76); the annual change in real GNP (in billions of dollars), ΔGNP; a dummy variable set equal to 1 in 1972 and zero otherwise, *DUM72* (to capture the effect of Phase II wage controls); and the estimated annual change in the number of workers covered by expiring major-union agreements (agreements covering 1,000 or more workers), ΔEXP, measured in thousands of workers. This last variable was estimated by subtracting the number of workers receiving deferred adjustments in a given year in the major-union sector from an estimate of the total number of workers in that sector, and taking the annual first difference.[2]

It appears from table C-3 that strike activity does contain a cyclical component. The annual increment of workers involved in stoppages in-

1. A wage, hours, or benefits issue is defined as falling under the following headings used by the Bureau of Labor Statistics: general wage change, supplementary benefits, wage adjustments, hours of work, other contractual matters.

2. Data on workers receiving deferred adjustments and the number of workers in the major union sector were taken from various issues of the *Monthly Labor Review*. Before 1967, the data on the number of workers receiving deferred adjustments omitted the finance, insurance, and real estate sectors. Data for prior years have been adjusted upward by 200,000 workers, based on the estimated effect of this omission. See Cordelia Ward and William Davis, "The Wage Calendar for 1968," *Monthly Labor Review*, vol. 91 (January 1968), p. 23, n. 1. Data on the number of workers in the major-union sector can be obtained as far back as 1969. For years before 1969, these data were spliced onto total non-Canadian union membership excluding government union membership. Data on total union membership were taken from Bureau of Labor Statistics, *Handbook of Labor Statistics, 1975—Reference Edition*, bulletin 1865 (Government Printing Office, 1975), p. 389. Data on government union membership are available only for even-numbered years; estimates for odd-numbered years were made by interpolation. Government union membership data appear in the 1975 *Handbook*, pp. 382–86.

creases in periods of economic boom relative to periods of recession—
that is, the coefficient of *RGNP* is positive. But periods of recovery tend to
reduce the number of workers involved in stoppages. The change in the
number of workers under major expiring agreements is an important influence on the dependent variables. The magnitude of the coefficient of
ΔEXP is in line with the coefficient of *EXP* in table C-7 (discussed below). It suggests that, for every hundred workers in the major-union sector whose contract expires, thirty to forty workers under all sizes of agreements actually become involved in stoppages. (Table C-7 suggests a range
of twenty to forty workers.) Since the major-union sector constitutes
roughly half the total union sector, these estimates should be cut approximately in half if the object is to estimate the probability that a worker
under an expiring contract will become involved in a stoppage.

Finally, the variable *DUM72* suggests that controls in 1972 had a
calming effect on industrial relations. The form in which the dummy is
entered is consistent with the hypothesis that the effect was permanent.
That is, the increment of workers involved in 1972 was smaller than would
otherwise have been predicted and in subsequent years was not offset by
a bigger increment.[3] Note that the equation, taken literally, suggests that
in the steady state (where $RGNP = 1$, $\Delta GNP = 0$, $\Delta EXP = 0$, and
$DUM72 = 0$) the number of workers involved in strikes would increase.
This result is implausible over a long period of time but reflects the relatively short period for which the estimates were made.

Determinants of Wage Sensitivity across Industries and across Time Periods

Cross-Industry Evidence

Table C-4 presents three sets of regressions obtained from a cross-
industry study based on the industries listed in table A-1.[4] A series of

3. The equations presented in table C-3 are derived from regressions appearing
in Arnold R. Weber and Daniel J. B. Mitchell, *The Pay Board's Progress: Wage
Controls in Phase II* (Brookings Institution, 1978), p. 443; and Daniel J. B. Mitchell
and Ross E. Azevedo, *Wage-Price Controls and Labor Market Distortions* (UCLA
Institute of Industrial Relations, 1976), p. 139. A dummy for 1973 in the latter
study remained negative but fell below significance. Note that the equations appearing in these two studies employ somewhat different data and units of measurement.

4. One industry, ordnance, was eliminated because data were not available for
the variable *KLDEP*.

regressions was run for each of the ninety-two industries in the form $\dot{W} = A + B\dot{P}_{-1} + CU^{-1}$, where $\dot{W}$ is the percentage annual change in average hourly earnings, $\dot{P}_{-1}$ is the percentage annual change in the consumer price index lagged one year, and U^{-1} is the inverse of the unemployment rate. The regressions were run over the period 1956–76 or 1959–76, depending on the availability of earnings data.

A series of cross-industry regressions was then run to explain the regression coefficients B and C as well as the R^2 obtained for the time-series equations. These three parameters were explained by one of the three unionization rates used in chapters 2 and 3 (the contract file [UNE76], the compensation survey [UNEEC], and the current population survey [UNCPS]); BLK76, the ratio of nonwhite workers to total employment in the industry; ESSIZ, the mean establishment size in the industry; PFEM, the proportion of female workers in total employment in the industry; KLDEP, the ratio of depreciation to total employment in the industry; and ED, weighted median educational attainment in the industry. Details of the construction of these variables can be found in appendix B.

An important question is the degree to which industry wage setting responds to changes in real economic conditions as measured by the unemployment rate. Columns 1–3 of table C-4 suggest that unionization is negatively related to C, the regression coefficient of the inverted unemployment rate. Heavily unionized industries are thus less likely to show wage–unemployment responsiveness, even after other factors (reflected in the other four explanatory variables) are considered. Heavily capitalized industries and industries with relatively high proportions of nonwhite workers are also less responsive in their wage setting to unemployment, as are industries in which the workers have high educational attainment. In two of the three equations, the proportion of female workers is positively and significantly associated with unemployment sensitivity.

Variations in the degree of price sensitivity (the B coefficient for $\dot{P}_{-1}$) are not well explained in columns 4–6 of table C-4. In particular, in two of the three equations presented there seems to be no clear distinction between heavily and lightly unionized industries in price sensitivity. In table 4-3 a very mild positive association between price sensitivity and unionization was found, but no standardization for other industry characteristics was attempted in that table. The results thus reinforce the conclusion that wage determination is price-sensitive in all sectors but that in the union sector—particularly where escalators apply—it is somewhat more sensitive to price changes. Some of this difference in sensitivity may be due to other factors correlated with unionization.

Two variables are consistently significant in columns 4–6 of table C-4. Capital intensity, as measured by *KLDEP*, is positively associated and educational attainment is negatively associated with price sensitivity. The proportion of female workers in the work force has a significant negative effect in two of the three equations, probably reflecting the concentration of female workers in such industries as apparel and shoes, which did not maintain real hourly earnings during the high inflation rates of the 1970s. However, the impact of *PFEM* is not large in an absolute sense. The coefficients in columns 4 and 5 suggest that the price coefficient for an industry that employed only females would be only 0.2 point below that for one that employed only males.

Finally, it is possible to ask whether the variables used in table C-4 can predict what type of industry is likely to yield a good-fitting wage equation as measured by $\bar{R}^2$. Columns 7–9 suggest that there are no systematic relationships between a good wage equation and industry characteristics. None of the variables produce consistently significant results in the three equations and none of the three are particularly good at forecasting goodness of fit.

Comparative Time Periods

Although regressions of the type shown in table C-4 attribute significance to some variables and not to others, these variables are intercorrelated. There may well be a nexus of industry conditions that contributes to wage sensitivity to a particular economic variable. Unionization is one industry condition that existed on a comparatively small scale before the mid-1930s. Hence the 1920s and the early 1930s can be examined for evidence of the structure of wage determination before unionization. Of course, such historical evidence is inevitably contaminated by other changes in economic structure that have taken place. Moreover, the availability of good data before the mid-1930s is severely limited.

Despite these limitations, a crude comparison of wage-change determination in the 1920s and early 1930s can be made with wage-change determination in the post–Korean War period. Table C-5 presents a series of wage equations for production workers in manufacturing in both periods. As it turns out, the coefficients of U^{-1} in the earlier period and that in the later period are similar (except for skilled males in the earlier period). However, because the unemployment data upon which the regressions for the early period rely are based on fragmentary evidence, the similarity should not be stressed. What table C-5 does indicate is that the preunion period was not characterized by a labor force that responded to the market in accordance with the simple textbook model. While table C-4 suggests that wage responsiveness to unemployment is reduced by unionization, table C-5 indicates that even without unionization responsiveness of this type is limited. Unionization, with its long-term contracts and concepts of equity, may reduce the responsiveness. But apparently the union effect is simply to intensify the propensity to downplay real business conditions as a factor in wage setting. This propensity is already latent in the labor market.

One puzzling result of table C-5 is that wages were not as responsive to prices in the earlier period as they were in the later period. Table C-4 indicates that such responsiveness is not strongly associated with unionization. Yet in the earlier (nonunion) period the reaction of wages to price changes was not like that in the later (unionized) period. It is possible that unionization did bring about price sensitivity but that its effects are hidden by a post–Korean War spillover of this sensitivity into the nonunion sector. However, it may also be that wage setters in the 1920s and early 1930s were less confident that they could predict future price changes from past ones. Prices during this period could rise or fall abruptly from year to year.

Post–Korean War Time Series

The evidence from table C-4 that union wages after the Korean War were less sensitive to unemployment than nonunion wages is supported by table C-6, which divides the ninety-three industries of appendix A into groups with above-average and below-average unionization rates. Separate wage equations for these two sectors, for the two sectors combined, and for the entire private nonfarm economy are presented in the table for each index of unionization (*UNE76, UNEEC,* or *UNCPS*) in 1960–76. It is clear from the table that the nonunion sector is more unemployment-responsive in its wage setting than the union sector and that there is little difference in wage responsiveness to price change across the two sectors —the coefficient of $\dot{P}_{-1}$ is about the same in all equations. Table C-6 supports the evidence presented for manufacturing in table 4-6.

Contract Expirations and Work Stoppage

Chapter 4 discusses the proposition that public policy ought to aim at discouraging long-term contracts, since such contracts are less responsive to real business conditions than short-term contracts. Apart from questions of causality, shortening contract durations would increase the number of workers under expiring contracts in any given year, which would lead to more workers being involved in work stoppages.

Table C-7 presents a pooled cross-section analysis of workers involved in work stoppages resulting from contract renegotiations. Its data base was drawn from twenty-seven private nonfarm industries for the years 1968–75. Data on workers (measured in thousands) involved in stoppages were taken from Bureau of Labor Statistics figures appearing in selected annual issues of *Analysis of Work Stoppages*.[5] The number of workers involved in renegotiation stoppages was regressed against the number of workers estimated to be covered by expiring major-union agreements in each industry and year (*EXP*). These estimates are from the wage calendars published periodically in the *Monthly Labor Review* and are measured in thousands of workers.

Also included in some of the regressions are dummy variables for certain industries that seemed either much more or much less stoppage-prone than other industries and dummy variables for certain years that seemed significantly above- or below-average in the number of workers involved in strikes. The dummies enter the regressions in an interaction format with the *EXP* variable.

The regressions represent the following model:

$$(1) \qquad SWKR_{iy} = A + BEXP_{iy},$$

where *SWKR* is the number of workers involved in a work stoppage arising from a contract renegotiation, *EXP* is the number of workers under major expiring contracts (*EXP* has been adjusted for open-ended contracts in railroads and airlines), and i and y represent the industry and year, respectively. The constant A allows for the possibility of underlying friction in labor-management relations that could give rise to a minimum number of workers being involved in disputes. The B coefficient could be regarded as a fixed parameter, as in column 1 of table C-7, or could be a function of other variables. One hypothesis is that B is a function of in-

5. The industries covered are ordnance, food, tobacco, textiles, apparel, lumber, furniture, paper, printing, chemicals, petroleum, rubber, leather, stone-clay-glass, primary metals, fabricated metals, nonelectric machinery, electrical machinery, transportation equipment, instruments, miscellaneous manufacturing, mining, construction, transportation-communications-utilities, wholesale and retail trade, finance-insurance-real estate, and services.

dustry conditions and economic and other conditions that prevail in particular years. This hypothesis can be expressed as:

(2) $$B_{iy} = C + D_i I_i + E_y Y_y,$$

where I and Y are industry and year dummies.

Finally, it is possible that the propensity to be involved in work stoppages is heightened if real wages have lagged or if wages in a particular industry have lagged relative to other industries. Two variables, $REAL$ and $RELW$, were created to test for this effect. Thus expression 2 above is expanded into:

(3) $$B_{iy} = C + D_i I_i + E_i Y_y + REAL_{iy}$$

or

(4) $$B_{iy} = C + D_i I_i + E_y Y_y + RELW_{iy}.$$

The variable $REAL$ was defined as the ratio of current real hourly earnings to real hourly earnings lagged two years in each industry minus one. Thus an industry in a given year whose real wage had risen 3 percent relative to the level two years before would have a value of 0.03. The variable $RELW$ was created by taking the ratio of nominal hourly earnings in each industry and year to the level of earnings two years before. This ratio was then divided by the mean value of these ratios for all industries in the given year. The resulting ratio was adjusted by subtracting one from it. Thus an industry in a given year whose nominal wage had risen 10 percent in two years at a time when other industries had generally experienced an 8 percent wage increase would have a value of $RELW$ of about 0.02. The formulas for the two variables are as follows:

$$REAL_{iy} = \left[\frac{AHE_{iy}/CPI_y}{AHE_{iy-2}/CPI_{y-2}} \right] - 1$$

and

$$RELW_{iy} = \left[\frac{AHE_{iy}/AHE_{iy-2}}{\sum_{i=1}^{27} \dfrac{AHE_{iy}/AHE_{iy-2}}{27}} \right] - 1.$$

It should be noted that $REAL$ and $RELW$ are highly correlated ($R = 0.88$) so that a choice between the two approaches cannot be made statistically.[6]

---

6. If both $REAL \times EXP$ and $RELW \times EXP$ are put in the same regression, neither appears significant because of the intercorrelation.

Two conclusions can be drawn from table C-7. First, the number of workers under expiring major agreements and the total number of workers involved in work stoppages from renegotiations in a given year are closely related. The coefficient of *EXP* varies between 0.22 and 0.36 in table C-7, in general accord with the results from table C-3. Hence it appears that for every hundred workers under a major expiration twenty to forty became involved in renegotiation work stoppages during 1968–75. Since the major-union sector is roughly one-half of the total union sector, these estimates should be cut approximately in half—that is, for every hundred workers under expiring contracts, ten to twenty ultimately ended up being involved in a stoppage related to renegotiation.

A second conclusion is that fewer workers are involved in work stoppages in industries that have provided relatively large real wage increases or that have moved their workers up in the interindustry wage hierarchy. That is, the coefficients of *REAL* × *EXP* and of *RELW* × *EXP* are negative. The evidence on this point is tentative, since when all industry and year dummies are included in the regressions (columns 5 and 6), the negative coefficients are significant only at the 10 percent level.[7] Labor disputes are the product of a management-union interaction, so it is not evident a priori which party's preferences are most reflected in the generation of work stoppages. Table C-7 indicates that the union's preferences tend to dominate.

Agreements Covered in the Regression Analysis of Table 4-7

Table 4-7 presents a series of regressions based on the wage outcomes of seventeen bargaining situations from the mid-1950s to the mid-1970s.

---

7. The *REAL* and *RELW* variables test for the effect of industry conditions on worker involvement in stoppages. A different hypothesis is that when the interindustry wage structure is "disturbed" the propensity for stoppage involvement should increase. This hypothesis is sometimes used to explain wage movements—a disruption of wage differentials "excites" wages throughout the labor force to move upward. For example, see Arnold H. Packer and Seong H. Park, "Distortions in Relative Wages and Shifts in the Phillips Curve," *Review of Economics and Statistics*, vol. 55 (February 1973), pp. 16–22. The strike version of this hypothesis could not be tested directly with the data in table C-7, but an interindustry wage dispersion variable—both in absolute form and as a first difference—was introduced into the regressions of table C-3. No statistically significant relationship was found.

The names of the employers and the unions in the contract file are listed below.[8]

1. Aluminum Company of America (Alcoa)—United Steelworkers of America
2. Anaconda Company (Montana Mining Division)—United Steelworkers of America
3. Armour and Company—Amalgamated Meat Cutters and Butcher Workmen of North America
4. Atlantic Richfield Company—Oil, Chemical and Atomic Workers International Union
5. Berkshire Hathaway, Inc.—United Textile Workers of America
6. Bituminous Coal Mine Operators—United Mine Workers of America
7. Boeing Company (Washington plants)—International Association of Machinists and Aerospace Workers
8. Dan River Inc.—United Textile Workers of America
9. Firestone Tire and Rubber Company—United Rubber, Cork, Linoleum and Plastic Workers of America
10. Ford Motor Company—International Union, United Automobile, Aerospace and Agricultural Implement Workers of America
11. General Electric Company—International Union of Electrical, Radio, and Machine Workers
12. International Paper Company (Southern Kraft Division)—United Paperworkers International Union
13. Lockheed Aircraft Corporation (California)—International Association of Machinists and Aerospace Workers
14. Council of North Atlantic Shipping Associations (CONASA)—International Longshoremen's Association
15. Pacific Maritime Association—International Longshoremen's and Warehousemen's Union
16. Trucking Employers, Inc.—International Brotherhood of Teamsters, Chauffeurs, Warehousemen and Helpers of America
17. United States Steel Corporation—United Steelworkers of America

8. Information on the base earnings used for these situations can be found in Daniel J. B. Mitchell, "Union Wage Determination: Policy Implication and Outlook," *Brookings Papers on Economic Activity, 3:1978*, pp. 581–82.

Table C-1. *Annual Regression Equations Relating Charges of Unfair Labor Practices Filed with the NLRB to Business-Cycle Factors*

Explanatory variable	Number of charges filed against employers[a]	Number of charges filed against unions[b]
Constant	51,248*	13,923*
RFISGNP	−49,634*	−13,393*
Δ*RFISGNP*	33,003*	(2,139)
TIME[c]	816*	420*
rho	0.75	0.67
$\bar{R}^2$	0.99	0.99
Standard error	520	333
Durbin-Watson	1.86	1.79

Source: Data on unfair labor practices drawn from National Labor Relations Board, *Annual Report*, various issues, 1955–76.

Coefficients in parentheses not significant at 10 percent level. Period of observation is fiscal years 1955–76.
* Significant at 5 percent level or better.
a. Under section 8(a) of the Taft-Hartley Act as amended.
b. Under section 8(b) of the Taft-Hartley Act as amended.
c. *TIME* = 1 in fiscal year 1954, 2 in 1955, 3 in 1956, and so on.

Table C-2. *Annual Regression Equations Relating Number of NLRB Elections and Union Win Rate to Business-Cycle Factors*

Explanatory variable	Number of elections			Union win rate		
	Total (1)	Manufacturing (2)	One union (3)	Total (4)	Manufacturing (5)	One union (6)
Constant	(−1,144)	(−2,841)	(−2,691)	26.68*	28.43	(19.34)
RFISGNP	(5,456)	6,110	(6,095)	39.81*	38.96*	42.12*
ΔRFISGNP	7,572	4,224	6,251	(17.86)	(14.00)	(6.65)
TIME	224*	50	236	−0.74*	0.87*	−0.60*
rho	0.74	0.81	0.68	...	...	0.30
$\bar{R}^2$	0.95	0.82	0.96	0.91	0.92	0.87
Standard error	368	229	314	1.56	1.73	1.60
Durbin-Watson	1.68	1.82	1.73	1.99	2.03	1.87

Source: Election data from NLRB, *Annual Report*, various issues, 1955–76. Period of observation for equations estimated with autocorrelation correction (rho) is fiscal years 1955–76. For other equations, it is 1954–76. The variables are defined in the text. Coefficients in parentheses not significant at 10 percent level.
* Significant at 5 percent level or better.

Table C-3. *Regression Equations Relating Annual Change in the Number of Workers Involved in Work Stoppages to Business-Cycle Factors*

Explanatory variable	$\Delta WAGWK$ (1)	$\Delta RENWK$ (2)	$\Delta ALLWK$ (3)
Constant	−10,936	−8,920*	−9,992*
RGNP	11,356*	9,251	10,369*
ΔGNP	−1.10*	−0.78†	−0.90†
ΔEXP	0.36*	0.36*	0.31*
DUM72	−768*	−900*	−954*
$\bar{R}^2$	0.70	0.85	0.71
Standard error	383	276	355
Durbin-Watson	2.24	2.56	2.34
Period of observation	1958–75	1962–75	1958–76

Source: Strike data from Bureau of Labor Statistics, *Analysis of Work Stoppages*, various annual issues, 1959–77. The variables are defined in the text.
  * Significant at 5 percent level or better.
  † Significant at 10 percent level.

Table C-4. Cross-Section Regression Equations Relating Industry Time-Series Coefficients to Selected Variables

Explanatory variable[a]	Coefficient of U^{-1}			Coefficient of $\dot{P}_{-1}$			Coefficient of determination ($\bar{R}^2$)		
	(1)	(2)	(3)	(4)	(5)	(6)	(7)	(8)	(9)
Constant	108.03*	121.74*	126.72*	1.51*	1.36*	1.45*	(0.33)	(0.41)	0.63
UNE76	−9.09*	...	...	(0.02)	...	...	−0.25*	...	...
UNEEC	...	−15.94*	...	...	0.14	...	...	(−0.11)	(−0.20)
UNCPS	...	...	−21.59*	...	...	(0.17)	...	...	(0.07)
BLK76	−38.41*	−29.12	−36.39*	(0.11)	(0.11)	(−0.08)	(0.20)	(0.03)	(0.07)
ESSIZ	(0.00)	(0.00)	(0.00)	(0.00)	(0.00)	(0.00)	(−0.00)	−0.0001	(−0.00)
PFEM	11.69*	8.15*	(5.53)	−0.22*	−0.18*	(−0.13)	0.15*	−0.15	(−0.09)
KLDEP	(−0.00)	(0.00)	(−0.00)	0.00001*	0.00001*	0.00001*	(0.00)	(0.00)	(0.00)
ED	−7.78*	−8.57*	−8.77*	−0.07*	−0.06*	−0.07*	(0.03)	(0.02)	(0.01)
$\bar{R}^2$	0.49	0.50	0.50	0.19	0.25	0.20	0.28	0.10	0.05
Standard error	7.04	7.06	6.82	0.14	0.13	0.15	0.13	0.15	0.16
Mean of dependent variable	12.26	12.11	12.38	0.67	0.67	0.67	0.60	0.60	0.62
Number of observations	92	87	68	92	87	68	92	87	68

Coefficients in parentheses not significant at 10 percent level.
* Significant at 5 percent level or better.
a. Variables are defined in appendix B.

Table C-5. *Annual Regression Equations Relating Changes in Hourly Earnings of Manufacturing Production Workers to Past Price Change and Unemployment, Selected Periods, 1920-76*

	Hourly earnings changes					
Explanatory variable	All workers (1)	Skilled males (2)	Unskilled males (3)	Males (4)	Females (5)	All workers[a] (6)
Constant	-5.77	(-2.03)	-5.33	-4.52	-5.41	(-1.08)
$\dot{P}_{-1}$	(0.39)	(-0.17)	(0.42)	(0.41)	(0.32)	0.61*
U^{-1}	23.44	(10.77)	22.89*	20.53*	20.99*	20.19*
rho	...	-0.37	0.13	0.25	0.50	0.57
$\bar{R}^2$	0.27	0.40	0.64	0.66	0.69	0.77
Standard error	6.30	3.14	3.66	3.23	2.98	1.02
Durbin-Watson	1.97	1.55	2.02	2.06	1.83	1.76
Period of observation	1920-32	1922-32	1922-32	1922-32	1922-32	1954-76

Sources: Columns 1-5, data from a survey of twenty-five manufacturing industries published in Bureau of the Census, *Historical Statistics of the United States: Colonial Times to 1970* (GPO, 1976) pt. 1, p. 172; column 6, Bureau of Economic Analysis, *Business Statistics, 1977* (GPO, 1978), pp. 43, 69, 81.

Coefficients in parentheses not significant at 10 percent level.

* Significant at 5 percent level or better.

a. Hourly earnings excluding overtime.

Table C-6. Annual Regression Equations Relating Percent Change in Hourly Earnings to Past Price Change and Unemployment, 1960–76

| | | Annual percent change in hourly earnings[a] | | | | | | |
| | | Heavily unionized sector[b] | | | Lightly unionized sector[c] | | | Annual percent change in hourly-earnings index[d] |
Explanatory variable	Union and nonunion sectors (1)	Contract file (2)	Compensation survey (3)	Current population survey (4)	Contract file (5)	Compensation survey (6)	Current population survey (7)	(8)
Constant	(1.33)	(2.33)	(2.56)	(2.40)	(0.43)	(0.21)	(0.11)	(0.95)
$\dot{P}_{-1}$	0.50*	0.55*	0.45*	0.53*	0.57*	0.58*	0.58*	0.51*
U^{-1}	10.75	(6.79)	(6.30)	(5.91)	13.46*	14.68*	15.47*	12.58*
rho	0.66	0.60	0.77	0.69	0.38	0.26	0.22	0.75
$\bar{R}^2$	0.89	0.78	0.87	0.86	0.88	0.85	0.86	0.91
Standard error	0.61	1.13	0.78	0.87	0.60	0.66	0.62	0.60
Durbin-Watson	1.94	1.82	1.91	1.84	1.79	1.76	1.76	1.89
Mean of dependent variable (percent)	5.39	5.76	5.52	5.59	5.28	5.33	5.34	5.41
Number of industries included	93	34	49	34	59	39	35	...

Coefficients in parentheses not significant at 10 percent level.
* Significant at 5 percent level or better.
a. Weighted by production and nonsupervisory employment in 1976.
b. Industries with above-average unionization rates as determined from the contract file, compensation survey, or current population survey.
c. Industries with below-average unionization rates.
d. Adjusted for overtime in manufacturing and interindustry employment shifts.

Table C-7. *Pooled Cross-Section Regression Analysis Explaining the Number of Workers Involved in Work Stoppages Arising from Renegotiations in Twenty-seven Private Nonfarm Industries, 1968–75*

Explanatory variable[a]	Number of workers involved in renegotiation stoppages (thousands)					
	(1)	(2)	(3)	(4)	(5)	(6)
Constant	(5.58)	11.14	(9.72)	(10.08)	13.80*	13.76*
EXP	0.36*	0.27*	0.32*	0.28*	0.25*	0.22*
I5 × EXP	...	−0.26*	−0.26*	−0.27*	−0.21*	−0.22*
I15 × EXP	...	−0.15	−0.18*	−0.17*	−0.20*	−0.20*
I22 × EXP	...	0.89*	0.88*	0.91*	0.83*	0.83*
I23 × EXP	...	0.32*	0.30*	0.32*	0.43*	0.43*
I24 × EXP	...	(0.08)	(0.08)	0.11*	0.10*	0.10*
Y70 × EXP	...	...	...	...	0.25*	0.26*
Y71 × EXP	...	...	...	...	0.29*	0.30*
Y72 × EXP	...	...	...	...	−0.16*	−0.16*
Y73 × EXP	...	...	...	...	−0.12*	−0.15*
Y74 × EXP	...	...	...	...	−0.09*	−0.07
Y75 × EXP	...	...	...	...	−0.32*	−0.27*
REAL × EXP	...	...	−1.24*	...	−0.76	...
RELW × EXP	...	...	...	−2.44*	...	−0.83
$\bar{R}^2$	0.54	0.63	0.66	0.67	0.85	0.85
Standard error	84.84	75.91	73.24	72.40	48.41	48.40
Number of observations	216	216	216	216	216	216

Sources: Given in the text.
Coefficients in parentheses not significant at 10 percent level.
* Significant at 5 percent level.
a. The variables *I5*, *I15*, *I22*, *I23*, and *I24* are dummies for apparel; primary metals; mining; construction; and transportation, communications, and utilities, respectively. The variables *Y70*, *Y71*, *Y72*, *Y73*, *Y74*, and *Y75* are dummies for 1970, 1971, 1972, 1973, 1974, and 1975, respectively. Two coefficients, *REAL* and *RELW*, were created to test for lagged effect of wage changes (see the text).

Regression Equations Relating to Wage Spillover Effects

The Sensitivity of Previous Estimates to Specification

Two empirical studies, one by Robert Flanagan and the other by George Johnson, have attempted to measure the degree of wage spillover from the union to the nonunion sector, and vice versa.[1] Both studies found that nonunion wage decisions appear to influence union wage decisions, but neither found evidence of a reverse flow. It seems, however, that alternative specifications of the model, data sources, and periods of observation can produce contradictory results.

For example, table D-1, column 1, shows the results of an estimated regression explaining nonunion effective wage rate changes in manufacturing (Flanagan's dependent variable). Instead of using Flanagan's specification, Johnson's index of the union-nonunion earnings differential is employed with a one-year lag ($DJOHN_{-1}$). The equation of column 1 explains nonunion wage change in manufacturing with the annual change in the consumer price index lagged one year ($\dot{P}_{-1}$) and the inverted official unemployment rate (U^{-1}), plus the Johnson variable. In this format, $DJOHN_{-1}$ has a positive and significant coefficient, implying that, if the union sector's wage level rises relative to that of the nonunion sector, nonunion wage change speeds up. Such a result contradicts the findings of the Flanagan and Johnson papers.

An alternative specification is presented in columns 2 and 3. The ninety-three industries listed in appendix table A-1 are divided according to their unionization rates, using the three unionization indexes previously applied in this study. Annual changes in hourly earnings for industries with above-average (below-average) unionization rates were weighted by

1. Robert J. Flanagan, "Wage Interdependence in Unionized Labor Markets," *Brookings Papers on Economic Activity,* 3:1976, pp. 635–73. George E. Johnson, "The Determination of Wages in the Union and Non-Union Sectors," *British Journal of Industrial Relations,* vol. 15 (July 1977), pp. 211–25. The variable referred to as *DJOHN* below in the text appears on page 217 and is called *"D"* by Johnson.

1976 production and nonsupervisory employment, producing earnings change indexes for the heavily (lightly) unionized sectors. These indexes were then explained by $\dot{P}_{-1}$, U^{-1}, and $DJOHN_{-1}$ in regressions shown in columns 2–7. The variable $DJOHN_{-1}$ has the wrong sign and is not significant for the three definitions of the heavily unionized sector in columns 2–4. This suggests that there was no spillover from the nonunion to the union sector. However, a positive and significant coefficient is found for the three definitions of the lightly unionized sector, implying a spillover from the union to the nonunion sector. Again, the evidence of table D-1 contradicts the Flanagan and Johnson studies.

The point of this exercise is simply to demonstrate that econometric tests of spillover must be approached cautiously and with skepticism. Wage changes are highly intercorrelated among virtually all industries. This intercorrelation makes it difficult statistically to sort out differences in the mechanisms that cause those wage changes across industry groups.

Regressions Pertaining to Pay Relations between Clerical and Skilled Maintenance Workers

Normally, white-collar workers are less likely to be unionized than blue-collar workers. But it is often believed that the white-collar workers in firms with unionized blue-collar work forces have their wages increased in line with the union workers. Such a linkage would represent a wage spillover from the union to the nonunion sector *within* firms. Various Bureau of Labor Statistics *Area Wage Surveys* were used to gather straight-time pay change information for skilled maintenance workers (males), unskilled plant workers (males), and clerical workers (males and females) in twenty-four metropolitan areas where the unionization rate for plant workers was reported to be 75 percent or more during 1971–74.[2] Only areas for which complete data were available were included. Data were also gathered on the unionization rates for office workers in these areas (CU_i).

If employers were mechanically tying pay raises for nonunion clerical workers to unionized skilled maintenance workers or unskilled plant

2. For clerical workers, the data refer to weekly earnings for a standard week. For the other groups, the data refer to hourly earnings excluding overtime and other shift differentials. The twenty-four metropolitan areas are listed in footnote 24, chapter 5.

workers, the degree of office-worker unionization would be irrelevant to the pay raises received by clerical workers—the unionization of clerical workers would not change the rate of pay increase for such workers. However, the regression equations of table D-2 do not support this hypothesis.

In table D-2, regressions are presented explaining the annual rate of clerical pay change by the annual rate of skilled maintenance pay change or the annual rate of unskilled plant worker pay change and CU_i across the twenty-four metropolitan areas. In the periods 1971–73 and 1973–77 especially, clerical workers could expect to receive larger pay raises if they were unionized, according to these estimates. Moreover, the size of the coefficient of the pay change of the comparison group (skilled maintenance or unskilled plant workers) declines over the 1967–77 period, suggesting that the effects of the pay raises of the heavily unionized blue-collar groups on clerical wages declined statistically. This indicates that the degree of intrafirm union-nonunion pay spillover is a variable rather than a constant. The overall results suggest that employers did not feel compelled to keep clerical pay apace with union pay unless pressured by clerical unionization. Throughout the economy during the period covered, union pay gains were generally larger than nonunion pay increases, and employers were apparently willing to let this difference be reflected in their internal pay structures as well.

Table D-3 uses the data underlying table D-2 to estimate the effect of unionization on the absolute wages of nonproduction workers, given the wage levels of production workers in manufacturing. As noted in chapter 5, estimates from the 1960s suggest that white-collar unionization had little effect on white-collar pay levels at that time. Since it is known from table D-2 that white-collar unionization accelerated the pay increases of white-collar workers in the 1970s, it is possible for the effect of unionization on absolute white-collar pay to be visible by the late 1970s.

Average annual earnings of nonproduction workers in 1971 in each of the twenty-four areas ($NPRE_{i, 1971}$) were estimated by dividing the nonproduction worker payroll by nonproduction worker employment. An analogous procedure was followed to estimate average annual earnings in 1971 for production workers in each area ($PRE_{i, 1971}$).[3] The rates of change of clerical pay over 1971–77 (from the sources used for table D-2) were applied to these base annual earnings to estimate annual earnings of

---

3. Hourly rather than annual earnings would be a better measure. However, hourly data were not available for nonproduction workers.

nonproduction workers in 1977 ($NPRE_{i,\,1977}$). Then $PRE_{i,\,1971}$ was adjusted to estimated 1977 levels by using rates of pay change of skilled maintenance workers or unskilled plant workers ($PRES_{i,\,1977}$ and $PREU_{i,\,1977}$, respectively). Regressions were then estimated explaining $NPRE_{i,\,year}$ by $PRE_{i,\,year}$, $PRES_{i,\,year}$ or $PREU_{i,\,year}$, and CU_i.

In chapter 3 it was noted that the coefficient of a unionization rate in regressions such as those of table D-3 can be considered an estimate of the union-nonunion pay differential. The coefficient of CU_i in the 1971 equation (column 1) is positive but not significant. This nonsignificance confirms the results cited in the text for the 1960s. The 1971 coefficient, taken at face value, is about 16 percent of the annual wage of nonproduction workers. But by 1977 the estimate rises to 23–25 percent of the annual wage and is significant at the 10 percent level when $PRES_{i,\,1977}$ or $PREU_{i,\,1977}$ is used as an explanatory variable. This 23–25 percent estimate is within the 20–30 percent range suggested in chapter 3 as a reasonable estimate of the union-nonunion differential for production and nonsupervisory workers. In summary, white-collar unionization was thought to be redundant in the 1960s in its effects on white-collar pay. In the late 1970s, however, the widening gap between union and nonunion pay may have made this conclusion invalid.

Table D-1. *Selected Annual Pay-Change Equations Including a Spillover Variable, 1959–74*

| | | Annual percent change in hourly earnings[a] | | | | | |
| | *Effective nonunion manufacturing wage change* | *Heavily unionized sector*[a] | | | *Lightly unionized sector*[a] | | |
Explanatory variable	*(1)*	*Contract file (2)*	*Compensation survey (3)*	*Current population survey (4)*	*Contract file (5)*	*Compensation survey (6)*	*Current population survey (7)*
Constant	−4.84*	(0.89)	(0.82)	(1.21)	(−1.39)	−2.05	−1.80
$\dot{P}_{-1}$	0.88*	1.02*	0.97*	0.99*	0.80*	0.78*	0.77*
U^{-1}	25.90*	(5.31)	(5.91)	(4.01)	17.24*	20.39*	19.87*
$DJOHN_{-1}$	0.31*	(0.10)	(0.07)	(0.07)	0.14*	0.18*	0.15
$\bar{R}^2$	0.90	0.69	0.79	0.78	0.91	0.90	0.91
Standard error	0.56	1.17	0.86	0.93	0.46	0.50	0.47
Durbin-Watson	2.58	1.83	1.85	1.86	2.41	2.34	2.24
Mean of dependent variable (percent)	3.96	5.27	5.06	5.12	4.89	4.94	4.99

a. See footnotes to appendix table C-6.

Table D-2. *Cross-sectional Regressions Relating to Pay Change of Clerical Workers in Manufacturing, Twenty-four Metropolitan Areas, 1967–77*[a]

	Annual rate of change of clerical pay					
Explanatory variable	1967–71 (1)	1971–73 (2)	1973–77 (3)	1967–71 (4)	1971–73 (5)	1973–77 (6)
Constant	2.23	(2.14)	4.46*	2.11*	3.46*	6.21*
Rate of change in pay of skilled maintenance workers						
1967–71	0.53*	...	...	...	...	...
1971–73	...	0.40	...	...	...	...
1973–77	...	...	0.37*	...	...	...
CU_i[b]	(0.42)	(2.09)	2.30*	(−0.11)	3.18	2.44*
Rate of change in pay of unskilled plant workers						
1967–71	...	...	...	0.57*	...	...
1971–73	...	...	...	...	(0.18)	...
1973–77	...	...	...	...	...	(0.17)
$\bar{R}^2$	0.26	0.22	0.41	0.39	0.16	0.32
Standard error	0.76	0.83	0.45	0.69	0.87	0.48
Number of observations	24	24	24	24	24	24
Mean of dependent variable (percent)	5.75	5.09	8.11	5.75	5.09	8.11

Coefficients in parentheses are not significant at 10 percent level. All variables are expressed in percentage points, except CU_i, which is expressed as a ratio.

* Significant at 5 percent level.

a. The cities selected reported plant-worker unionization rates in manufacturing of at least 75 percent during 1971–74 and had complete data available for 1967–77.

b. Clerical workers' unionization rate.

Table D-3. *Cross-sectional Regressions Relating to Annual Earnings of Nonproduction Workers in Twenty-four Metropolitan Areas, 1971 and 1977*[a]

Explanatory variable	$NPRE_{i,\ 1971}$ (1)	$NPRE_{i,\ 1977}$ (2)	$NPRE_{i,\ 1977}$ (3)
Constant	3,818*	(3,898)	4,903
$PRE_{i,\ 1971}$	0.91*	...	...
$PRES_{i,\ 1977}$	...	0.98*	...
$PREU_{i,\ 1977}$	...	...	0.89*
CU_i	(1,865)	4,036	4,435
$\bar{R}^2$	0.62	0.63	0.62
Standard error	595	1,031	1,052
Number of observations	24	24	24
Mean of dependent variable (dollars)	11,625	17,556	17,556

Coefficients in parentheses not significant at 10 percent level.
* Significant at 5 percent level.
a. See the text for definitions of the variables.

Index

Aaron, Benjamin, 67n
Abowd, John M., 105n, 108n
Addison, John, 183n
Adelman, M. A., 46n, 47n
Aerospace industry: engineers' organization, 6n; escalator clause, 50n; Pay Board action on contracts, 50n, 153n
AFL, 4
AFL-CIO, 26
Alexander, Kenneth, 183n, 191n
Aliber, Robert Z., 19n, 43n, 47n
American Motors Corporation, 146n
Annable, James E., Jr., 163n
Apparel industry, 73–74
Arbitration: NLRB policy toward, 27n; on union contracts, 228; wage and benefit changes from, 29n
Arnow, Philip, 47n
Ashenfelter, Orley C., 80n, 91n, 101n, 105n, 107, 108, 110, 116n, 117n, 128n
Automobile industry: collective bargaining, 32, 46, 47, 57; strikes of *1930s*, 4n. *See also* United Automobile, Aerospace, and Agricultural Implement Workers
Auto Workers. *See* United Automobile, Aerospace, and Agricultural Implement Workers
Average hourly earnings. *See* Hourly earnings
Azariadis, Costas, 226n
Azevedo, Ross E., 49n, 224n

Bailey, William R., 103n
Bain, George Sayers, 116n
Bain, Trevor, 32n
Baldwin, Stephen E., 103n
Barber, Randy, 209n
Becker, Brian, 199n
Becker, Gary S., 226n
Behman, Sara, 121n
Bell, Carolyn Shaw, 38n
Bernstein, Irving, 25n, 184n
Bird, Monroe M., 69n
Blacks: pay differentials for whites and, 80n, 96; union effect on earnings, 100–01, 112

Block, Richard N., 137n
BLS. *See* Bureau of Labor Statistics
Bolton, Lena W., 28n, 193n
Borstein, Tim, 57n
Boskin, Michael J., 103n
Bosworth, Barry, 21n, 191n
"Boulwarism," 56n, 77n
Bowlby, Roger L., 8n, 31n
Boyle, W. A., 58n
Briggs, Vernon B., Jr., 47n
Brinker, Paul A., 200n
Bronfenbrenner, Martin, 46n
Brooks, Harold E., 59n
Bureau of Economic Analysis, 119n, 158n, 218n, 221n
Bureau of Labor Statistics (BLS), 23, 24–25, 26n, 27n, 28n, 53n, 78, 97n, 103, 115n, 175, 177n; employment cost index, 114; hourly earnings data, 39, 94; industry wage surveys, 42, 80, 104, 179n; life-of-contract wage adjustment data, 148–49; manufacturing wage series, 129, 130, 131; union contract wage data, 138, 139, 190–91; unionization data, 41, 180, 181
Bureau of National Affairs, 130n
Bureau of the Census, 73n, 125n, 158n, 179n
Burke, Donald R., 51n
Burton, John, 183n
Business cycles: effects on wages, 11, 16–18, 157–58; and labor-management relations, 116–17; and union-nonunion wage differentials, 9–10, 29, 211–12

Capital: human, 97, 226; in primary labor market firms, 124; putty-clay model of, 108; substituted for labor, 67, 68, 75, 97; in unemployment-sensitive industries, 123; union versus nonunion, 85
Capital-labor index, 85
Caples, William G., 34n
Carter administration: wage "deceleration" program, 33, 119n, 202; wage

283